ABOUT THE EDITOR

Bill Fawcett is the author and editor of more than a dozen books, including *You Did What?*, *It Seemed Like a Good Idea . . .* , *How to Lose a Battle*, and *You Said What?* He is also the author and editor of three historical mystery series and two oral histories of the U.S. Navy SEALs. He lives in Illinois.

HOW TO LOSE
WWII

Also by Bill Fawcett

HOW TO LOSE

WWII

BAD MISTAKES
OF THE GOOD WAR

Edited by

Bill Fawcett

HARPER

NEW YORK • LONDON • TORONTO • SYDNEY

HARPER

HarperCollins books may be purchased for educational, business, or sales promotional use. For information, please write: Special Markets Department, HarperCollins Publishers, 10 East 53rd Street, New York, NY 10022.

FIRST EDITION

Library of Congress Cataloging-in-Publication Data is available upon request.

ISBN 978-0-06-180731-2

13 14   OV/RRD   10 9 8 7 6 5 4 3 2

For my father who flew a B-29 in this war
and all those who served and fought in it.
Thank you for our world today.

CONTENTS

INTRODUCTION

There had never been a war on the scale of World War II. The sheer size of the conflict, and even the immense scope of the extended battlefields, multiplied the effects of both brilliant and bad decisions. With millions of men attacking in a Russian offensive or thousands of aircraft dueling in the skies over Europe, every key decision had important consequences.

In this book you will find a collection of the mistakes made by the military and political leaders in the European Theater. Decisions, it should be understood, that were often made with limited information and little time. Some slowed victory, others ensured defeat. There is only so much space in a single volume, and literally millions of decisions were made in combat and by national leaders in the six years of war. We limited the scope of this book to presenting for you a range of important decisions that actually directly affected the Allied victory and Axis defeat. Although many other lost battles were just as significant, the battles included here had more immediate effects on the final result of the war. This means many bad decisions on both sides—decisions that often lost thousands of lives—were not included. Hundreds of lost opportunities and what-if scenarios, prime examples being the botched attempts to assassinate Hitler, are not included. Each blunder in this book is in itself a significant and complicated event. If you find yourself interested in reading more about one there are entire books, occasionally libraries' worth, on each mistake and battle. Many of these are firsthand accounts that can shed light into the thinking, or lack of it, that went into the decisions discussed here.

In 1941 the Axis controlled virtually all of continental Europe and in it an immense amount of manufacturing production and resources. The German army had easily overcome all opposition and its scientists had successfully developed both guided missiles and jets. Any leader, or even interested citizen, most certainly did not see the defeat of the Axis as inevitable or even likely. Yet a few years, and millions of casualties, later Adolf Hitler committed suicide as the Red Army approached his Berlin bunker. There is a military axiom that is really the basis for this book: In war, the side that makes the least mistakes wins.

Bill Fawcett
2010

HOW THE WESTERN POWERS PAVED HITLER'S ROAD TO WAR

Europe, 1936–1939

BY DOUGLAS NILES

> *All that is necessary for the triumph of evil is that good men do nothing.*
>
> —Edmund Burke

Nothing can assuage the guilt of Adolf Hitler, the Nazi Party, and the millions of Germans who supported both for their role in history's march toward the massive calamity of World War II. Hitler's aggressiveness and his appeals to national pride were certainly part of the political rise that carried him to office when, at least nominally, Germany was still a democracy—albeit a dying one. His appeals to fear, his scapegoating of non-Aryan peoples (most notably the Jews), and his sneering taunts against his political foes all found willing ears. Crippled by the massively punitive Treaty of Versailles that had ended World War I, the German economy virtually moribund because of catastrophic inflation augmented by the worldwide Great Depression, many citizens of Germany embraced a vocal champion in the proud, nationalistic Hitler.

The Nazi leader's aims and intended methods were not a secret. As early as the 1920s he had laid out the key concept in his book, *Mein Kampf*: Germany needed room to grow in population and strength, room to farm and produce, room to mine and to harvest, for a vibrant nation with a mighty destiny. This space, called lebensraum, would have to come from other countries, countries that, most likely, lay to the east of Germany. He made the case that they were occupied by peoples of less-deserving ancestry—indeed, such ancestry as to render them as somewhat subhuman when compared to the pure Aryan stock of the Teutonic ideal (of which stock, ironically enough, the Austrian Hitler was most definitely *not*).

Hitler ascended to the chancellorship by election, in the fading days of the German republic. By the mid–1930s the state had been converted into a Nazi dictatorship while the rest of Europe watched nervously. On March 16, 1935, Hitler publicly renounced the disarmament requirements of the Versailles treaty, declaring that his nation had as much of a right to its own military defense as any other country. The rest of the world, struggling through its own economic morass, took note but did nothing. A year later, in March 1936, Hitler put his words into action when he ordered troops of the budding Wehrmacht to reoccupy the Rhineland— German territory adjacent to France that, under terms of the Versailles treaty, were to remain demilitarized.

France merely watched, with leaders such as Pierre Laval and Edouard Daladier voicing only a weak protest. The German general staff, a professional group of senior officers, all of them veterans of World War I, actually objected to the reoccupation far more strenuously than did any foreign country. There is evidence to suggest that German military commanders such as Colonel General Baron von Fritsch and General Werner von Blomberg would have been willing to overthrow the Nazi regime if any other European power—France being the most obvious based on proximity and military strength—had indicated any willingness to go to war over this issue.

Such willingness was nowhere to be found. At this point, Germany had only begun the process of rearmament. It had no air force or mechanized ground forces to speak of, and even the infantry was understrength, comprised of units formed mainly of veteran survivors of World War I. France, in contrast, was in a strong position, with a large army and vastly superior strength in artillery—but not superior, alas, in military spirit and daring.

There is no question that French timidity did a great deal to embolden Hitler and to cause his generals to question their own assertions even as they feared that the Nazi dictator was leading them to calamity. One Wehrmacht high commander would later characterize the military's objections as "straws in the wind" compared to the strength of Hitler's will.

With each subsequent success, the führer would become more convinced of his own infallibility and more aggressive in his behaviors, ambitions, and plans. The population of his country, seething with resentment after two decades of punishment for the "War to End All Wars," increasingly united behind Hitler's explanations. These racist and xenophobic appeals were artfully articulated by Joseph Goebbels, the Nazi minister of propaganda, and repeatedly pounded home the simplistic lies that the Jewish people were to blame for most of Germany's problems and foreigners bore the fault of the rest.

Hitler's international presence grew in stature in October 1936,

when he signed a treaty with his fellow dictator, Benito Mussolini. The Rome-Berlin Axis established a solid barrier of fascism
across the middle of Europe, from the Mediterranean Sea to the
borders of Scandinavia. Mussolini's ambitions were already directed to the south, where he coveted parts of North and East
Africa, and the east toward Albania and, eventually, Greece. With
his determination to forge a new Roman Empire, he was a perfect
partner in crime to Hitler's megalomaniacal ambitions toward
the rest of the Europe.

It was a little more than a year later that Hitler crystallized
those goals on paper, informing his closest advisers in a secret
meeting on November 5, 1937, exactly what his idea of lebensraum entailed. He would begin by reclaiming Germany's "ancestral" territories—that is, those lands around the borders of
the Fatherland that were populated with significant numbers of
people of German ancestry. (If he made note that these territories also contained significant numbers of non-Germans, that
note is lost to history.) These border regions included Austria, the
Sudetenland portion of Czechoslovakia, and enough of Poland
to reestablish a connection between Germany proper and East
Prussia—meaning the elimination of the "Polish Corridor."

After that, his ambitions included vast regions to the east,
most notably the fertile grain-growing steppes of the Ukraine
and other parts of the USSR, as well as valuable oil fields in Romania and, possibly, farther to the east. He expected France and
England to stand on the sidelines during these adventures, and he
anticipated a continued flow of valuable resources—most notably
iron ore, but also including timber—from a neutral Sweden.

Most of the generals who were privy to these plans were, privately, aghast, convinced that Hitler was leading the nation to a
ruinous repeat of World War I. Once again the idea of a military

revolt simmered just below the surface, but fear—Hitler's favorite stepchild—prevented any decisive action. Even as Europe held its breath, waiting to see what would happen next, the führer tightened his grip on the Fatherland, and the Nazi Party, through propaganda and the terrorizing reach of the Gestapo, instilling even greater fear and obedience throughout the German population.

In March 1938, Germany claimed Austria—aided by numerous Austrians who saw the Third Reich as a route to the return of Hapsburg glory—as its territory in a bloodless coup known as the Anschluss. When not even the Austrians visibly opposed this takeover, there wasn't much the rest of the continent could do about it. With its strategic position in the Alps, south of Germany and north of Italy, the addition of Austria firmly cemented the hold of the Axis throughout the center of Europe.

In fact, it seems that the nations of western Europe were not all that dismayed by Hitler's ambitions, as long as they felt that his goals lay to the east. Both France and England considered Stalin's USSR as a major threat to the democratic and capitalistic way of life—not unreasonably, as history was to illustrate. But they erred in thinking that Germany could be a useful buffer against the danger of Soviet expansionism. In the late 1930s, a lone voice warning about the Nazi menace was the British foreign minister, Anthony Eden. He repeatedly disagreed with Prime Minister Neville Chamberlain's stance of appeasement, so much so that at one point the prime minister told him to "go home and take an aspirin."

In February 1938, Eden resigned, to be replaced by Lord Halifax. Halifax wasted no time in traveling to Germany to assure the Nazis that England would take a very practical view of matters. The clear impression given to Hitler was that, so long as his ambitions were directed eastward, Great Britain would have no strong objection. This inept and indirect communication has to be regarded as one of the greatest mistakes made by any diplomat in the years leading up to World War II. (A little more than a year later, the Chamberlain government would reverse itself, but by that time it was too late.)

By the end of the summer of 1938, Hitler was publicly demanding the return of the Sudetenland to Germany. This territory had been a part of the nation of Czechoslovakia since that country's borders had been drawn at the end of World War I. Possessed of a large, relatively modern army and stern political will that was unusual during these latter years of 1930s Europe, Czechoslovakians were willing to fight to hold on to lands that they believed were rightly theirs.

At last, the leaders of western Europe were stirred from their slumber to at least voice opposition to one of Hitler's ambitious claims. An international conference was arranged in September 1938, to be held in Munich, Germany. Hitler would meet personally with Chamberlain, as well as Prime Minister Daladier of France, the leaders of Poland, and a few other interested parties. Notably shunted aside was the Soviet Union.

Despite Czechoslovakia's willingness to resist, the French and British agreed to Hitler's demands regarding Sudetenland. Even Poland, in a remarkably shortsighted bit of diplomacy, made no protest—its interests were assuaged slightly, and very temporarily, with a German agreement to give Poland a small bit of the territory that was taken from Czechoslovakia. In return for Western acquiescence, Hitler promised that the occupation of the Sudetenland would be the last of his territorial ambitions. Everyone was eager to believe him.

Neville Chamberlain returned home to memorably boast that his agreement had won "peace for our time." Apparently he believed his own press for, despite the agitation of other British leaders, including the pugnacious Winston Churchill—a rival leader in Chamberlain's own Conservative Party who urged that England began immediately arming for war—Chamberlain declined to take any immediate steps to upgrade his understrength military. In particular, the Royal Air Force—which could have greatly benefited from a rearmament program starting in fall of 1938—was left to languish under a peacetime budget and strategy for several crucial months.

As late as March 10, 1939, Chamberlain was privately expressing his confidence in the prospects for peace. Ironically enough, that was the day the Germans—less than a half a year after the Munich conference—put the lie to Hitler's pledge. Moving swiftly, the Germans gobbled up the rest of the Czech lands, including Bohemia and Moravia. Slovakia, the eastern half of the country, was left for the time being as a quasi-independent German ally.

By March 16, the deed was done, another virtually bloodless conquest for Nazi Germany. On April 1, Chamberlain publicly reversed his policy of appeasement, belatedly ordering the mobilization of British forces in anticipation of war. France did the same.

But it was already too late.

BETWEEN A HARD PLACE AND ANOTHER EVEN HARDER PLACE

Poland, September 1939

BY DOUGLAS NILES

When it comes to disadvantages, there is the win-lose situation, the lose-lose situation, and then Poland in 1939, which might best be analyzed as being in a lose-lose-*lose* situation. With its geographical position exactly between Nazi Germany and Soviet Russia, its resources coveted by both, and its physical attributes— borders, mountains, coasts, rivers, and so forth—almost diabolically placed to aid an attacker and deny their use in defense, Poland had virtually no chance of standing against an onslaught from either the west or the east.

As it happened, it was attacked from both directions—first by the Germans and sixteen days later by the Soviets—and it collapsed at the end of one month of battle. The Polish army, while manned with valiant men and dedicated officers, was outmaneuvered by speedier, mechanized attackers. The Polish air force numbered some two hundred planes and was mostly destroyed on the ground during the opening hours of the war. The speed of the conquest, and the complete defeat of all aspects of Polish arms, have led to the common conclusion that nothing Poland did would have had any impact on the course of the campaign.

This is not entirely true.

Admittedly, the great bulk of Poland's disadvantages in this short, brutal campaign cannot be categorized as mistakes so much as inherent and unsolvable problems of the historical circumstances. In the context of the situation in 1939, there was little way to neutralize several intrinsic disadvantages of the Polish military situation.

These problems began with the very layout of the national borders. These had been established at the conclusion of World War I. Most significant to this campaign was the creation of the Polish Corridor. This was a stretch of land that had been German territory until the end of the war. Created by the Treaty of Versailles, the Polish Corridor gave Poland access to a port on the Baltic Sea, Danzig, by slicing off the part of Germany known as East Prussia from the rest of the country. This stinging territorial punishment was a gouging thorn in the side of German pride throughout the intervening years, and one of the main examples listed by Adolf Hitler of the unjust manner in which his countrymen had been treated by the victorious Allies in 1918.

In practical military terms, however, the existence of East Prussia meant that German armies could attack Poland from the north as well as the west, where the bulk of Germany proper lay. Furthermore, Hitler's incursions into Czechoslovakia, accomplished by the early part of 1939, meant that much of Poland's southern border was now also adjacent, and accessible to, German arms. In essence, the whole of western Poland was now a salient, threatened by the Nazis on three sides.

Yet the Poles, prideful and stiff-necked to the last, were undeterred. The Polish foreign minister, Colonel Józef Beck, refused to consider any negotiations with the Germans that would have eased the thorny issue of the Polish Corridor. At the same time, the commander in chief of the Polish army, Marshal Edward Smigly-Rydz, displayed a vast confidence in the capability of his forces to defend their homeland. This sanguine view of the situation drew its foundation from several facts. First, the Polish army had performed very well in a short, violent war against the Soviets from 1919–1921, driving the aggressive communist armies back as far as Minsk. Poland had a long tradition of military valor, and this most recent campaign encouraged the view that its substantial armies were as capable as any in Europe. Second, the British and French had guaranteed Polish sovereignty after Hitler's occupation of Czechoslovakia. They made this promise because they thought it would *prevent* war, but when the Hitler attacked anyway there was literally no way, physically, for these western European nations to come to the aid of a Poland in eastern Europe, at least not during a war that would only last a few weeks.

Finally, and most significantly, however, the Polish high command had utterly failed to anticipate the changes to tactics and strategy brought about by the technological developments of the twentieth century—or, indeed, in the latter part of the nineteenth century. As far back as the American Civil War (1861–1865), the effectiveness of massed infantry fire had proved to be a complete deterrent to the massed cavalry charge that had been a hallmark of the great wars of Europe up to, and including, the campaigns of Napoléon. Despite the invention and proliferation of the machine gun, all of the major armies of Europe had maintained horse cavalry forces during World War I, vainly hoping for that one crucial breakthrough that would allow a light, mobile force to sweep around the enemy's rear to secure victory.

While the other nations that had been so bruised by the Great War had finally cast aside their cavalry formations in favor of more infantry and, slowly but surely, a gradual increase in motorized and mechanized divisions, the Poles had clung gallantly to their belief that massive, splendidly trained, highly courageous forces of horse-mounted soldiers would once again prove invaluable during war. This belief would show its utter fallacy in September 1939.

Yet it was not just in its reliance on the horse that the Polish military high command displayed a failure to grasp the nature of modern warfare. Though the Poles did in fact possess a moderately respectable air force, and they had a very large army by the standards of the 1930s, they neglected to mechanize any part of that army. Furthermore, the offensive-minded Polish generals refused to authorize the construction of defensive works, intending instead to go on the attack if the country was invaded. There were even boasts of a cavalry charge that would sweep all the way to Berlin!

Nor did the Poles see antiaircraft guns, or any kind of antitank weaponry, as worthy investments during the prewar period. The soldiers of their large army were armed mainly with single-shot carbine rifles and old-fashioned artillery that relied upon horses to transport the guns. Large troop movements were to occur by railroad.

There is a common belief that the German army at the outbreak of World War II was a highly mechanized formation outfitted with lots of heavily armored, cannon-equipped tanks. Winston Churchill himself, in his memoirs on the Polish campaign, suggested that Germany utilized more than a thousand "heavy tanks." Yet the fact is that the German high command was ill prepared for the war in Poland, and that it only committed to the invasion at the insistence of its führer. At the outbreak of war, Germany only had six panzer (armored) divisions, and about an equal number of motorized or mechanized infantry divisions. Of the sixty German divisions that participated in the invasion, these twelve accomplished far more than all the rest of the German army combined. And they were not equipped with anything resembling the tanks that came to prominence later in the war. The German tanks were indeed tracked vehicles, which gave them great mobility, and they were armored enough to protect their crews from machine-gun fire, but they were not armed with powerful cannons—indeed, most of them boasted only a machine gun in the turret, and none possessed a gun that could have knocked out an enemy tank. Of course, in this campaign, there were no enemy tanks to be found.

The fatal flaw inherent in the construction of the Polish army was further exacerbated by the initial deployments made by Smigly-Rydz when it became clear that war was on the horizon. Faced with the political necessity of defending his entire country, instead of just the industrialized heartland—which was at least partially screened by several major river lines—the Polish high command dispersed its army widely, with most of it concentrated along the borders, and fully a third of it in the vicinity of the Polish Corridor, where it was subject to attack from the east and the west.

The Polish commanders based their plan on reacting to the German attack, and moving their divisions—by rail, if necessary—into position to block the enemy advances and to vigorously and aggressively counterattack.

The German attack, and the true outbreak of World War II, began before dawn on September 1, 1939. Following the deception of a propaganda mission, in which the Nazis claimed that the Poles had crossed the border and initiated the war, the Luftwaffe began a series of vigorous attacks. Their first targets were the aircraft and air bases of the Polish air force, which was virtually obliterated during the first three days of the war. Even before this victory was attained, German aircraft were bombing rail and other transportation centers, completely paralyzing the ability of the Polish army to move anywhere except on foot.

France and Britain, who had boldly declared their support for Poland against Nazi Germany, were utterly unable to intervene in the campaign. The French, of course, were positioned strategically on Germany's western frontier, but they showed a complete lack of resolve in coming to their erstwhile ally's defense via any kind of diversionary attack. In fact, the French mobilization proceeded so slowly that Poland would be conquered long before most French soldiers even reported to their units. The Poles were on their own.

Within a matter of days, those few German armored divisions sliced cleanly through the Polish infantry. Vast pockets of surrounded armies were left with no mission, not even the capability of fighting their way out of the encirclement. Compressed by the slow, if relentless, pressure of the plodding German infantry, the surrounded Poles could only hold out for a few days, or a few weeks, and then surrender.

By the time Stalin's Red Army attacked eastern Poland on September 17, the issue was already decided. The Poles—valiant and courageous until the end—fought for the rest of the month and watched as their beautiful and historic capital, Warsaw, was cruelly bombed. The last resistance by an organized military formation (a force of less than twenty thousand men) ceased by October 5. Poland was divided by Germany and the USSR, and the rest of the world would dither and delay for the next six months while Adolf Hitler decided what to do next.

THE SILENT CATASTROPHE OF THE SITZKRIEG

October 1939–April 1940

BY DOUGLAS NILES

Watching and waiting seemed to be the new strategy. There were many reasons for why the French and British were unprepared for, and unwilling to wage, a war that neither nation sought or wanted. However, once Germany invaded Poland and the Western powers declared war on Germany, that war was a reality. (In fact, Hitler was profoundly shaken when these declarations were issued—after calling the Allied bluffs over Czechoslovakia, he had really not expected them to seriously come to war in Poland's defense.)

Yet Poland fell by early October 1939, and from that point until Germany embarked on its sudden campaign against Norway and Denmark in April 1940, there was virtually no land combat fought between the Western Allies and their Nazi enemies. Why, then, did France and England take such few, hesitant, and feeble steps to prepare for and to wage the war?

The scars of World War I, which had ended only two decades earlier, were still fresh across the entire continent of Europe. In

Germany's case, it had lost that war, and those scars had been exploited by a new breed of rulers to build within a sizable portion if the citizenry a thirst for revenge. This was not the case in the Great War's most prominent victors, France and England. Like Germany, those nations had lost the bulk of an entire generation of young men in the trenches of France and Belgium, and despite their victory, the people did not see that they had gained much in the waging of that massive struggle. Consequently, they were appalled at the prospect of another war in Europe, and this resulted in an almost universal unwillingness to accept the reality. There was neither necessary political nor military will to take the offensive.

Indeed, one of the primary lessons of World War I had been the primacy of defense, as the system of trenches, defended by barbed wire, machine guns, and thousands of pieces of artillery, had proven almost impossible to breach. While casualties in every battle had been tremendous on both sides, the attacker always bore the greatest brunt of the losses. This lesson had sunk in so deeply that the Western nations, as the next war began, decided to rely on their defensive positions and to force the Germans into a costly—and hopefully futile—attack. Though the Polish campaign would seem to have indicated that this was a new era, neither of the leaders of the Western powers was ready to absorb that lesson. (There were a few younger officers, such as Charles de Gaulle in France and Basil Henry Liddell Hart in England, who loudly advocated for the primacy of the armored forces, but they were essentially ignored by their superiors.)

The French placed a great deal of trust in the Maginot Line, a tremendously expensive and extensive network of fixed fortifications that began at France's border with Switzerland and continued about halfway to the watery flank of the English Channel.

Every mile of the common border between Germany and France was protected by this mighty bastion, which included countless pillboxes and vast coils of barbed wire. About every five miles along the line the French built a massive fortress, capable of withstanding attack from all sides, stocked with provisions and ammunition enough to support a garrison for many weeks, if it should be cut off from supply.

However, the rest of France's northeastern border faced not Germany, but Belgium, and it was felt that the erection of a permanent fortress along the frontier of a neutral, and essentially friendly, state would have been too provocative. Thus, the French-Belgian border was defended by a line of field armies. Even so, this was not inherently disastrous; for one thing France possessed was a very large army. Some fourteen divisions were posted in the fortifications of the Maginot Line by January 1940, while eighty-eight more divisions were available for mobile operations.

The English contribution to this great defensive effort was the British Expeditionary Force (BEF) under the command of General Lord Gort. Four divisions crossed the Channel in October 1939, and by the next May the number had been increased to nine. The combined forces of France and England had more than three thousand tanks and some two thousand aircraft ready to face the German onslaught. In addition, the French, in particular, were very well equipped with heavy artillery.

However, neither nation seemed willing to accept any of the lessons that the Germans had learned, and displayed for the rest of the world, in their swift conquest of Poland. While some of the British tanks were gathered in an armored brigade, the rest were scattered thinly throughout the infantry divisions, where they were regarded as something like mobile pillboxes. The French had more tanks than the Germans, including many that were more heavily armed and armored—though slower moving—than the enemy's. However, they still viewed the tank as an infantry support vehicle, whereas the Germans had begun to concentrate their tanks in armored divisions. (The French were in the process of forming a single armored division under the command of General de Gaulle as the war began.)

The same lack of foresight applied to the use of the air forces. While both the French and British possessed some modern fighters—the Supermarine Spitfire was every bit the equal of Germany's premier fighter, the Messerschmitt Bf–109—and each country had a respectable force of fast, long-range bombers, neither nation spent much time trying to coordinate its air units with its ground operations. Germany, meanwhile, had made good use of this tactical cooperation in Poland, and used the lessons of that campaign to further refine its operations. Luftwaffe officers and radiomen traveled with army headquarters units, and were able to request air strikes against specific positions during the course of a battle, while neither France nor England had anything approaching this level of coordination between the two arms.

The greatest natural barrier between Germany and its western targets was the Rhine River. Though the Germans had nothing like the Maginot Line on their side of the river, the water barrier itself was a powerful deterrent to any French attempt to attack Germany along the southern flank. However, the border runs away from the Rhine north of the city of Strasbourg, and this salient—the Rhineland—was very lightly garrisoned by German armies, especially during the Polish campaign. A French advance into the Rhineland could, in all probability, have pushed the Germans back to the river, and across it, but no such offensive was seriously contemplated by the French.

A further complication of the defensive position, strategically speaking, was the position of the Low Countries (the Netherlands, Belgium, Luxembourg) between France and Germany, and west of the Rhine. These small countries were resolutely neutral, refusing even to plan for combined operations with France and England, for fear of antagonizing Germany. The Western powers were understandably reluctant to violate that neutrality by moving into these countries, but there is no denying that they could have done so, and if they had they would have been able to form a defensive position along the Rhine extending all the way from Switzerland to the North Sea.

As it was, they were left to utilize a series of much smaller rivers, most notably the Meuse, upon which to base their defense. It should be noted that Belgium was protected by a rather extensive series of fixed fortifications, much of it based along the Meuse and the Albert Canal, and anchored by a huge, modern fortress known as Eben Emael. This mighty emplacement was designed to be defended against attack from east, west, north, and south—though not, unhappily as it turned out, from above. Southern Belgium and all of Luxembourg were further protected by a rugged range of rocky hills and narrow valleys, all heavily forested, called the Ardennes. The roads through the forest were narrow, twisty, and steep, and it was taken as a matter of faith that the region would be virtually impassable to a mobile army. The much flatter terrain of northern Belgium and Holland, it seemed, would surely provide the main route for the German attack.

So the Western Allies formed a strategy to meet this anticipated German attack, which they assumed would be based very much on the infamous Schlieffen Plan that the Kaiser's forces had used to such good effect in the early months of World War I—before the static lines of trenches had scored the continent from

Switzerland to the sea. The French commander in chief, General Maurice Gamelin, proposed an operation called Plan D. The key element of this plan was that the French and British forces in northern France would advance into the Low Countries as soon as Germany attacked, creating a shorter and straighter left flank to be supported by the Maginot Line in the south.

And, indeed, a repeat of the previous war's strategy was exactly what the Germans planned. Their operation was code-named Fall Gelb ("Plan Yellow") and it was a virtual repeat of the Schlieffen Plan. It called for the great bulk of the German army to advance through the Netherlands and Belgium, sweep into northern France, drive southward through Paris, and finally wheel around to take the Maginot Line from behind. The assumption was that the presence of armored spearheads would let the advance progress so quickly that the Allies would be unable to dig trenches and create a bloody stalemate such as had existed during much of World War I.

In the years and months leading up to the war, and during its opening campaign, Adolf Hitler's ambitious audacity had served him well, even as the most powerful generals of the German high command—notably Walther von Brauchitsch, commander in chief of the army, and Franz Halder, chief of the general staff— had resisted his plans and counseled caution on every step of the way. Buoyed by his unbroken string of successes, Hitler was determined to continue his breakneck pace, and insisted that the attack against France begin in November 1939. Once again, his generals pleaded that they needed more time, and the führer met these objections with ranting temper tantrums and accusations of cowardice.

However, this time the generals were right. Though they could not convince Hitler of this, the weather intervened, with rain, snow, and muddy conditions forcing a delay of the offensive through December and into January 1940. This delay turned out to be very fortunate for Hitler and very disastrous for the Western Allies. On January 10, Hitler ordered that the offensive against the West begin on January 17, but on the same day he issued that order, an event occurred that, while it seemed fortunate for the Allies and not so for the Germans, all but sealed the fate of the campaign even as it forced its postponement for several more months.

On January 10, a major working on the staff of General Kurt Student, who commanded all of the German airborne (paratroop and air-mobile) forces, was flying from Münster to Bonn for a routine meeting to discuss the upcoming operation. The details of the meeting itself were relatively trivial, but the major was carrying a folder containing the complete, detailed version of Fall Gelb. His plane encountered bad weather and strong winds, and he was blown off course and forced down in Belgium. He was unable to burn his papers before the Belgians picked him up, dusted him off, and politely returned him—and his papers—to German authorities.

However, the Germans suspected that their plan had been reviewed by the Belgians, as in fact it had. Following a long phone conversation between King Leopold III of Belgium and the Queen of Holland, the Belgians passed their intelligence bonanza on to the French and English—who took no action in response to the information. In Berlin, and contrary to his usual temperament, Hitler reacted to the news with certain equanimity. He supported the idea that the plan had likely been compromised, and so it should be changed. But to what?

Plan Yellow had called for the main attack, in the north, to be made by Field Marshal Fedor von Bock's Army Group B. Von

Bock's force was to include most of the armored divisions, while to the south Army Group A, under General Gerd von Rundstedt, would play a supporting role on the flank. Von Rundstedt's chief of staff was an able and visionary younger general, Erich von Manstein, and von Manstein had a revolutionary idea. He had already presented it to Halder and von Brauchitsch, who had nixed it, but von Manstein wasn't ready to give up. With von Rundstedt's support, he described it to Hitler—and it was just the kind of audacious, daring idea that could stir up the führer's interest.

Von Manstein proposed a new variant of Plan Yellow, called Sichelschnitt ("cut of the scythe"). He suggested that the bulk of the panzer divisions be transferred to von Rundstedt and Army Group A. Von Bock's Army Group B would advance into the Low Countries on the northern flank, triggering the advance of the French and the BEF in Holland and Belgium. In the meantime, the tank columns would make their way through the Ardennes, which would presumably be lightly defended, and slice right through the heart of the Allied line. The scythe would then slice north all the way to the English Channel, resulting in the encirclement and destruction of perhaps half of the enemy's army. (Von Manstein consulted Colonel General Heinz Guderian, one of the early masters of tank warfare, for advice on whether or not the panzers could pass through the rugged Ardennes, and Guderian—who would be commanding an armored corps in the assault—was certain that they could.)

As a result, Hitler authorized a delay in the offensive, until May 10 as it turned out. He was worried about the morale of his men because of this long delay, but in the end it was the morale of the French that suffered most drastically. As the months passed, the French made no significant modifications to their plans, simply waiting with a fatalistic sense of resignation for the campaign that the enemy would eventually commence.

After the fall of France that summer, the Germans went over plans captured from the French high command, and discovered that the Western Allies had been brainstorming about many wild schemes, ranging from an invasion of Scandinavia to threaten Germany's northern flank, to a raid against the Soviet oil fields in the Caucasus—the source of the bulk of the enemy's fuel—to a strike through Greece against Germany's southern border. None of these plans had even the remotest hope of being successful, and it is a testament to the Western Allies' unwillingness at this point in the war to face the reality of their situation that they even considered them at all.

BLITZKRIEG IN THE NORTH

Scandinavia, April–June 1940

BY DOUGLAS NILES

Even before making his move against his most powerful neighbor, France, Adolf Hitler was aware of a key vulnerability to his economy and his defensive position, and—together with the advice of some of his more visionary planners—he devised a way to turn a theater of weakness into the northern flank of what would become his continent-wide bastion, Fortress Europa.

The countries of Scandinavia, including Denmark, Norway, and Sweden, remained uneasy observers of the developing strife on the mainland to their south. Although Denmark had been a part of the Kaiser's Germany during World War I, the Danes were a proud people who retained their own king and, following the conclusion of the Great War, had taken a progressive path that diverged further and further from the route taken by their fascist neighbors to the south.

Sweden was adamantly neutral and had a large, well-trained army. However, it was also the primary source of the iron ore upon which nearly all of Germany's industrial activity depended. About half of this vital resource was shipped from Swedish ports, over a short crossing of the Baltic Sea, to be unloaded in German ports. The other half of German-bound iron ore pulled from Swedish mines traveled by rail to the northern Norwegian port of Narvik. In this remote settlement, which despite its Arctic environment was able to keep its port open all year round, the ore was loaded aboard freighters and shipped south, following a long, exposed route along the Norwegian coast until it made its way to German ports on the North and Baltic seas. This required a voyage of more than a thousand miles, and the merchant ships were tremendously exposed to interdiction by British naval and air units, but because they stayed in Norwegian territorial waters, any attack on them would have violated Norway's neutrality and been considered an act of war.

Still, British interest in a Norwegian campaign began as early as December 1939, after the USSR attacked Finland on November 30 in what became known as the Winter War. Britain was eager to send aid to the Finns, but Norway's determined neutrality prevented the mission from landing. The intended port of debarkation for these troops was Narvik. France also supported the idea of a campaign in Norway, primarily because Norway was a long way from France. None of the early schemes got off the ground, but the British Admiralty (the command staff of the Royal Navy) kept a wary eye on the nation's neighbor across the North Sea. The steady stream of iron ore haulers steaming southward through Norwegian waters until they could cross to German ports was a particularly thorny burr under the British saddle.

In February 1940, a German supply ship, the *Altmark*, attempted to return to Germany by sailing far to the north of Great Britain, then slipping down the Norwegian coast to its home country. The *Altmark* had been in the South Atlantic, where it provided ammunition and other supplies to the Nazi pocket battleship *Graf Spee* and other warships that had been busily raiding Allied nautical commerce. Although it had dispensed most of its supplies, the *Altmark* carried a number of British seamen as prisoners of war (POWs). When its presence was discovered, the Admiralty determined to try to free those captive sailors. A destroyer, HMS *Cossack*, chased the *Altmark* into a fjord near Stavanger, on the southwest coast of Norway.

Norway protested the violation of its neutrality by the British, but when the crew of the *Cossack* boarded the *Altmark* and rescued 299 British seamen, the Norwegian objections rang hollow, since there was now clear proof that the country had allowed an armed enemy ship to seek refuge in Norwegian waters. Relations between Norway and Britain grew increasingly testy, and in early April the Admiralty decided to send a task force to the waters off of Narvik, where it would lay mines to deter the shipping of ore south to Germany. This, of course, would be regarded as an act of war by Norway under international law, but the British were ready to take that drastic step.

Though the British had gathered a small landing force in its eastern ports in preparation for the earlier land intervention, the soldiers were left at home as a force of destroyers and minelayers, escorted by larger ships—including the battleships HMS *Warspite* and *Renown*, and the aircraft carrier HMS *Glorious*—steamed toward Norwegian waters. In one of the bizarre coincidences of military history, the Germans, who had decided to invade Denmark and Norway to secure their northern flank, launched their invasion with an intended landing date one day after the British minelaying fleet moved into Norwegian waters. Thus the British ships, which had no troops aboard, would find themselves in a firefight with determined Kriegsmarine (German navy) destroyers, cruisers, and battlecruisers, all tasked with protecting the transports carrying the landing parties.

As usual, once Hitler had made a decision and the plans had been drawn up, the Germans wasted little time. At the very outbreak of the campaign, the Nazis moved quickly and decisively against their small neighbor on the Jutland Peninsula. Unfortunately, Denmark had a mere shell of an army and an easy land connection in proximity to Germany that made the tiny, peninsular country an almost certain victim of Nazi aggression—if for no other reason than that it was in the way of Hitler's more grandiose ambitions.

Even so, the Germans used a little subterfuge to aid their conquest. Three merchant ships sailed into Copenhagen harbor and berthed at the docks, quickly disgorging a battalion of infantry that marched through the streets of the Danish capital and took the military barracks without a shot being fired. Other German units crossed the border and quickly overcame the brief resistance of the defending army. By the end of the first day of the campaign, Luftwaffe units were moving to airfields in northern Denmark, which would put short-ranged fighter planes within range of Oslo and Stavanger, the main invasion targets in southern Norway.

Norway itself was not without resources. The Norwegian army consisted of 12,900 trained regulars, organized into six infantry brigades that would quickly be augmented by 120,000 reserves. Furthermore, it had a small air force, a navy that included a number of destroyers, and numerous militia cadres and local defense forces that could be mustered in an emergency.

To face this force, and any Allied reinforcements that might arrive, the Germans dispatched pretty much the whole of the Kriegsmarine, including the two fast, powerfully armed battle cruisers *Gneisnau* and *Scharnhorst*, several heavy and light cruisers, and a number of fast, modern destroyers. In addition, twenty-four U-boats were assigned to support the operation. Eight divisions of infantry, including several battalions of paratroops, and five hundred aircraft would also take part in the campaign. As usual, the Germans would strike suddenly and with the element of surprise.

In the foggy waters off of Norway, the two fleets, attempting two different missions, ran into each other and started shooting. The first firefights were confused affairs. The German heavy cruiser *Hipper* sank the destroyer HMS *Glowworm* off the coast of Trondheim, in central Norway, almost before the British knew what was happening. The Germans had the advantage of continuing with their assigned mission, and their ships plowed on to their assigned targets. The British, on the other hand, were forced to change the mission from minelaying to fighting surface battle over the course of a matter of hours.

And indeed, the Admiralty was stunned by the audacity of the German move. British command of the seas had for so long been taken as a matter of unchallenged fact that they found it almost inconceivable that Hitler would take such a risk. The First Lord of the Admiralty was no less than Winston Churchill (he would not become prime minister for another two months), and in an address to the House of Commons he declared, "Herr Hitler has committed a grave strategic error." On the face of it, it seemed that the Royal Navy should have been able to smash up the Kriegsmarine and strand the landing forces without supply or reinforcement.

Several things would prevent that from happening. Certainly the weather, which was foggy and rainy, hampered the attempts of one fleet to find the other. (Though the British had radar, that new technology was still in its infancy in early 1940.) But the primary difficulty seemed to be that German audacity and daring consistently outmaneuvered the British plodding, conservative, and confused response. This was a campaign the Royal Navy should have won, but it made so many mistakes that it did not. Prominent among them was a sudden timidity to expose British ships to enemy air attack. Though the Admiralty, during the pre-war years, had sniffed disdainfully at the notion that airpower could ever supersede the might of fast, heavily armed battleships, now that push came to shove, it became very cautious.

The initial German objectives were the main ports of Norway, which included all of the major cities. These began with Oslo, the capital, but included the other southern ports of Kristiansand, Bergen, and Stavanger, as well as the centrally located Trond-heim. Most daring of all was a mission to land nearly two thou-sand troops at Narvik, more than a thousand miles away from the German ports of embarkation. (This landing was so audacious that, when the Admiralty received intelligence about the mission, it assumed that it were seeing a spelling error—surely its sources were telling them about an attack on Larvik, a city near Oslo!)

The attacks occurred on April 9, 1940. Despite their complete surprise, not everything went smoothly for the Germans. The harbor at Oslo was protected by several large shore batteries, and the Norwegian gunfire and shore-launched torpedoes were enough to sink the German heavy cruiser *Blucher* and drive the transport fleet away from the landing zones. However, a force of *fallschirmjäger* (German paratroops) landed at Oslo airport and, after a stiff battle, overcame the antiaircraft unit assigned to pro-tect the crucial objective. Junkers Ju—52 transports immediately began to fly in more troops, landing them on the newly captured runways, and as the force built up, it began to move south, ap-proaching the capital city overland. Meanwhile, the naval land-ing forces that had been driven away from the harbor put their troops ashore outside of the city, and these closed in to make a pincer attack in combination with the airlanded troops. By the second day of the campaign, the Norwegian capital was in German hands.

The attacks at Kristiansand and Bergen came from the sea, and both landings were hotly contested by the Norwegian army. At Kristiansand, the cruiser *Karlsruhe* was damaged by shore batteries and subsequently sunk by British bombers. On April 10, the cruiser *Konigsberg* was sunk by the Royal Air Force off the coast at Bergen. Despite suffering heavy casualties against stiff Norwegian opposition in the attacks, the Germans fought their way ashore and managed to secure both ports. At the same time the key city of Stavanger, between the other two, was captured in a daring paratroop attack. With these quick, violent strikes, nearly all of Norway's southern coast fell into German hands.

Infantry units moved out from the ports to secure the inland territories, and gradually advance northward with the relief of the landing forces at Trondheim and, eventually, Narvik as their objective. Air units of the Luftwaffe wasted no time in setting up forward airbases on captured airfields, and these allowed the Germans to maintain consistent air superiority during the ongoing battles.

Trondheim, too, was captured on the first day of the campaign by naval forces screened by the heavy cruiser *Hipper*. For the time being, these forces were isolated from the other ports seized by the Germans, but they held an airfield that was quickly turned into a Luftwaffe base, and were prepared to hold out until relief could arrive.

The most dramatic encounters occurred at the city in the far north that was, in so many ways, the key objective of the whole campaign. If the Germans could not capture and hold Narvik, they would lose the port where so much of their iron ore was loaded aboard ship. Situated as it was some four hundred miles north of Trondheim, Narvik in Allied hands would very well negate the whole reason for invading Norway in the first place.

Narvik was the intended target of a naval force of ten destroyers, called Group I. The flagship was *Wilhelm Heidkamp*, and the force was under the command of Commodore Friedrich Bonte. Each destroyer carried nearly two hundred Austrian mountain troops (*gebirgsjäger*), with a total landing force of nineteen hundred men. Two Norwegian coastal defense frigates intercepted the German fleet as it approached the fjord leading to Narvik, but these were quickly destroyed. The troops were put ashore on April 9, and secured their objective, while the destroyers remained in the Narvik fjord to guard against attack from the sea.

On April 10, a small fleet of British H-class destroyers approached, with the flagship being HMS *Hardy*. These ships were smaller than the Kriegsmarine's destroyers, but managed to sink several German ships in their first attack. They were driven off after a spirited gun battle that cost the British two destroyers, including the *Hardy*. On April 14, the British returned, and this time the destroyers were accompanied by the battleship HMS *Warspite*. Its big guns proceeded to blow apart many of the remaining German destroyers, and the rest were scuttled by their crews after exhausting their fuel and ammunition. This battle completely obliterated the landing fleet, though some twenty-six hundred sailors were able to take small boats or swim to shore, and they would form an ad hoc infantry battalion in the subsequent fighting.

Even with the loss of their fleet, the Germans in Narvik were not cut off from resupply. They held an airfield, and with all of southern Norway quickly falling into German hands, they were able to bring in provisions via air with virtually no opposition. However, the British realized the importance of Narvik, too, and were finally beginning to take steps to mount a campaign there.

On April 14, British army units under the command of Major General Pierse J. Mackesy were put ashore outside of Narvik, with orders to liberate the port. During the next few days, an even larger British force was landed on both sides of Trondheim. They tried to recapture that central Norwegian city, but the Germans—aided by furious dive-bombing from the Luftwaffe that forced the British navy out of the area and severely demoralized the ground troops—held firm. Some of the British troops advanced inland and joined the Norwegians in trying to defend Lillehammer, but they were quickly pushed back by the advancing Germans. At the end of the month, the British were forced to withdraw from the Trondheim area, leaving, for a short time, Narvik as the only theater of war in Europe where Allied and German troops faced each other in combat.

On land at Narvik, the German commander of the Austrian mountain troops was General Eduard Dietl. In addition to the stranded sailors, he was reinforced by several hundred German troops who surreptitiously rode in by train from Sweden (having disguised themselves as medical troops) as well as about three hundred more troops brought in by air. In total, Dietl command-ed about five thousand men.

The Norwegian Sixth Division, commanded by General Carl Gustav Fleischer, included more than eight thousand men. It was reinforced by the three British battalions that arrived on April 14, and later by a French brigade and three Polish battalions. By early May, the Allies had some twenty-five thousand men ashore in the vicinity of Narvik, so they held a significant numerical advan-tage. Nevertheless, they were slow to move out and acted with little coordination between the four nations (each with its own language) as they pressed in on the Germans. General Mackesy proved to be extremely cautious, and was repeatedly urged by his commanders to move out. His naval counterpart, Admiral William Boyle, advocated a landing directly at the city of Narvik, but Mackesy preferred an indirect approach overland—an approach that was retarded by the bad weather, rough ground, and the general's overly wary nature.

Finally, Mackesy was replaced with Admiral Boyle, who was given overall command of the Allied forces, and the units of the four nations closed in more quickly, each force approaching Narvik from a different direction. The British forces were transported by ship directly into the city's harbor, and the fighting grew hot.

By the end of May the pressure grew to be too much for General Dietl, and he was forced out of Narvik by the combined soldiers of Britain, France, Poland, and Norway. He began retreating up the railroad line toward the Swedish border, which was not far away in this very narrow stretch of Norway. Having lost his airfield, Dietl was denied a source of resupply and was in a very bad predicament. Admiral Boyle's men were in control of the key port and its airfield, which remained out of range of the Luftwaffe fighters, based four hundred miles away in Trondheim.

This was the first Allied land victory of the war, but it was already overshadowed by events far to the south. On May 10, the Germans invaded the Low Countries and France, and by the end of May things were going very badly for the Allies on the Continent. Even as Narvik was falling to the Allied offensive, the British high command was contemplating a decision to withdraw all troops from Norway, in case they were needed to defend England. The Norwegians reacted with shock and indignation when this decision was announced, but they lacked the resources to carry on by themselves.

Timidity, caution, and outright fear had demoralized the British military leaders so much that they simply abandoned a strategically vital position, one that had been gained over more than a month of hard fighting. Certainly the situation on the Continent was bleak, but they had a substantial force in Norway, one which the Germans would have had a tremendously difficult time dislodging. A squadron or two of fighters could have been dispatched to the Narvik airfield, ensuring that the Allies would have air superiority there for the foreseeable future. (Germany had no aircraft carriers, even in the unlikely event it tried to challenge England for control of the North Sea.) The value of Narvik would have had an immediate impact by completely blocking off the port as a position on the enemy's iron supply route. Furthermore, though this could not have been foreseen at the time, it would have dramatically eased the horrific risks suffered by the Murmansk convoys when Britain and the United States started sending Lend-Lease supplies to the Soviet Union in 1941.

Instead, over the course of June 4–8, all of the Allied troops were pulled out of the Narvik area. The king of Norway and the government sailed into exile in England, while General Dietl and his scrappy force moved back into Narvik, putting the final cap of success on the dramatic, and strategically decisive, Norwegian campaign.

INVADING NORWAY

April 1940

BY ROBERT GREENBERGER

A wide-ranging war was becoming a dreaded certainty across Europe as countries watched with paralyzing horror the speed with which Germany had rebuilt itself under the mesmerizing control of Adolf Hitler. As a result, the larger countries were quickly allying themselves with one another, which meant that when Hitler invaded Poland on September 1, 1939, France and England honored their pact and declared war on the Nazis.

For months, neither side mounted much of an attack and it was considered a "phony war," a phrase first uttered by Winston Churchill. During those months, though, both sides were seeking some place with which to engage the other, testing their mettle. It soon became obvious that the neutral country of Norway was perfectly positioned for such a contest.

Germany sought to secure the continued export of iron ore from the port of Narvik. Sweden annually provided Germany with 10 million tons of ore by then, and without it Germany's desire for military expansion would have been severely hampered. During the harsh winter months, the Baltic Sea could freeze over, effectively trapping 9 million tons and leaving just the Narvik route and its million tons of ore as the final option. To the Allied forces of France and England, the Norway routes meant they could prevent a total German blockade of the seas, allowing them access to needed supplies from unoccupied countries.

Germany risked its U-boats to ferry the ore via the Straits of Dover or north of Scotland. As far back as 1929, Vice Admiral Wolfgang Wegener wrote in his book *The Sea Strategy of the World War* that his country should capture Norway as a safer route to the Atlantic Ocean.

Admiral Erich Raeder did not support that particular notion, but was especially concerned over the Allies taking control of the North Sea, hampering Germany's plans. As it was, ore production had been reduced and its transportation suspended at the war's outbreak, and Germany needed those routes cleared for when production resumed. On September 19, 1939, Churchill advised the British cabinet that Germany must be prevented from receiving iron ore from Norway and Sweden. By October 10, German intelligence had been made aware of Churchill's efforts to control sea traffic around Norway.

Russia's invasion of Finland on November 30 forced the Allies to partner with Norway and Sweden in support of their neighbor, opening up a new front they were ill prepared to support. Finland's proximity threatened these countries' safety, so when Allied troops in the region began to total 150,000, Hitler was motivated to take decisive action. The führer was hampered, though, by the recently signed Molotov-Ribbentrop Pact (officially known as the Nazi-Soviet Non-Aggression Pact), obligating Germany to remain neutral on matters pertaining to Finland.

Hitler was ready to begin planning by December 10. He and Raeder met with Norway's sympathetic defense minister, Vidkun Quisling. The man promised Hitler that Norway would support German occupation and that the people would support Axis forces at their docks and borders. Raeder was pleased because this meant keeping the British away from the docks that he wanted for the U-boats. Satisfied with Quisling's comments, the führer ordered invasion plans to be drawn up.

A week later, Hitler told Quisling he was inclined to keep Norway neutral unless the Allies forced his hand by moving into Scandinavia. It had become clear the diplomat had lied, overstating the Norwegian government's willingness to work with Germany, hoping to personally benefit from German occupation. He no longer had Hitler's ear, but Germany continued to covetously eye Norway. Quisling would later be a key player in Germany's control of the country, but at this time, he was out of favor with Berlin.

The *Altmark*, a boat carrying 299 British POWs, was boarded by British forces in a Norwegian fjord on February 16, 1940, killing five of the captors, wounding four others, and freeing their brethren. This was a direct violation of neutrality laws, and it angered the Norwegian government. It also showed Hitler that the British would not abide by international law and he instructed General Nikolaus von Falkenhorst to accelerate invasion planning. He had every right to be concerned since First Lord of the Admiralty Winston Churchill had already begun advocating Operation Wilfred, mining the waters to thwart the enemy. To Churchill, invading Norway would keep German forces away from France and England and take the way to Hitler from the north. Various plans were debated until Wilfred was scheduled to be initiated on April 8.

The Germans had their own plan, Operation Weserübung, which would secure the ports and the vital ore for their use. To accomplish this, it was decided to place troops aboard the faster warships, moving them into position to occupy the ports before resistance could be mounted. A simultaneous attack on multiple ports caught Norway by complete surprise.

Hitler framed this as a way to protect Norway's neutrality through German troops. The plan was expanded to take Denmark by force, also keeping it away from Allied control. With the nights growing shorter as spring approached and the need for the troops to complete their work in Norway before turning their attention to France, Weserübung was scheduled for the morning of April 9.

Oslo, Kristiansand, Egersund, Bergen, Trondheim, and Narvik were the six main objectives for the German navy, with paratroops tasked to take control of the airfields at Fornebu and Sola. This was the German equivalent of shock and awe. The plan was designed to quickly overwhelm the Norwegian defenders and occupy these vital areas before any form of organized resistance could be mounted. Two brigades would be dispatched to take control of bridges, while the Luftwaffe was tasked with taking Copenhagen and paratroopers would commandeer the northern airfields.

With the plans in place, both sides began moving their pieces on the global chessboard, with Germany beginning to maneuver its ships on April 3 and the British moving its forces a day later. Admiral William Whitworth, commanding HMS *Renown*, led twelve destroyers for the Vestfjords.

Bad weather and thick fog hampered the British, while the conditions screened the German forces, giving them an advantage. The following day, the approaching German ships were spotted, and sorties by the Royal Air Force gained valuable intelligence, though they could not inflict damage. The Allied command assumed the Axis was trying to break the blockade.

Admiral Sir Charles Forbes, commander in chief of the British Home Fleet, was dispatched that evening to stop its approach.

Neither side had proper intelligence of what its opponent was up to, so the first contact was inadvertent and somewhat of a surprise. On the morning of April 8, HMS *Glowworm* came upon the Z11 *Bernd von Arnim* and the Z18 *Hans Lüdemann*. While the German ships fled in panic, they sent out a call for help. As the *Glowworm* sought a man overboard, it was located by the *Admiral Hipper*, a cruiser responding to the SOS. As the fight continued, the *Glowworm* broke radio silence to inform the Admiralty of the situation, but wound up being lost soon after.

Ships were pulled from their positions to come to the *Glowworm*'s aid, and in the end, ten German destroyers, forming Gruppe 1, managed to enter the Ofotfjord leading to Narvik unmolested. As the various vessels deployed, three remained at Narvik, overwhelming the two aging Norwegian guard ships.

Gruppe 2 was equally successful at Trondheim while Gruppe 3's *Königsberg* and the artillery training ship *Bremse* took damage before securing Bergen. By lunchtime, much of Norway was surrounded by the Germany forces.

While Norway's ports were quickly secured, the inland forces encountered problems and delays that allowed Norway's king, parliament, and the national treasury to escape north to Elverum, where the king was willing to negotiate with the Germans in order to buy his people more time. No fool, he ordered Colonel Otto Ruge, inspector general of the Norwegian Infantry, to be prepared, and sure enough, seventy miles from Oslo, Ruge encountered a small force trying once more to capture the king. As commandeered private trucks were loaded with the treasury, each sped away until the vaults were empty, just avoiding capture by the Nazi forces. The negotiations with the Germans went nowhere, and on April 10, King Haakon VII adamantly refused to recognize the new government, which was to be led by the traitorous Quisling. Soon after, the Norwegian governement arrived in Great Britain. Although occupied by Germany, Norway never formally surrendered.

A day earlier, on April 9, the Wehrmacht entered Denmark to further secure their routes to the ore of Sweden and Norway, disembarking at Copenhagen, while paratroops took Aalborg Airport.

Shortly thereafter, King Christian X received the German ambassador and was told to surrender or face torrential bombing courtesy of the Luftwaffe. Recognizing the superior forces arrayed against his land, the king agreed to the surrender while reserving control over domestic matters. The country remained under German control until May 5, 1945.

While Germany acted swiftly, they still faced British resistance.

Captain Bernard Warburton-Lee, commanding the ships that were to support Operation Wilfred, gathered intelligence of the enemy force in Narvik and telegrammed the Admiralty his findings and desire to attack in the morning. He had swift approval, and in the morning, his vessel, HMS *Hardy*, led four destroyers, hidden by the morning fog and snow, toward the German ships. Soon after opening fire, the Allied forces managed to sink two destroyers, disabled another, and sank another six tankers and supply ships. The First Battle of Narvik was a British triumph until fresh ships, commanded by Commander Erich Bey, arrived and dealt the four destroyers crippling blows. The British managed to escape and the Germans, low on fuel, could not pursue.

Over the next several days, the Germans regrouped away from Norway's shores, letting the Luftwaffe harass the British vessels. Both sides re-formed their forces and once more headed for Narvik. The Second Battle of Narvik began on April 13 as airplanes, submarines, and boats all clashed in a larger, bloodier battle. In the end, the German side ran out of both fuel and ammunition, forcing commanders to order their ships be abandoned and scuttled. As night fell, the British commanded the Rombaksfjord.

So began a battle that saw Allied and Axis forces crawl around and through Norway until May 28, when the British finally retook Narvik. Unfortunately, by then France and the Low Countries had been invaded by the Germans. This meant relocating their dwindling resources away from protecting the ore transportation routes in order to actively engage the Axis forces. By then a plan for retreating, Operation Alphabet, was approved May 24, and finally on June 8, the Allied forces left Norway a torn-up country. Their enemies activated Operation Juno to help the garrison at Narvik but wound up chasing the departing British, sinking the aircraft carrier HMS *Glorious* and two destroyers.

It was time to pick up the pieces and assess the damage in what became known as the Norway Debate. The failure of the British planning to take control of Norway is said to have contributed to the resignation of British prime minister Neville Chamberlain, to be succeeded by Churchill.

As for the Germans, they were required to post 150,000 men in Norway to protect the supply line. While seen as a clear German victory, the tallied losses told a different story. While the Nazis lost just 3,800 men and another 1,600 wounded, they took bigger hits in the air and at sea. The Luftwaffe lost 100 aircraft, 10 percent of the force used; the navy lost a heavy cruiser, 2 of its 6 light cruisers, 10 of its 20 destroyers, and 6 U-boats.

Earl F. Ziemke wrote in 1959's *Command Decisions,*

> *To return to the firmer ground of tangible gains, WESERUE-*
> *BUNG brought Germany control of its supply line for Swedish iron*
> *ore (later also for Finnish nickel), a number of new naval and air*
> *bases, and some other economic advantages. The naval and air bases*
> *somewhat improved the German position with respect to the British*
> *Isles, increased the chances to break out into the Atlantic with raiders,*
> *and later made possible air and sea attacks on the Allied Murmansk*
> *convoys. However, a decisive improvement, particularly in the naval*
> *situation, was not achieved. Germany could still be shut off from the*
> *open sea, and for the Navy the advantages gained in the [newly gained*
> *Scandinavian] bases were offset by the losses in ships sustained during*
> *WESERUEBUNG.*
>
> *In the further course of the war Norway became the staging area*
> *for an advance across Finland to Murmansk [in Russia] and the Mur-*
> *mansk Railroad. That attack bogged down in the summer of 1941 short*
> *of its objectives, and thereafter the fronts in Finland and Norway*
> *stagnated, tying down more than a half million men and tremendous*
> *amounts of materiel. Although Hitler insisted to the very last that Nor-*
> *way was the strategic key to Europe, the expected Allied invasion never*
> *came; and on 8 May 1945 the German Army in Norway surrendered*
> *without having fired a shot in the decisive battles of the war.*

Germany could and did coerce other neutral countries through bullying diplomacy to give it what it wanted. Rather than commit men and equipment to taking control of Norway, could Hitler not have used this approach?

As many as 400,000 men were posted to secure the country by 1944, all for iron ore—not a strategically sound investment of precious but by then dwindling resources.

THE BLITZKRIEG COMES OF AGE

France, May–June 1940

BY DOUGLAS NILES

Finally the waiting was over. Having been granted better than a half a year to make his plans, build his forces, and train his troops following the fast conquest of Poland, Hitler's Nazi armies were ready to wage war against the West. They had learned many things from the new tactics they'd employed in September 1939. The invasion of Norway produced further lessons, particularly regarding the use of paratroops. Now the Germans were ready to put those refinements into action.

The French and, to a lesser extent, the British might as well not have been paying attention. After the long, slow winter of the sitzkrieg, followed by the shock of Germany's lightning strike against Norway, French civilian and military morale was at a low ebb. The British were not in much better shape, and the government of Prime Minister Neville Chamberlain was on very shaky ground. Both nations had fully mobilized their reserves, and they had large armies in place, waiting—and worrying.

The Germans, meanwhile, were flushed with their success,

bolstered and encouraged by the skillfully delivered propaganda of Doctor Goebbels. The troops were confident in their abilities and in their führer's instincts. Even though the German general staff still felt a great deal of trepidation about its dictator's schemes—it continued to fear a replay of World War I—it was unwilling to stop him, and in the end its fears didn't really matter.

Despite all the waiting and the planning, the invasion of France in May 1940 proved to be one of the most shocking, world-altering events of military history. In effect, Hitler's armies accomplished more in six weeks than the entire nation had been able to achieve in four and a half bloody, expensive years of World War I. They did this by exploiting new equipment, most notably armored vehicles and aircraft, and by creating and utilizing tactics that maximized the effects of those weapons. They were considerably abetted by their opponent's failure to make any similar adaptations.

In looking back on history, military and otherwise, it is easy to view certain events as essentially inevitable, ordained by the circumstances that preceded them. The utter mastery of the German blitzkrieg is one such event, and it is a common assumption that France was simply doomed by its outmoded understanding of warfare and the advanced, modern equipment of the Nazi armies. This assumption, however, is far from the truth.

For one thing, as the campaign loomed in the early weeks of May 1940, the German army was actually outnumbered by the defending armies—a direct contradiction of the military dictum that urges an attacker to always have a significant numerical advantage over the foe. For this attack, the Germans had mustered some 2.5 million men, organized into three army groups on the Western Front. These armies included some one hundred infantry divisions, nine motorized divisions, ten armored divisions, and less than one complete airborne division. Army Group B (von Bock) was in the north, facing the Netherlands and northern Belgium. Army Group A (von Rundstedt), with most of the Germans' twenty-five hundred tanks, was in the middle, facing southern Belgium and Luxembourg. The longest stretch of the frontier, including the entire German-French border, was faced by Army Group C, under General Wilhelm Ritter von Leeb. The two flanking army groups included two armies each, while von Rundstedt's Army Group A, on the narrowest frontage, included four armies and a powerful panzer formation—almost the strength of an entire army on its own—under General Paul von Kleist.

The French and British armies facing the border numbered a little over 2 million men, also organized into three army groups, though the total reached 3 million when the armies of the Low Countries were factored in. The northernmost was the First Army Group, under General Gaston Billotte, and included five armies—one of which was the British Expeditionary Force. With a left flank resting on the English Channel, it covered the borders of the Low Countries, except for Luxembourg. The Second Army Group, under General André-Gaston Prételat, included three armies and was curiously stationed behind the Maginot Line, where it would be of little use until the divisions could be moved, by rail, to where they were needed. (Another thing that failed to sink in to the French was the effect of air superiority on rail transport.) The Third Army Group was just a single army under General Antoine Besson, and it occupied the Maginot Line emplacements themselves. The Allies possessed more than thirty-six hundred tanks, including many that were better than the best German tanks, but these were dispersed through three armored divisions and a number of small tank battalions designated for infantry support.

Although the Low Countries had remained strictly neutral,

it was understood by everyone that they would throw their lot in with the Western Allies should Germany initiate attack. Belgium could muster 600,000 men and Holland another 400,000, though neither nation had fully mobilized by May. Still, each country had sturdy defensive positions in place, with the Belgian fort of Eben Emael a centerpiece, while the Dutch had a series of wide river barriers (including the Rhine). However, both of these Low Countries, in a vain effort to preserve neutrality, had resisted every effort of France and England to discuss, even informally, plans for mutual defense. This failure would prove to be a fatal flaw before the first week of the campaign was concluded.

One key area where the Germans had a real advantage in numbers was aircraft. The Luftwaffe was bringing some thirty-five hundred combat planes to the party, and these were mostly modern types, highlighted by the Bf–109 fighter, the Bf–110 long-range twin engine fighter, medium bombers well-suited to ground support, and the lethal and accurate Stuka dive-bombers. In contrast, the French air force numbered some fourteen hundred machines, while the British had dispatched just under three hundred Spitfire and Hurricane fighters to the Continent.

In the early morning hours of May 10, the Germans commenced Operation Sichelschnitt (see chapter 4) according to plan. As they had done in Poland, they opened the attack with surprise air strikes against the airfields of the French and Royal air forces. Because of the watchful state of the Allies, these attacks did not succeed in destroying a lot of aircraft on the ground, but they did disrupt all subsequent air operations by seriously damaging the bases from which the Allied aircraft needed to fly.

As dawn was breaking on the tenth, the next phase of the blitzkrieg went into effect. The parachute troops under General Kurt Student numbered only 4,500 men, organized into six battalions; they were backed up by one 12,000-man light infantry division that was air mobile—that is, it could be transported by plane to captured airfields. Of the paratroopers, 4,000 (five battalions) of them were used in the attack on Holland. One battalion was dropped directly into The Hague, where they attempted to capture the Dutch government. They failed in this objective, but their presence caused immense confusion in the Dutch high command. The other four battalions were dropped to capture bridges across the several mouths of the Rhine, at Rotterdam, Dordrecht, and Moerdijk. They were successful in every case—at one point attacking *fallschirmjäger* charged into a guardhouse and put out the lit fuse of a demolition charge just before the bridge was blown. Not only did the paratroops capture every one of their objectives, but they were able to hold them for several days, until von Bock's ground forces arrived on the scene.

This left only one parachute battalion for the attack on Belgium, but it played perhaps the most crucial role of any small unit in the entire campaign. Because the Germans would have to pass through a corner of Holland before reaching the main Belgian defense line, they knew that the defenders would have ample time to blow up the key bridges across the Albert Canal. This deep, formidable water crossing was protected by the batteries of heavy guns in the fortress Eben Emael.

While most of the battalion dropped onto the bridges themselves, a small force—some seventy-eight parachute engineers—landed directly atop the fortress, which was garrisoned by twelve hundred men, and quickly overcame the antiaircraft troops that were stationed there. They then employed a new and highly secret explosive compound to blow up the cupolas and casemates of all the heavy guns within Eben Emael. The garrison troops were held at bay by these *fallschirmjäger*—who only lost six men in the battle—for a full twenty-four hours, until German infantry arrived to relieve them.

Also on May 10, Chamberlain's government finally fell, and the formidable, stubborn, bellicose, and eloquent Winston Churchill became Britain's new prime minister. Although his tactical and strategic ideas were not always sound, Churchill's attitude, charisma, and confidence would prove very valuable to British morale throughout the upcoming years of the war. In fact, he would personify the spirit of plucky courage in the face of terrible odds that became so well known around the world.

By May 11, German ground forces were driving into the Low Countries. Army Group B in particular advanced quickly and aggressively, fulfilling its role of drawing the Allies' attention. The Dutch would last only four days, finally surrendering under the shadow of Hitler's threat to destroy all of Holland's cities with a brutal terror bombing campaign. In fact, the entire heart of Rotterdam was destroyed as a demonstration, even while the surrender negotiations were going on.

The Belgians put up a little more fight, falling back from their initial defensive positions as these were overrun. They were quickly reinforced by the rapidly advancing French First Army and the BEF. By May 15 there were thirty-five Allied divisions in Belgium being hard pressed from the front by von Bock's Sixth Army and hammered on the left flank by the Eighteenth Army, moving southward after sweeping through Holland. About the same time, the Allied commanders were just beginning to realize the enormity of the disaster that had occurred south of Belgium, through that "impassable" region of mountain and forest known as the Ardennes.

There, the key stroke of von Manstein's Sichelschnitt plan was being executed to perfection by Heinz Guderian's panzer corps and other formations, including General Erwin Rommel's Seventh Panzer Division. Because the terrain itself was thought to be so rugged, this section was the most lightly defended area along the entire front. The French relied on light cavalry formations to hold those narrow roads, but these were easily swept out of the way by the onrushing juggernaut of German tanks. By May 13, Rommel had reached the Meuse River near Dinant, and in another day his leading tanks were across.

Meanwhile, just to the south of Dinant, the main breakthrough was targeted for Sedan. Here Meuse flows through a wide bend, with a low salient on the west bank and high ground on the east bank, which had heavy forest for cover. Guderian's leading armored units also reached the river on the thirteenth. This area was defended by the Ninth French Army, under General André Georges Corap. Though he had been warned by his picket units about the advance through the Ardennes, Corap was slow to react and was unable to meet the Germans east of the river. It rapidly became clear to the Allied commanders that a crossing of the Meuse by a force as powerful as Guderian's would have disastrous consequences.

French troops rushed to man artillery positions that would cover the river, but these positions were shattered by vicious air attacks, prominently featuring Stuka dive-bombers equipped with sirens—the sirens used for no other purpose than to terrify the defenders. Allied aircraft made a valiant attempt to protect the ground positions, but Luftwaffe fighters brushed them aside as Guderian's *panzergrenadiers* (infantry accompanying the panzer troops), in rubber rafts, boldly paddled across the river. They seized the low ground on the west bank and, within another day, established a bridge so that the panzers themselves could start pouring across.

Now the German tanks had a front some fifty miles wide to the west of the Meuse River—the barrier that the Allies had depended upon to make a strong defensive stand. The Germans completely destroyed the Ninth French Army and began a relentless drive northwest, toward the Channel coast. If they succeeded in reaching the shore, the entire Allied presence in Belgium—all thirty-five divisions—would be cut off from the rest of France. The French army, under General Gamelin, tried to counter the breakthrough by bringing up troops from Army Group Two, but they were hampered by their horrible preinvasion position, far to the south, and by the fact that Luftwaffe air strikes had paralyzed the rail system. The lack of vehicles in these infantry-heavy formations doomed them to arrive on the scene far too late to do any good.

The lone French armored division, under the command of Brigadier General Charles de Gaulle, made three successive attacks against the left flank of the panzer corps (May 17–19), and actually made some progress in what were the only successful French offensives of the entire campaign. But his tanks were too few to make a difference, and eventually his brave men were plastered by German dive-bombers and counterattacking panzers.

The British, in the meanwhile, quickly realized their peril. On May 21, Lord John Gort ordered a counterattack against the panzers, utilizing two infantry divisions and the Royal Army's lone tank brigade. In effect, this became a thrust led by two understrength tank battalions, supported by two understrength infantry battalions, striking the flank of Rommel's Seventh Panzer Division. After making a little progress in the vicinity of Arras, the attack ran out of steam—though not before it had thrown a real scare into the German high command. One can only wonder what a significant armored force, such as two or three divisions, might have been able to accomplish.

In reality, the main obstacle slowing up Guderian and the other panzer leaders during this bold thrust came not from the Allies, but from his own commanders. The conservative masters of the general staff, Halder and von Brauchitsch, were very concerned that the panzer spearheads would get isolated and destroyed. They were already advancing far ahead of the rest of the army—much farther than any of the senior commanders had envisioned at the start of the campaign. Indeed, Guderian came very close to getting fired for insubordination as he kept advancing, exploiting the gap that his audacity had earned. He was frequently ordered to slow down, but he always found a way just short of direct disobedience to keep pressing ahead.

By May 22, German tanks had reached the coast, and the BEF—together with many French divisions—was cut off and trapped. Belgium finally surrendered on May 25, over Churchill's protests, but most of the country was already in German hands. Still, the surrender completely exposed the left flank of the BEF, now fighting for survival with its back against the English Channel and one lone port, Dunkirk, available as an escape route. In his one grave mistake of this campaign, Hitler ordered his units to halt instead of destroying the British (see chapter 7).

By June 4, the Dunkirk pocket had been evacuated, and the Battle of Flanders was over. With amazing discipline and precision, the Germans regrouped in a broad front and reversed their facing from north to south. Von Bock's Army Group B now anchored its right flank on the English Channel at Abbeville. With four armies now under his command, he would make a strong attack to the southwest, with Paris—among other objectives—as his target. Von Rundstedt now commanded three armies, and he was tasked with the main effort, which was to sweep southward and then swing east, taking the Maginot Line from the rear. Von

Leeb's two armies, as before, remained positioned against the front of the Maginot Line, and were merely there to keep the French pinned down in their positions—he was not ordered, nor expected, to break through the front of that vast series of entrenchments.

By now, French morale was completely shattered. The combination of the deadly air attacks—particularly the lethally accurate Stuka dive-bombers—and the fast-moving panzer formations had utterly sapped the will of the still-very-large French army to resist. General Gamelin had been replaced by General Maxime Weygand as commander in chief, and Weygand's wild orders for maneuvers and attacks proved to have no basis in the real capabilities of his troops. As the next phase of the blitzkrieg began, with von Bock moving out on June 5, the Germans advanced everywhere they attacked. Army Group A attacked on June 9 with similar success. By June 10, the French government was moving out of Paris, which was declared an open city (that is, it would not be defended) on June 13, 1940. Also on the tenth, Mussolini decided the time was right for Italy to get involved, and the Italian army attacked the French (for the most part unsuccessfully) along the border they shared between Switzerland and the Mediterranean Sea.

By June 17, the French were seeking an armistice, and on the twenty-first, in the same railway car where the Treaty of Versailles had been signed nearly twenty-two years earlier, the surrender of France became official.

Hitler was hailed by his people as the undisputed master of the continent of Europe. (Though Joseph Stalin and the USSR had yet to weigh in on the matter . . .)

ONE THAT GOT AWAY

Dunkirk, May–June 1940

BY DOUGLAS NILES

Following the breakout from the Ardennes, the stabbing drives of German armored columns sliced cleanly through the Allied lines. Even as the bulk of the French forces fell backward in chaos and confusion, hundreds of thousands of troops in the British Expeditionary Force and the French First Army found themselves surrounded by the enemy, cut off with their backs to the English Channel and with no realistic hope of survival. The fact that they got away and lived to fight another day is due squarely to the intervention of Adolf Hitler himself, and constitutes a huge mistake on the führer's part—even if the ramifications of that mistake wouldn't become obvious for months and even years to come.

When Guderian's panzers reached the coast of the Channel at Abbeville on May 22, he succeeded in isolating some 400,000 Allied soldiers, including almost the entire BEF, the First French Army, and the Belgian (and even a few Dutch) soldiers that had continued to fight on after their small countries had surrendered (Belgium finally giving up on May 28). With his usual drive, Guderian turned north, quickly capturing the small port at Boulogne and isolating Calais (which would fall on the twenty-seventh).

This left only the little harbor at Dunkirk as a place where the trapped British troops could escape aboard ships.

Guderian continued up the coast to Gravelines, which was barely ten miles short of Dunkirk. The British were still oriented to face Army Group B's attack from the north and east, and had yet to form any kind of defense against the attack from the rear. Clearly the panzers could have continued forward against very little opposition, and Guderian wanted to do so. At the same time Army Group B kept up relentless pressure from the east, the massive infantry formations under von Bock's command steadily pushing the Allied survivors out of Holland and Belgium, toward the coast and apparently imminent destruction.

Then, on May 26, Hitler issued the firm order that all of his panzer formations were to stop where they were, and were not to close any farther on Dunkirk—though if the port could be captured quickly, the stranded BEF would have no choice but to surrender. (Apparently this order was delivered with enough force that even the rambunctious Guderian was compelled to obey.) The reason for this colossal blunder is not known for certain. One common explanation holds that Air Marshall Hermann Goering, commander of the Luftwaffe, wanted to demonstrate the might of his airplanes to his führer, and beseeched Hitler to let the aircraft annihilate the British pocket. There is evidence to support this theory in the way subsequent events developed, but no one knows for sure if Goering made such a plea.

Another possibility suggests that Hitler was worried about a French counterattack into the southern flank of Guderian's position, and that the order to halt was simply a cautionary command to make sure his troops were prepared and available to face a new threat. Certainly Hitler had many moments of doubt during the campaign, and most of them were related to the reckless speed of the advancing panzers. Several times during the drive to the coast he and the general staff had issued Guderian orders to slow down—orders that Guderian usually obeyed technically, even as he continued to send out "reconnaissance elements" that in effect continued his advance.

In the case of the Dunkirk pocket, however, Guderian was sternly ordered to stay put, and he did. The command is known to originate from Hitler, so the blame for the mistake must lie squarely on his shoulders.

In the event, when the panzers stopped, the Luftwaffe did make a furious effort to destroy the Allied troops, the ships that were coming to rescue them, and the port of Dunkirk itself. However, Dunkirk was pretty close to southeast England, and there were a lot of RAF fighter bases there. Hundreds of Hurricanes and Spitfires flew the short distance to Dunkirk, and they waged fierce air battles for control of the skies over the crucial port. Both sides suffered losses, but the British fighter cover went a long way toward disrupting the Luftwaffe's attempt to wipe out the forces on the ground. Troops gathered there, exposed on the beaches, but it turned out that the soft sand actually dampened the effects of the high-explosive bombs that rained down on their positions.

From May 26–28, the British began to dig in, forming a strong defensive perimeter around their precious port. Lord Gort, commander of the BEF, had already decided to retreat to the sea, and on the twenty-seventh the British cabinet authorized the War Office to telegram Gort and order him to evacuate as much of his force as he could.

On May 20, Churchill had had the foresight to order the Royal Navy to assemble a force of small boats in readiness to rescue small elements of the BEF that might become trapped along the coast. At the time, it was assumed that the British forces would be moving south, and the prime minister feared that isolated units might get cut off and have to be evacuated by sea. By May 26, of course, this plan had already been overtaken by recent events. Admiral Bertram Ramsay, commanding the operation from Dover Castle, started to collect the ships and boats under the code name Operation Dynamo (since his headquarters was in a large bunker that had housed the electrical generator for the castle during World War I).

On the twenty-sixth, even before Gort had been ordered to evacuate, Ramsay ordered Operation Dynamo into effect. By this time it was clear that Dunkirk was the only port that could be used. Ramsay expected to bring some forty-five thousand men out of the pocket over the course of a couple of days, after which it was assumed the Germans would have overrun the position and taken the rest of the BEF as captives.

On May 28, Hitler lifted his halt order, and the panzers attacked again. But now the British defenses were stiff, and Guderian's tanks faced three British infantry divisions that had had time to form a defense in depth. Those two precious days made all the difference, and German progress slowed to a crawl.

Yet neither was the evacuation proceeding as quickly as possible. Despite his hope of pulling out forty-five thousand men in two days, Ramsay's transports were only able to rescue a little more than half that number by the twenty-eighth. The problem was obvious: Dunkirk's small port only allowed a few ships to dock at a time, so most of the escaping men had to be brought out over the beaches. The water was too shallow for large ships to approach the shore, and there were not enough small boats to transfer the evacuating soldiers to the transports anchored a quarter mile or more out to sea.

The call went out across southern England, and even as far away as Scotland, and an amazing thing happened. Over the next few days, more than eight hundred small boats, ranging from fishing vessels to yachts to ferries to pleasure boats, made the voyage across the Channel to the coast of France. While the few larger craft embarked troops and brought them all the way back to England, most of the smaller boats simply served as shuttles, picking up the soldiers who—good Englishmen that they were—patiently queued up on the beaches and in the shallows, waiting sometimes for hours in shoulder-deep water before they got a ride out to the transports.

The rate of evacuation picked up rapidly. By May 29, 47,000 men were brought away, followed by 54,000 on the thirtieth, and 68,000—including Lord Gort—on the last day of the month. On June 1, 64,000 were rescued, though increasing German air attack forced a suspension of daylight loading.

At the same time the German ground forces relentlessly chewed away at the steadily shrinking perimeter. Though some French, such as General Weygand, viewed the British withdrawal as some kind of betrayal, the gallant troops of the French First Army fought a courageous rearguard action, allowing virtually all of the British troops who had reached the Dunkirk pocket to escape.

By the end of June 2, 224,000 soldiers of the British army had been rescued from Dunkirk. The relief effort continued, until some 95,000 additional Allied troops—mostly French, though many Belgians and a few Dutch were numbered among them— had also been rescued. On the morning of June 4, Operation Dynamo was finally suspended, with several thousand French soldiers still left in the pocket, doomed to become prisoners of war. Of course, these evacuated troops had been forced to leave all of their heavy equipment, and even many of their personal weapons, behind as they made their escape. But the effort had rescued and carried to England some 338,000 veteran soldiers, a cadre of personnel that would go a long way toward keeping Great Britain in the war.

SURE, HAVE THE UNCOMMITTED RUN GERMAN MILITARY INTELLIGENCE

Germany, 1935–1945

BY PAUL A. THOMSEN

Nazi Germany is largely remembered as one of the most ruthless and oppressive reigns in the history of the world. The Reich's black-and-white images of jackbooted soldiers against traditional European settings were designed to convey the rise of a new and strong order. Similarly, the dark silhouette of men dressed in black uniforms, often emblazoned with the twin lightning bolts of the Schutzstaffel (SS), or wearing trench coats and fedoras, standing in doorways, on street corners, in the background at photo opportunities, were intended to evoke the ever-present watchfulness and strength of Germany's intelligence community. While no one ever doubted the prowess of Nazi soldiers, the same could not be said for the reality behind their Nazi intelligence public relations image. In fact, the German intelligence community and much of the Reich's policy actions were a mess, because Adolf Hitler mistakenly picked

Wilhelm Canaris as the head of the Abwehr ("Defense"), the German military intelligence organization.

The Abwehr served as the frontline defense of German national security policies. Created in 1921 as one of the few German national security initiatives permitted under the Treaty of Versailles, the intelligence organization started as small and effectively impotent office that was so deeply divided by army-navy bickering that many considered the agency a professional dead end. Under the early-1930s stewardship of naval officer Captain Konrad Patzig, it rapidly developed into one of the nation's most potent weapons. Fostering a close-knit group of learned intelligence offices, Patzig won the respect of both army and navy servicemen by supplying his superiors with a steady stream of accurate intelligence extracted from encrypted communiqués between a host of nations. Patzig, however, was not much loved by the Nazi Party. While signal intelligence and decryption were legitimate tools of spycraft, many among the party leadership found the reports far too boring to be fully appreciated. Instead, they challenged Patzig to engage in the more virtuous and exciting field of human intelligence. Yet when Patzig modified the Abwehr's capabilities to meet the Nazi's desires, the intelligence chief once more fell under the sharp criticism of Adolf Hitler's men for now attempting to encroach on the territory of the Gestapo and the Sicherheitsdienst (SD). As a result, the conflict between Patzig and seemingly every other office in the Reich became a never-ending struggle to protect the Abwehr from the Nazis.

The bureaucratic war raged many years against the Abwehr's German competitors, including the SS, SD, and Gestapo. Every month there seemed to be a new slight, assault, or crisis caused by its sister organizations for the Abwehr to fix, then one day, Patzig was suddenly challenged by the Nazis for allowing reconnaissance flights over Poland. In one of Hitler's classic administrative moves, Poland had recently become the new playground for several of Heinrich Himmler and Reinhard Heydrich's secret SS programs. As a result, Patzig was relieved of his duties by Adolf Hitler and, quickly replaced by a personal friend of Nazi Party member Admiral Erich Raeder, Wilhelm Canaris.

On paper, Wilhelm Canaris looked like the very personification of German nationalism. Born in Aplerbeck, Germany, in 1887, Canaris joined the navy at age eighteen as a cadet and rapidly rose through the ranks to become one of the most celebrated U-boat captains of World War I. Perceived as a charming fellow by the high command, Canaris seemed to be Patzig's antithesis. He brought an affinity with foreign languages (speaking English, Spanish, French, and some Russian) and cultures, a history of field work in covert operations, and a certain likability to the job that, at times, even seemed to disarm the usually standoffish SS leadership. Furthermore, while the new German government under Hitler aggressively encouraged its staffers to serve their nation as Nazi Party members, in the late 1930s, the German chancellor was beginning to fear his Nazi officers (most notably, SS leader Heinrich Himmler) might eventually accrue enough power to challenge even himself. Canaris, on the other hand, had the timely benefit of being perceived as apolitical. As a result, in 1935, Adolf Hitler made the mistake of appointing Wilhelm Canaris to be his perfect political foil as the new head of the Abwehr.

If only Hitler had read between the lines of Canaris's dossier, he would have seen what a colossal blunder he had just made.

In his first few months as Abwehr's chief, Canaris completely reorganized the intelligence organ, dividing the organization's departments into three distinct sections: (1) Abwehr, which ran largely HUMINT counterintelligence operations, (2) the foreign office, which targeted operations in other nations, and (3) the central office, which coordinated the activities of the other two, disbursed monies, and engaged in cryptography (most well known for their use of the Enigma machine). He also pioneered many long-term espionage rings, which ran throughout the British Empire, France, Spain, Latin America, and the United States, netting armament blueprints, production numbers, diplomatic messages, as well as a veritable host of well-placed resident turncoats throughout the world. Canaris, likewise, made certain that both branches of German military received pertinent intelligence to meet their needs. He was everything military intelligence needed to launch a war.

Unlike others in the Reich, Canaris also managed to remain unswayed by the increasingly cultish environment of Hitler's retinue. He never told the high command what it wanted to hear. Instead, he consistently reported intelligence analysis supported by the hard facts of what his staffers found. In several instances, for example, he characterized the invasion of Russia as a senseless waste of men and machinery in the pursuit of the unobtainable. At one point, he even asserted that the venture would be the death of the Reich. In his spare time, Canaris, conversely, did his best to woo the other intelligence organs, giving the Gestapo intelligence, offering joint covert operations programs with the SD and SS, and making friends with Reinhard Heydrich and even paying regular visits to the man's home on weekends to ensure the two men appeared to be on the same page. While the SS could and often did complain at length about the spymaster's in-

terference and dubious loyalty, Hitler could not argue with his
track record of success.

Perhaps He Should Have . . .

It seemed Canaris was too good to be true, and he was. While
seeming to be everything Germany and the Nazis needed, Wilhelm Canaris was secretly doing everything he could to undermine the German government and its racially motivated plans.
An arch anti-Nazi, Canaris helped many Jews stay hidden, escape
Germany using Abwehr passports, and even employed many
others as purported Nazi agents. Similarly, he recruited other anti-
Nazis as Abwehr agents, lending assistance to several resistance
cells (including German theologian Dietrich Bonhoeffer and his
friends) in the pursuit of assassinating Hitler and/or deposing the
Nazi government. Furthermore, when Hitler considered invading
Switzerland, Canaris furnished the chancellor with fraudulent intelligence reports, arguing that such an invasion would be against
the interests of the Reich.

It's one thing to undermine policy, but it is entirely another
matter to wreck entire strategies, which Wilhelm Canaris also
managed to pull off without getting caught. When the German
high command contemplated invading Gibraltar through Spain,
Canaris flew to Spain and persuaded Francisco Franco to forbid
the passage of Nazi troops through his territory. When Hitler
believed the Allies would invade Anzio, Italy, Canaris changed
Hitler's mind, thereby pulling away much needed defensive assets
from the region at a critical moment for the Allies. Finally, when
the high command demanded Canaris slow down the progress of
the United States, the spymaster organized Operation Pastorius,

in which two teams of haphazardly trained and highly uncommitted Abwehr agents were inserted into the United States by U-boat. Within days, two of the men turned themselves, their teams, and several dozen previously undetected Nazi sleeper agents over to the federal government. Best of all, Canaris had plotted his moves so well that Hitler never suspected the old naval officer was anything less than a loyal servant of Nazi Germany with just a string of bad luck.

Yet, as every spy knows, all luck eventually wears out. When a group of Abwehr agents were linked to the SS breakup of an anti-Nazi group (the Frau Solf Tea Party) in 1943 and subsequently defected to the British Empire, the SS and the Gestapo finally had justification to kill the Abwehr. In their subsequent investigation, several of the agency's misdeeds were uncovered and many anti-Nazi agents were exposed, but, for all his savvy and political connections, they could not touch Canaris himself. Instead, Hitler reassigned the aging spymaster to a do-nothing administrative position where the old sailor might await retirement.

Instead of taking the hint and giving up the life of clandestine operations, Wilhelm Canaris returned to his old ways to finish that which he could no longer do as a spymaster. Shortly after his reassignment, Canaris heavily invested his knowledge, skills, and assets in Claus von Stauffenberg and his co-conspirators' plot to remove Hitler by placing a bomb under the meeting room table at the führer's Wolf's Lair complex. On July 20, 1944, the plan, called Operation Valkyrie, was initiated, and, like clockwork, the bomb exploded. Yet, in a cruel twist of fate, Hitler managed to escape harm. The conspirators were soon discovered and Canaris was subsequently arrested. On April 9, 1945, he and several former Abwehr agents were forced to strip naked, marched into a prison courtyard before the harangues SS officers, hanged, and left to decay.

In just a few years, Wilhelm Canaris made Hitler rue the day the chancellor had ever considered him an ideal choice to run the Abwehr. As the intelligence chief, the naval-officer-turned-spymaster had single-handedly undermined numerous opportunities for Adolf Hitler to achieve his goals and, moreover, actively contributed to the demise of the Nazi Party to a greater extent than any anti-Nazi cell or member of the German resistance.

WE'VE ALMOST WON, SO LET'S CHANGE THE PLAN!

The Battle of Britain, August–September 1940

BY DOUGLAS NILES

The war in the air is a crucial part of any serious look at the campaigns of World War II. Many people understand that the Battle of Britain was one of the keystones of the air war, and that Britain's narrowly won victory was absolutely essential for its continuing to wage the war. But there are a lot of misunderstandings about that battle, which a lot of people tend to picture as the "Blitz," with brave Londoners seeking shelter in the subways and whole swaths of the capital city, and other great British cities, burning under the relentless onslaught of Luftwaffe bombs.

The Blitz very much occurred, of course, and was the source of massive destruction and large loss of life across much of southern England and the Midlands. But the Blitz occurred after the Battle of Britain, and was only made possible because the skilled and valiant pilots of the Royal Air Force *had already defeated the Luftwaffe* in the first battle fought exclusively between the flying forces of two great powers.

The Battle of Britain is a historical watershed for another reason: it was the first German strategic campaign that failed to accomplish its objective. It was a true turning point, before which the Germans seemed unstoppable and after which they did not. True, there were many terrible battles, other nations would fall to the Nazi storm, and four and a half bloody years would pass before Hitler's regime was destroyed—but the Battle of Britain was the hinge that allowed the drastic shift in the war's momentum to begin.

Germany faced many obstacles in the battle, but in the end was defeated because of two mistakes—one that dated back almost a year, to the start of the war. Great Britain declared war on Germany on September 3, 1939, yet at no time between that declaration and the fall of France in June 1940 did the German political or military leadership give much thought to the problem of defeating the English foe. It seems likely that Hitler truly expected the British to sue for peace after he completed his conquest of the Continent. Perhaps, under other leadership, this might have happened, but it soon became clear that Winston Churchill would entertain no such notion.

Finally, at the beginning of July 1940, Hitler reluctantly ordered a study of the problems inherent in invading England. By the middle of that month, he ordered his forces to prepare for that invasion, which would be called Operation Sea Lion. It was initially scheduled for the middle of August, but even after the date was decided, the führer was distracted and unenthused, as he was already thinking ahead to the problem of Russia. (In late July he told General Halder that, if at all possible, he wanted to attack the Soviet Union in the autumn of 1940.)

Neither the Wehrmacht nor the Kriegsmarine was enthusiastic about the prospects of a cross-Channel invasion. The navy warned of the dangers presented by the British fleet, which included many battleships, any one of which could blast apart an anchored invasion fleet. (The Germans at this point had no battleships, and their largest battlecruisers, *Gneisnau* and *Scharnhorst*, had been damaged during the Norwegian campaign and had yet to be prepared.) The army, at the same time, felt that it would need many divisions, including at least three panzer units, to successfully win a land campaign in England. Moving this many troops and their equipment would require a massive sealift capacity and sufficient command of the waters to allow safe passage back and forth to maintain a supply line.

Only the Luftwaffe—in the person of Reichsmarschall Hermann Goering—embraced the notion of a contest with its British counterpart, the Royal Air Force. The army and navy were both more than willing to let Goering's forces make the attempt, since a command of the air was a clear prerequisite for both sea and land operations against Great Britain.

Unfortunately for Germany, Goering's Luftwaffe had not been designed with a campaign like this in mind. While its fast medium bombers and accurate Stuka dive-bombers were ideal for supporting an army in battle, they were poorly designed for a strategic air campaign. The twin-engine Dornier, Heinkel, and Junkers bombers couldn't carry a heavy enough bomb load to inflict massive damage, while the Stukas and twin-engine Bf-110 fighters were so slow and unmaneuverable that they would prove easy prey to British fighters. The fast, well-armed Bf-109 was better in air combat than the British Hurricane and approximately equal to the top-of-the-line Spitfire. But it was hampered by a short range—even from bases just across the Channel, in Calais, it could fly only as far as London, and once there could engage in only a few minutes of combat before it needed to head home to refuel.

Yet Goering was determined to go to battle with the RAF, and Hitler believed that he could win. His aircraft were organized in three great air fleets: Luftflotte Two, in northern France (Air Marshal Albert Kesselring); Luftflotte Three, in Belgium and Holland (Air Marshal Hugo Sperrle); and Luftflotte Five, in Denmark and Norway (General Hans-Jürgen Stumpff). Air fleets two and three, together, began the battle with 875 twin-engine bombers and 316 dive-bombers, supported by about 700 Bf–109s and 225 Bf–110s. Luftflotte Five had another 125 bombers, but its bases were too far from England to allow the use of fighters.

To counter these numbers, the RAF had about 650 fighters, with slightly more than half of these Hurricanes. Fighter production would be a key element during the battle and throughout the year, as losses had to be replaced. When Churchill became prime minister (May 10, 1940) he created a new office, the Ministry of Aircraft Production, and appointed Lord Beaverbrook to the post. Under his touch—Air Chief Marshal Sir Hugh Dowding, commander in chief of Fighter Command, described his influence as "magical"—Britain had been able to replace the four hundred fighters lost in the Battle of France during the last months of summer. The production of fighters had been more than doubled since his appointment, and in fact reached a total of nearly forty-three hundred for all of 1940, a year in which Germany only produced three thousand.

Another advantage the British possessed was the new technology of radar. A series of towers along the coast allowed them to scan the skies around the country and even over northern Europe. The Germans were very slow to understand the impact of radar, much to their detriment. At the same time, the RAF had a unified command and control system, extending from the radar stations to centralized sector stations, where incoming attacks were studied and interceptions planned, to the wide network of small airfields across the country. This high level of command and control even extended into the cockpit of each fighter, since every aircraft was equipped with a reliable high-frequency radio. Thus, the British aircraft were managed about as efficiently as possible, while the Germans didn't even attempt to coordinate the attack plans of Luftlotten Two and Three, which occupied adjacent sectors on the Continent.

In fact, the Luftwaffe's intelligence department was under the command of a lowly major, and he and his staff routinely underestimated British production capacity. For example, the intelligence department suggested the British produced about two hundred fighters in August, at the height of the battle, when the real number was more than twice that. In the middle of that month, it claimed that nearly a dozen British airfields had been completely destroyed—yet only one, at Manston, had been incapacitated for more than a few days.

The air struggles between Germany and England began in earnest during July and the first week of August, with the Germans making damaging raids against British ports and installations on the English Channel. However, these objectives were not crucial to Britain's war effort, so Fighter Command held back from all but the most tempting engagements, marshalling its forces for the more important battles that Hugh Dowding, and others, expected in the near future.

These commenced in earnest on August 8. For the next ten days the Luftwaffe flew more than a thousand sorties (individual aircraft missions) every day, including 1,485 on August 8 and a high of 1,786 sorties on August 15. They went after radar installations and the many fighter bases scattered across the country, mostly with small groups of bombers escorted by fighters. The

RAF fought back, using radar and central control to zero in on the enemy formations. German losses were much higher than the RAF's. After a few attacks, Germany realized that the lumbering Stukas were easy meat for the speedy British fighters, and pulled the dive-bombers from the battle.

Theorizing that the strong British fighter presence in southern England meant that the Midlands had been stripped of squadrons, Luftflotte Five made a bomber-only attack from Norway on August 15, suffering heavy losses when the theory proved false. This would be the only day Stumpff's air fleet saw action; as the battle progressed, the bombers based in Scandinavia were recalled to France and the Low Countries to replace losses suffered by the other two air fleets.

All told, on August 15, the Germans lost seventy-five aircraft, the British thirty-four. The savage action across the whole of central and southern England inspired Churchill's famous quote: "Never in the field of human conflict was so much owed by so many to so few." By the eighteenth, a period of inclement weather suspended operations for a few days, allowing both sides time to regroup. The brutal fighting and heavy losses also caused Goering to rethink his strategy.

Clear weather returned on August 24, and the Luftwaffe returned to the battle with a new focus: the attacks would be made by large formations (hundred-plus bombers) and would concentrate on key Fighter Command bases and installations around London. Formations of bombers took off and flew circles over France, confusing the radar operators who had a hard time telling these dummy formations from the actual bombing raids. Huge numbers of fighters accompanied each raid, and RAF losses spiraled higher than the rate of replacements. On August 31, Fighter Command had its worst day, losing thirty-nine fighters against forty-one German losses. By September 5, many forward airfields had been rendered at least temporarily unusable, and total British losses numbered more than four hundred fighters in the previous nine days.

At this point, Fighter Command was near the breaking point, and the Luftwaffe was on the verge of gaining air superiority over England. And then Hitler and Goering made the mistake that would cost them the battle and, arguably, the war itself. The reasons for the mistake were not found in military tactics, but rather in the psychology of these two men, aided perhaps by an intentional goad from the feisty Winston Churchill.

Thus far throughout the war, the British and Germans had refrained from intentionally bombing each other's cities, fearing retaliation—a notion that now seems almost quaint, considering how strategic bombing and rocket attacks were employed by both sides later in the war. But when Goering shifted his efforts during the Battle of Britain to RAF installations around London, a small formation of bombers went off course on August 24. Lost in the clouds and anxious to return home, the crews jettisoned their bombs—which happened to fall on London.

Churchill seized the chance, and immediately ordered reprisal raids against Berlin. For a week, RAF bombers roamed over German skies in nighttime attacks, using the darkness as protection against German antiaircraft. Virtually untouched, they bombed Berlin three times, and also struck Düsseldorf, Essen, and other industrial cities. By early September, Goering was humiliated and angry, and Hitler was in a ranting fury. Both men agreed: these raids must be avenged!

So the focus of the Battle of Britain shifted again. Beginning on September 7, and continuing for the rest of the month, the Luftwaffe sent raid after raid against London, in direct retaliation for the bombing of German cities. The attacks, all occurring in day-light, reached their peak on September 15, when more than one thousand bombers and seven hundred fighters struck the great city. But the RAF knew where the Germans were going to attack, and Fighter Command's damaged bases had been repaired and were once again operational. Spitfires and Hurricanes harassed the German aircraft throughout that long day, inflicting fifty-six losses for only twenty-six RAF fighters. (And, as always during the battle, every German pilot and crewman who was shot down was either killed or captured, while about half of the British fliers survived unscathed and lived to fight another day.)

Now it was the Luftwaffe that was suffering unsustainable losses in this battle of attrition. Though the suffering of Londoners was real and extensive—more than ten thousand citizens lost their lives, and much of the city was destroyed during those September raids—the plucky British spirit remained undaunted, and the RAF was able to rebuild its strength. Operation Sea Lion was indefinitely postponed on October 12. As autumn progressed, the Luftwaffe abandoned daylight raids entirely and commenced the night missions known as the Blitz, which continued until the next May, when most of the German air strength was pulled east for the invasion of the USSR.

The Battle of Britain was over, and Britain's victory had assured its survival and paved the way toward the winning of the war.

SACRIFICING AFRICA
AND GREECE
September 1940–April 1941

BY DOUGLAS NILES

The African campaign waged in Egypt and Libya during World War II has achieved a nearly mythical status in the minds of amateur historians, storytellers, and military buffs. The dashing personalities—Erwin Rommel, Bernard "Monty" Montgomery, Claude Auchinleck—and the dramatic, mobile battles, with tanks dashing across trackless desert in vast encirclements and sweeping advances, are the stuff of pure, real-life drama. The stakes were high, being nothing less than the lifeline of the British Empire.

In the end, of course, the British and Monty prevailed over Rommel and his Afrika Korps, later known as PanzerArmee Afrika. But the campaign lasted for years and was a major drain on British resources. The battles were fought in a series of ebbs and flows, with an Italian advance into Egypt, a British counterpunch swiftly occupying half of Libya, Rommel pushing the British back into Egypt, and on and on. Furthermore, the existence of the Axis force in Africa undoubtedly prolonged the survival of Mussolini's Italian government significantly, even as it delayed the Allies' ability to strike against the European mainland.

That whole campaign, however, might never have been necessary—the Rommel legend of the "Desert Fox" might never have come to be—without one of greatest strategic blunders of World War II. It was a decision that cost the British many thousands of men, and opened up Egypt to the dire threat of Germany capturing the Suez Canal.

And it is a decision that rests squarely on the broad shoulders of Winston Churchill himself.

Egypt, and particularly the canal, which allowed passage between the Mediterranean Sea and the Indian Ocean, formed a key portion of the British Empire, and it would need to be protected. The presence of an Axis ally in Italy made this need all the more certain. The problem was that, in the summer of 1940, there were precious few resources available for the task. The commander in chief of Middle East Command was General Sir Archibald Wavell. He was responsible for the safety of Egypt, Palestine, and the British provinces, such as Sudan and Kenya, in East Africa. In Egypt itself he had only thirty-six thousand troops, and most of these were administrative and other noncombat soldiers. An understrength armored division, the Seventh, was his lone offensive force. Portions of Indian and New Zealand divisions formed the backbone of his infantry.

Facing him across the border in Libya was an army of 200,000 Italians, supported by a large, modern air force, under the command of Marshal Rodolfo Graziani. In September 1940, this large army advanced eastward into Egypt, following the coast of what the British called the "Western Desert" (because it lay to the west of Egypt's population centers) in a methodical advance. If unchallenged, this course of movement would have carried him through

Alexandria, Cairo, and eventually the Suez Canal. But Graziani only advanced fifty miles before setting up his own blocking position in a series of fortified camps anchored to the coast at Sidi Barrani, and extending southward into the desert.

The British moved out to establish a blocking position at Mersa Matruh, 200 miles west of the Nile and 120 miles from the Libyan border. This Western Desert Force, of some thirty thousand men, included the Seventh Armored Division, the Fourth Indian Division, and a brigade of New Zealanders. As his field commander, Wavell appointed a man who would turn out to be one of the more brilliant practitioners of blitzkrieg-like tactics during the early years of World War II. Major General Richard O'Connor assumed command of the Western Desert Force at the end of summer in 1940. His light forces were outnumbered approximately seven to one by his Italian foe—but he wasn't about to let a little detail like that stop him from taking offensive action.

Utilizing the Seventh Armored Division, soon to become famous as the "Desert Rats," as his mobile force, O'Connor approached the rear of the first line of Italian camps by the simple expedient of moving through a wide, unguarded gap between them. (The camps were too far apart to allow for mutual support.) The fortified position at Nibeiwa was his first target. It was laid out in a pattern that was repeated by Graziani's forces throughout the Western Desert: it had a minefield to the east, which was backed up by trenches and barbed wire. These defensive emplacements curved around to protect the north and south flanks of the camp, with a gap at the ear—shaped sort of like a backward C.

With a spearhead formed by the Matilda tanks of the Seventh Royal Tank Regiment, followed by the well-trained and fiercely combative infantry of the Fourth Indian Division, O'Connor's men charged through the gap at the rear of the Italian camp. The surprised Italians, four thousand of them, quickly surrendered. British casualties were negligible. In short order the attack was repeated, using the same tactic, against camps called Tummar West and Tummar East, while the Seventh Armored Division moved on ahead to occupy the coast road and block the Italians' line of retreat.

The Italians were alerted now to the danger, and when O'Connor's men attacked the large camps near Sidi Barrani the next day, the enemy put up a spirited resistance in the middle of a blinding sandstorm. Some reinforcements were called back from the Seventh Armored, and by the end of the third day of combat, O'Connor's thirty thousand men had taken forty thousand prisoners. Since the attacks had been initially ordered as a mere raid, it was a truly stunning victory.

The rest of Graziani's force retreated from Egypt, many of them holing up in the border fortress at Bardia. They were quickly isolated there by the racing tanks of the Seventh Armored Division, but before O'Connor could press a follow-up attack, his Indian division was recalled by Wavell for use against an Italian attack in East Africa. It would be another three weeks before a replacement, the Sixth Australian Division, reached the front after having been ordered there from Palestine.

On January 3, 1941, O'Connor was authorized to resume the attack, and in a three-day battle the fortress was captured, along with 45,000 prisoners, 462 artillery pieces, and 130 tanks. Next up was the coastal fortress of Tobruk, which was sealed off by the Desert Rats and attacked and captured by the Australians on January 22, yielding 30,000 prisoners, 236 guns, and 90 tanks. Tobruk was a hugely important position, because it was the only good port between Egypt and central Libya. Possession of it, coupled with command of the sea, gave the British a splendid forward supply base.

The Italians were clearly on the run, with only two more ports—Benghazi and Tripoli—available to them on all the north coast of Africa. But Winston Churchill was starting to have a new idea, and it wasn't a good one, not for O'Connor, his men, or British fortunes in the war. Around the turn of the new year, Churchill had pressed the head of the Greek government, General Ioannis Metaxas, for permission to reinforce his Greek army with British troops—troops that would have to be pulled from O'Connor's tiny force. Metaxas and his army commander, General Alexander Papagos, politely declined, fearing that a British presence would make Greece more likely to be attacked by Germany. (Although at war with Italy, Greece was not yet engaged in hostilities with Hitler's Reich.) The Greeks even suggested that the British forces could best be employed to rid Libya of its Italian presence.

Churchill was not persuaded. He himself had participated in campaigns in Greece during World War I, and the region had a powerful fascination for him. (Later he would refer rather ludicrously to the rugged, mountainous peninsula as the "soft underbelly" of Hitler's Europe—a term he also applied to Italy.) In his desire to create a theater where British troops could challenge Germans, he was ever seeking fronts that did not involve a direct assault against the strong German armies in France.

Since the Greeks had turned down his generous offer, and Tobruk had been so fortuitously captured, Churchill and Wavell authorized O'Connor to continue his advance and capture Benghazi. Still, Wavell was ordered to hold on to any reinforcements that reached him in Egypt, so that they could be dispatched to Greece if the opportunity arose. Undeterred, the Western Desert

Force swept on, though the Seventh Armored Division was now down to just fifty Matildas, which had proven to be by far the most effective British tank so far. O'Connor was preparing to attack on February 12, but a week earlier he received reports indicating that the Italians were already pulling back, evacuating the "bulge" of Libya's coast along the road that curved north, west, then back south to a bottleneck at El Agheila. Many thousands of enemy troops were observed to be moving westward along the road.

Acting upon this knowledge, the British general conceived of his boldest stroke yet: he ordered the tracked and wheeled elements of the Seventh Armored to race in a straight line across the desert in an attempt to reach and block the coast road before the Italians, following the more circuitous route along the coast, could escape. After a magnificent cross-country race, in which British tanks and armored cars crossed some 170 miles of rugged ground in just about thirty hours, they arrived on the coast road just thirty minutes before the first of the retreating Italians marched into view.

Here, at Beda Fomm, a British force of some three thousand men blocked the road and refused to be budged. The Italians fought ferociously to get out. Both sides lost many tanks, but every Italian effort was checked by speedy armored cars and light tanks. In the end, the remainder of Graziani's men—20,000 of them—surrendered on February 7. All told, during the campaign O'Connor had lost some 2,000 men (only 500 killed) from a force that had never numbered greater than 30,000, and he had wiped out a field army of nearly 150,000, taking over 130,000 prisoners.

After Beda Fomm, the road to Tripoli—the last remaining Italian base in Africa—was wide open and undefended. O'Connor was eager to continue his advance, and if he had been allowed to do so, he would, in all likelihood, have cleared the Axis out of Africa even before the first tanks of Erwin Rommel's Afrika Korps had been put ashore. (Rommel himself didn't reach Tripoli until February 12, and his first tanks didn't follow until March.)

But fate, in the irresistible force of Prime Minister Churchill, threw this chance, and all the fruits of O'Connor's victories, away. On February 12, Churchill sent a message to Wavell, ordering him to halt O'Connor's advance, and stripping away the majority of the Western Desert Force for action in Greece. It seemed that General Metaxas had died suddenly at the end of January, and his successor was unable to resist Churchill's persuasions. On March 7, the first of some fifty thousand British troops landed in Greece, which was invaded by Germany on April 6. By April 27 the Nazis had overrun the country, capturing twelve thousand British troops and forcing the rest to abandon their guns and equipment as the Royal Navy evacuated them in a "Second Dunkirk." By the beginning of April, Rommel was also on the attack in Libya, and the war in Africa would continue for twenty-five more bloody months. And General Wavell? He was made the scapegoat for Churchill's blunder and was shunted off to the so-far quiet sector of India.

GOOD IDEAS TURN INTO DEAD ENDS

April 1941–December 1944

BY WILLIAM TERDOSLAVICH

The Romans called the Mediterranean Sea "Mare Nostrum"—
"Our Sea."

So did Great Britain.

The Americans didn't see it that way. They were at first reluctant to commit resources to the Mediterranean Theater, remaining convinced that the surest way to beat Germany was to invade France right away, even if the U.S. Army wasn't ready yet. Eventually they followed the British lead, sending forces to aid the conquest of North Africa, Sicily, and Italy. But the Americans would eventually designate the Mediterranean a secondary theater.

But that is not how the British looked at "the Med." It was a crucial link in the British Empire's line of communication, the shortcut that reached India via the Suez Canal in Egypt. Britain also controlled the Mediterranean's vital choke points of Malta, in the middle, and Gibraltar, its western gateway to the greater Atlantic.

Prime Minister Winston Churchill saw much of the British struggle in World War II in terms of controlling the Mediterranean. Eliminating Italy and Germany as players in that thoroughfare would free up 1 million tons of shipping that used to go around Africa to reach India or Egypt. The Allies could also use its naval superiority to bring more force to bear at any point along the Italian or Balkan coastlines, given that Italy, Greece, and Yugoslavia could only be reached from Germany by a single double-tracked rail line. And there was the possibility of bringing Yugoslavia, Greece, and Turkey into the war as British allies, thus threatening Germany's southern flank and threatening Romania's oil fields.

These were all promising ideas. But Churchill's strategic imagination often exceeded the capabilities of the British Empire. There were times when seemingly good moves turned into mistakes.

I'd Like Some Turkey with an Order of Greece

Churchill envisioned an anti-German alliance with Greece, Yugoslavia, and Turkey in 1941. Selling this proposition was not going to be easy, as these nations perceived Britain as weak and Germany as strong. Hitler's winning streak in Europe so far was proof versus Churchill's promise. Of the three, only Greece was at war, holding its own against an Italian invasion from Albania while maintaining a fairly conciliatory relationship with Germany.

Things became complicated when Yugoslavia suffered a coup d'état, discarding its pro-German foreign policy for a pro-British one. Eager to lance a threat to his southern flank on the eve of invading Russia, Hitler ordered his army to take out Yugoslavia and Greece. In April, the Germans attacked. Yugoslavia fell in one week.

Despite the need in North Africa, Churchill ordered six divisions to aid Greece. This could not have come at a worse time, as necessity was pulling British strategy in divergent directions. British and Commonwealth forces were needed to clear Italian troops out of Ethiopia and Somalia, then Italian colonies. British forces in Libya were in retreat before Rommel's Afrika Korps. Sending troops to Greece would only weaken the British at a time when they needed strength.

Britain's W Force was posted to face the Bulgarian border, the expected direction of a German invasion. But the German Twelfth Army had no trouble outflanking this line from behind as it staged its attack from Yugoslavia. A simultaneous attack by Rommel in Libya foreclosed any possibility of W Force getting more aid. W Force was pulled out of mainland Greece, a portion being sent to defend Crete, and the rest sent to Egypt.

Churchill could only promise too little and it came too late for Greece. After witnessing British defeat up close, Turkey was not keen on entering the war. President Ismet Inönü stuck to his policy of hardheaded neutrality. Churchill's Greek gambit only weakened British strength in the Mediterranean.

Turkish Delight at Club Med

With U.S. entry into the war in December 1941, Churchill got what he needed—massive aid and a strong ally that could help win the war. But he also inherited a headache. The Americans were not interested in operating in the Mediterranean, preferring instead to take a direct approach by invading France, then Germany.

Britain needed to gain control of the Mediterranean, plain and simple. Supplying an army in Egypt required a chain of merchant convoys going around Africa. Kicking Germany and Italy out of Libya, then Tunisia, would eliminate this drain on resources. But this meant persuading President Roosevelt and Army Chief of Staff General George Marshall that putting the Med first was worth it.

Reluctantly, the Americans went along with British strategy, which resulted in the invasions of Morocco and Algeria in late 1942. This strengthened the Allies in the Med, as Rommel's Afrika Korps and the Italian army beat a retreat from Egypt to Tunisia to avoid being strategically cut off from Europe. Churchill used this opportunity to woo Turkey again.

Churchill gave it his best shot in January 1943, paying a covert visit to Turkey's President Inönü, with concurrent military talks between Chief of the Imperial General Staff Lord Alanbrooke and Field Marshal Fevzi Cakmak. A Turkish entry into World War II would be a game changer, allowing the RAF to base bombers that could more easily hit the Romanian oil fields. The Turkish army was not on par with Germany's or Britain's, but aid and equipment would not hurt.

Churchill and Alanbrooke came away from the talks thinking that a deal was close. But German diplomats were closer, working on Inönü to stay out. They pointed to a significant German force in Bulgaria that could attack Turkey if it "chose the wrong side." The threat kept Turkey on the fence, even though this German force was more fiction than fact. At this time, Germany had about eleven divisions in occupied Yugoslavia. Another division was posted to Greece, which was largely occupied by the Italian army. Portions of northwestern Greece (Salonika and its vicinity) were given to Bulgaria.

Inönü understood his nation's army was no match for an enemy with a modern, mechanized army. Turkey suffered the loss

of the Ottoman Empire and near dismemberment as a result of
World War I. Those who ran the country during World War II
had direct experience in World War I and had no wish to repeat
it. Plus Germany had no trouble invading Yugoslavia in 1941. Despite being tied down elsewhere in Europe, Germany did show
some improvisational talent rushing major forces to trouble
spots. Inönü would have had good reason to heed a German
threat, especially since neutrality was enabling Turkey to survive
a continental war.

Dodecanese Debacle

Churchill followed up again shortly after Italy's exit from the war
in the fall of 1943. The Allies had already taken Sicily and invaded
Italy in two places. The Dodecanese Islands were Italian posses-
sions off of Turkey's southeastern coast that Churchill saw as ripe
for the taking if only he could get a division there. A demonstration of British strength so close to Turkey might get Inönü to stop
being "neutral," even though Turkey was selling chromium to
Germany and permitting some British air and naval movements
through its waters and airspace. The Americans wanted nothing
to do with the Dodecanese operation, being fixed now on invading France in 1944. Churchill would have to do this one alone. He
was depending on audacity in the face of the enemy, as well as
his cautious generals.

Sadly, only a British brigade could be spared for the effort,
along with an assortment of commandos and a flotilla of Royal
Navy cruisers and destroyers. The nearest RAF and Royal Navy
bases were in Egypt, so air and naval support was going to be
tenuous, not robust.

In less than two months, the British were ejected from Kos, Leros, and Samos by greater numbers of German infantry and paratroops. The Germans could reinforce their efforts thanks to the Luftwaffe flying from bases in nearby Greece. Small craft traveling at night eluded the British naval and air sweeps. The Germans suffered the loss of 4,000 troops, as well as 12 merchant ships and 20 ferry barges used to recapture the Dodecanese. In exchange, the British and Greek navies lost 6 destroyers, plus 4 cruisers and 4 destroyers damaged, plus another 10 coastal craft or minesweepers sunk. The RAF lost 115 aircraft, while an additional 4,800 troops were also lost, with many of this number captured.

Upon seeing this failure of British military prowess, Turkey wisely stayed out of the war. It was another failure for Churchill, but one that could have been avoided if his generals were better able to stand up to him. Alanbrooke was an exception. First Sea Lord Admiral Sir Dudley Pound was the rule, giving in to Churchill on sending two battleships to Singapore when Japan declared war (and losing them). Alanbrooke's predecessor, General Sir John Dill, disagreed with Churchill over strategy in Egypt and the Far East . . . and got fired. Wavell gave in twice, sending forces to Greece from Egypt and also launching a premature offensive. Auchinleck would also give in to Churchill, obeying an order to launch an offensive, also to lose. Many generals felt it better to do what Churchill wanted rather than risk being sacked for advocating caution over audacity.

The generals may be complicit for giving in to Churchill, but responsibility in the end must rest with the prime minister. Churchill, the amateur military historian, was ignoring past experience. Britain always got beat whenever it relied on audacious, small forces seizing key objectives in the face of greater forces. And this only got worse after the advent of airpower.

THE BATTLE OF CRETE

Eastern Mediterranean, May 1941

BY WILLIAM TERDOSLAVICH

It did not have to be a battle lost.

Crete is a skinny, mountainous island that sits like a speed bump guarding the approaches to the Aegean Sea, within easy bomber range of the Romanian oil fields and well placed to project naval power against Axis-held North Africa's long coast. That made Crete a prize worth having for the British, and a reason for the Germans to take it.

In May 1941, the remnants of a British army just evacuated from mainland Greece were diverted to Crete to make a belated defense. Their presence was augmented by the Royal Navy, which made any enemy seaborne invasion impossible. But Germany did have an air force. And it had paratroops.

Colonel General Kurt Student, founder of Germany's airborne forces, planned to airdrop an entire division to take at least one of Crete's three main airfields. Once secured, a light infantry division could be airlanded to help take the rest of the island. The Luftwaffe's bombers would make up for the lack of artillery and armor. This plan he named Operation Mercury.

Germany used paratroops before to seize tactical objectives

in Norway and Denmark, Belgium and the Netherlands. The airdrops were always within easy reach of relief forces on the ground, making the "vertical outflank" an effective tactic. This time the paratroops would be on their own.

Operation Mercury depended on surprise to obtain success.

There was only one problem: the British knew the paratroops were coming.

Enigma Without Mystery

The Luftwaffe was the sloppiest service to use the Enigma encryption machine. Mistakes made by signalers gave British code breakers in Bletchley Park the ability to crack the Enigma code used to transmit sensitive information. Classified as "Ultra," these decrypts usually stayed close to the top. Now that intelligence had to go to General Bernard Freyberg, commander of the New Zealand division and provisional defender of Crete.

Freyberg was a typical "muddy boots" general who was at ease with his men and good in a fight, but he was never a "big thinker." He had about thirty thousand British and Commonwealth troops, plus another eleven thousand armed Greek locals, to defend Crete. Ultra intelligence, wrapped under a plausible cover story, conveyed the exact time and place of the German air landings, but the list of expected enemy forces was larger than what actually arrived later. Freyberg took counsel of his fears and kept some of his forces defending beaches and ports, just in case.

Freyberg concentrated his remaining units on Canea, Crete's capital, and the three airfields of Maleme in the west, Retimo in the center, and Heraklion in the east. Sixteen tanks and forty-nine field guns were divvied up between the three forces covering the airfields. Radios were too few in number. This would prove to be a handicap later in the battle.

On May 20, the Germans struck.

Surprise! No Surprise!

The Luftwaffe used five hundred Ju–52 transports and about seventy gliders to transport the Seventh Parachute Division and the Assault Regiment of the Eleventh Air Corps to Crete. But there were not enough transports to drop the entire division at once. Half would jump in the morning on Maleme, the rest in the afternoon on Heraklion and Retimo.

To assault Maleme, Student planned to use gliders to land paratroops in the dry riverbed smack next to the airfield so they could see the objective. Another two thousand troops would parachute to the west of the riverbed, form up, and reinforce the attack. Key to taking Maleme Airfield was Hill 107. If the enemy held this height, the airfield could be fired on, making it useless for reinforcement.

Defending the airfield was the Twenty-second Battalion, Fifth NZ Brigade, Lieutenant Colonel Leslie Andrews commanding. He deployed D Company to cover the riverbed, posted C Company to protect the airfield, while placing A and B companies on the slopes of Hill 107. As soon as the gliders bringing in four hundred men of the Assault Regiment crash-landed in the dry riverbed, A and B companies opened fire, raking the position.

The paratroops of "West Group" suffered massive casualties in the battle's opening hours. They were expecting light resistance and friendly natives. They got a bunch of stubborn Kiwis out for blood. Each squad of German paratroops jumped with their weapons in a separate container, which they recovered upon landing. Squads that failed to recover weapons while under fire got mauled, their pistols not much use. It was not unusual for paratroop battalions to suffer 80 percent losses during landing.

That afternoon at Retimo, the Ju–52s flying in I and III battalions of the Third Parachute Regiment were shredded by British antiaircraft fire. Many of the remaining troops were shot while descending by British and Australian troops on the ground. First Parachute Regiments I and III battalions were slaughtered by the British prewar regulars posted at Heraklion. These two battles were decisively won with ease.

Meanwhile at Maleme . . .

Despite the massive losses being inflicted by the Twenty-second Battalion, the Germans had one advantage that the New Zealanders lacked—radios. The surviving leaders could coordinate their assault on Hill 107 and Maleme airfield with their tattered battalions. Lieutenant Colonel Andrews of the Twenty-second Battalion only had one radio, which linked him to brigade headquarters.

This lack of communication resulted in Andrews having an incomplete picture of his situation. He tried to reinforce his companies by launching an attack with two tanks, but one broke down and the other became embogged in the dry riverbed. Once night fell, Andrews assessed his situation based on what little he knew. He had no information from his front-line companies. He was getting no reinforcements from brigade. Andrews ordered his remaining units to pull back, assuming the worst had happened to his front-line companies. When the troops holding Hill 107 and the airfield found out that their comrades had fallen back, so did they, not wanting to be left out in the cold without support.

Without knowing it, Andrews handed Student the key to Crete. But the island would not be won until the Germans turned the key to unlock the battle in their favor. Student believed he had lost the battle, but was unwilling to give up. Scrounging up all available paratroops, Student formed a *kampfgruppe* ("combat formation") to drop on Maleme airfield. Coinciding with the paradrop would be the forced airlanding of a battalion of mountain troops (light infantry). The Ju–52s would come in, full bore, to land on the runway, flak and gunfire be damned.

The planned jump and forced landing was slated for the afternoon. That morning, the New Zealanders re-formed and launched an attack to take back the airfield and Hill 107. One battalion made it to the airfield, when the commander noticed no units coming up in support; he pulled back his force. Again, lack of radios undermined the tactical ability of the New Zealanders to coordinate their actions.

Then the Ju–52s came overhead. Fresh reserves of paratroops fell from the sky. Again, rifles and machine guns were pointed upward to plink at the paratroops, killing many in harness. While the Kiwis were shooting at live clay pigeons (or sitting ducks), the Ju–52s carrying the mountain troops came barreling in. Machine guns and antiaircraft guns blazed away at the tri-motor transports, hitting over twenty. Planes crash-landed but still managed to off-load reinforcing infantry. The wrecks were then pushed off the airfield by surviving paratroops using captured Bren Gun Carriers as bulldozers.

By day's end, a battalion of German mountain infantry made it to Maleme. Within three days, a shuttle of Ju–52s brought in the rest of their division. Freyberg's troops held the line in front of Canea, overlooking the main harbor at Souda Bay. But the Luftwaffe had air superiority. Student could reinforce his gains. Freyberg could not strengthen his defense. Reluctantly, Freyberg withdrew his remaining forces southward over the mountains to Sfakia, eventually to be evacuated. The Germans missed their chance to cut off Freyberg's retreat when they continued to drive east to relieve their shredded battalions at Retimo and Heraklion.

The High Price of a Cheap Operation

By May 27, Freyberg got his orders to pull his units off of Crete. Over the next four days, the Royal Navy managed to evacuate half his men, but the rearguards had to be sacrificed. British losses totaled 3,500 killed, 12,000 taken prisoner. Another day, another Dunkirk. The Royal Navy lost 2,000 men among the three cruisers and six destroyers sunk by the Luftwaffe. Four battleships, six cruisers, and seven destroyers took hits.

German losses were also grave, numbering 2,000 out of 8,000 paratroops; perhaps as many as 3,500 killed in action total. But worse was the loss of Hitler's confidence. Not until the Battle of the Bulge would German paratroops be allowed to make another combat jump.

The paratroops would later prove their worth fighting many defensive battles for the Third Reich in North Africa, in Italy (especially at Cassino), at Brest, and in the Low Countries. But that is not the same as winning.

GERMANY WON'T ATTACK US!

Moscow, Summer 1941

BY PAUL A. THOMSEN

While both Germany and Russia had suffered greatly in World War I, the two nations could not have been further apart from each other. In fact, the war, their close geographic proximity, and their embracement of different extremist political ideologies (one fascist, the other communist) had, indeed, made the two European powers the bitterest of interwar period enemies. They each decried the other as the proverbial hungry wolf at their door in newspapers and the public addresses of their leaders. Both governments regularly arrested, jailed, and often executed the other's political sympathizers. Both built war machines and regularly threatened to remove the other from the face of the earth. Yet, when Adolf Hitler, chancellor of Nazi Germany, proposed the two nations should grow closer together in peace, Joseph Stalin, a master of paranoia and murderer of upward of 20 million Russian citizens, actually believed Germany no longer had imminent designs on his homeland. Tens of millions more would pay the price for his folly.

The Soviet premier was never really a deep thinker, but he was cunning. Born the son of a poor shoemaker in 1879 in Gori,

Georgia, as Iosif Dzhugashvili, Joseph Stalin (renamed the "Man of Steel" by himself in adulthood) found Marxism in the Georgian Orthodox seminary at Tiflis. Thereafter, he joined Russia's Communist Revolution and eventually became one of Vladimir Lenin's leading lieutenants, writing for the Russian presses, raising money by robbing banks, and, occasionally, breaking legs. After several arrests, exiles, and two terms of imprisonment in Siberia, Stalin returned to western Russia. During the Russian Revolution of 1917 and the subsequent civil war, he served as one of Lenin's most aggressive army commanders. Although Lenin regularly used Stalin for "dirty jobs," the new Russian leader never entirely trusted his subordinate. Yet, before Lenin could neutralize the brute, a quirk of fate helped Stalin turn the tables on the Russian leader's plans. When Lenin suddenly fell gravely ill, Stalin thoroughly isolated the leader and neutralized his communist competitors. When Lenin died, every communist with intelligence ran for cover; Stalin became the last man standing and took on the mantle of leader of the Union of Soviet Socialist Republics (USSR).

Given his original line of work, the way he obtained the leadership, and the recent abbreviated histories of several European leaders, there was reason for Stalin to feel a little paranoid. Unlike others, however, Stalin had an entire nation (over 110 million citizens) and most world powers to fear and a national security state with which to manage his fears. Historical records have, in fact, proven that Joseph Stalin was a very efficient paranoid, both making and eliminating enemies with shocking regularity. When Stalin suspected someone might challenge him in any way, they were picked up by Soviet authorities, were questioned, and often "disappeared." When his land reforms failed in the 1920s and 1930s, the resulting mass starvation winnowed sections of the populace who might rise up against his rule. Still, Stalin was a special kind of person who seldom took chances. Fearing assassins in the night, Stalin never slept in the same bedroom twice in a row and never stayed in the same bed an entire night. Moreover, by many accounts, Stalin was his own worst enemy. After learning of a large ongoing secret operation by Russian intelligence to undermine Western opposition to the Kremlin, Stalin ordered the entire network immediately shut down, the personnel involved transferred, and intelligence head retired (Stalin had never authorized the operation, believed the intelligence to be intelligence service fiction, and feared the usurpation of his authority more than any potential Western threat.) In the 1930s, Stalin also "purged" the Communist Party several times, removing numerous political, economic, and military leaders (including Lev Kamenev, Marshal Mikhail Tukhachevsky, Aleksey Rykov, and secret police leader Genrikh Yagoda). As a result, when Adolf Hitler came to power in 1933, Joseph Stalin was left with few knowledgeable advisers, a country in gross economic disrepair, widespread starvation, a massive Siberian prison system, a lot of unmarked graves, and a handful of unseasoned lieutenants to nervously shepherd their responsibilities so as not to provoke Stalin into "purging" them for either their ingenuity or their incompetence.

With his mental stability tested daily and Russia perched in such a precarious position by a series of his policies, Joseph Stalin viewed the German Nazi Party's rise to power with equal parts interest and trepidation. Under Adolf Hitler's tutelage, Germany grew strong by bedeviling its political and social minorities, arresting in-country communist dissidents, and even threatening to remove communism from Europe by military force. It was apparent to Stalin that Nazi Germany's military was gearing up for war. While every Russian leader historically believed he could wear down any single invader by attrition and a little help from the Russian weather, in the mid–1930s, Stalin grew increasingly terrified of the prospect that Nazi Germany just might be able to neutralize Russia's advantages and bring the nation to its knees in one of two ways: (1) join with France and the British Empire in a combined declared war against Russia, or (2) enter into a nonaggression pact with those same nations to isolate the precarious Russian economy as a preemptive move to a Nazi invasion.

The choices of geopolitical poisons were enough to drive anyone mad, but Stalin was already there and he had other options. So Stalin surreptitiously asked the enemies of his enemies (ironically, also his enemies: France and Britain) if they would enter into a nonaggression pact with him. Rather than cozy up to the Big Red Bear, the two nations backed away from him very quickly.

Next, Stalin turned to Germany. Unable to remove his neighbor from power by the usual isolating or "disappearing" methods, the self-styled "Man of Steel" became the most endearing of diplomats, now hoping to get Hitler to strengthen Germany's ties with Russia. First, in May 1939, Stalin replaced his Jewish ambassador to Germany, Maxim Litvinov, with one of his few truly gifted zealots, Foreign Minister Vyacheslav Molotov. Second, Russia entreated Germany to initiate a few mutually beneficial trading agreements. Third, in light of a breakdown in tenuous diplomatic negotiations between the British, the French, and the Soviets, Stalin ordered his intelligence services to carefully monitor the diplomatic negotiations of the British and the French with Hitler. Finally, Stalin (demonstrating that not all paranoid feelings are unhealthy) ordered the Soviet army to prepare for war with all due haste. As a result, by the summer, Stalin was a nervous wreck, anxiously waiting for any signals of intent from the fascist state.

Adolf Hitler, of course, had his own plans. First, he would

reunify Germany by threat or, if necessary, by force of arms. Second, he would absorb Poland. Third, he would utilize these new eastern and western resources to maximize the potential of Germany's war machine and then conquer Europe. Germany also easily read Stalin's fears. Like Stalin, Hitler too had climbed his way to the top by both making and breaking enemies. If Russia could be duped into allowing him access to additional resources in the east (and, thereby, fuel Stalin's own demise), he reasoned, then so much the better. Hence, while Hitler played an anticommunist song in public diplomatic discourses, in private, the German chancellor accepted every proposal Russia put before him in due course. Consequently, on August 3, 1939, Nazi Germany soothed Stalin's fears with new entreaties (conducted through German foreign minister Joachim von Ribbentrop) designed to officially (if covertly) appear to mend the gap between the two neighbors, culminating in a secret Nazi-Soviet nonaggression pact.

For Stalin, the renewed German diplomatic interest in Russia had been a validation that his was the superior mind and, without further thought, he abrogated his nation's safety. After all, his nation did not need the other great powers. Russian trade would keep Germany from launching an attack on his homeland and aid in the rebuilding of the Soviet state. When the two nations signed the secret pact, Stalin gained an even greater boost to his ego when Hitler effectively gave away much of eastern Europe to Russia in the form of "spheres of influence" along with the ten-year nonaggression pact. Moreover, Germany would now move against the British and the French, leaving Russia considerable time before becoming Hitler's next target. Besides, no mere paperhanger could outwit Stalin! Well, it did sound good at the time . . . and those who might have objected would have wisely saved their nation the trouble of the interrogation, trial, and firing squad by blowing out their own brains. If anything, years of pogroms and purges had proved that Soviet premier Stalin did not tolerate pessimism. With the new buffer states, security, and the promised trade bonus, as far as the Russian leader could see, Hitler had effectively bought off Joseph Stalin at just the right price.

Time was now on Stalin's side . . . or so he thought. While feelings of suspicion and paranoia had served him well over the years, Stalin demonstrated confidence in the deal and his ability to handle prospective German aggression, failing miserably to appreciate the greater danger of Hitler over his nation's flagging economy.

One week after the signing, as Stalin set about purging the populace of dissenters in his new "spheres of influence," Nazi Germany moved troops into its new eastern territory, deployed its forces in positions that would facilitate a rapid offensive eastward when ordered, and continued to increase its presence in the area over the next several months. Hitler was more than willing to give a little land to expose Russia.

With Poland now redistributed between the two short-term partners, the Nazis, as expected, turned against the French and the British, but within a matter of months, Stalin once more lost all sense of security. In utilizing emergent technologies to mastermind blitzkrieg warfare, Adolf Hitler had managed to dominate most of Europe far sooner than anyone had expected and far more effectively than Joseph Stalin was willing to admit. Now his mistaken impressions were becoming clear: Hitler was no fool to be wooed by Stalin, Germany's military was a greater force to be reckoned with than previously estimated, and the Nazis had fatted Stalin's Russia up for the slaughter sooner than expected.

The facts were worse than Stalin knew. According to postwar

Allied interrogations of the Nazi leadership, as early as the summer of 1938, Hitler had toyed with invading the Soviet Union. While France had made a far more tempting first-strike target, the Austrian propagandist-turned-fascist-dictator had never once forgotten his rival to the east. Eleven days after the Soviet invasion of eastern Poland, Hitler initiated a two-pronged strategy that would leave the mighty "Man of Steel" with his red cape tied firmly around the Russian leader's head and the mighty Soviet army's tights around its ankles. With one hand, he had stroked Stalin's ego with robust economic proposals of association, promised mutual security procedures that would alert the other of problems brewing in their newly shared acquisition, and even the announced signing of the German-Soviet Boundary and Friendship Treaty, which granted Germany a greater portion of Poland and Russia a greater portion of the east, and replaced the Soviet Union with Nazi Germany as the clear and present threat to world stability. With his other hand, Hitler re-tasked his war planners (who had secretly been planning the war against the West for years) and industry to devise a means by which Nazi Germany could rapidly eliminate the Soviet Union by military force once and for all time.

It seemed that life could not get any worse for Joseph Stalin. Conventional military wisdom held that only an idiot would fight a war on three fronts, but now the Russian premier was the one apparently playing Hitler's fool. Worse, Stalin could not chance an uprising in his new acquisition, fearing that such a revolt would gobble up precious time, men, and supplies he did not have. Furthermore, fighting an uprising might encourage Nazi Germany to drop everything and attack Russia immediately in the hope of achieving as rapid a victory over the Soviet Union as it had gained against the French. Instead, Stalin initiated his own two-pronged strategy. While flexing what little might he could in the West to contrast the reality of an understrength Soviet military, he simultaneously placed Russia's heavy industry on a war production schedule and, in an act resembling truly poor comedy, covertly re-tasked his own military staff, already bled white by the purges, to hastily plan a preemptive strike against Germany, but by the summer of 1941, it was too late.

On June 22, 1941, Adolf Hitler authorized the final stage of his master plan against Russia, Operation Barbarossa, Nazi Germany's invasion of the Soviet Union. In just a few short weeks, the front lines of Russia's meager western defensive personnel and civilian populace, who had managed to survive for years under Stalin's own paranoia, rapidly fell before the might of Hitler's invasion force. They were ill prepared, ill equipped, and outgunned. Over the next several years, Stalin would send millions more to their deaths, trying to overcome the lost time and energy caused by his mistake in believing Hitler had been less of a threat than he truly was. Yet the Soviet leader was correct about at least one dismal strategic facet. Only the sheer number of sacrificed Russian lives and severest of Russian winters managed to slow down and drive back the German invader from Soviet soil. By 1945, an estimated 26 million Russians would pay for Stalin's mistake, but not a single Soviet citizen would challenge his leader's colossal blunder until long after his death in 1953. After all, unlike Joseph Stalin, they knew their true enemy and his capabilities. Too bad none of them had been Russia's leader.

BATTLE OF MOSCOW

September 1941–January 1942

BY WILLIAM TERDOSLAVICH

When invading another country, the goal is to capture the enemy capital.

Try telling that to Adolf Hitler.

Invading Russia in June 1941, Hitler wanted to seize Leningrad and the Ukraine, while his generals reminded him that the goal must be Moscow. To get all this, Hitler relied on 3.1 million German troops, aided by 500,000 Finns and another 150,000 Romanians, and backed by 2,130 aircraft and 3,600 tanks.

Army Group North, Field Marshal Wilhelm Ritter von Leeb commanding, pushed eastward with one panzer army and two infantry armies, and the support of one *luftflotte* (air fleet), and made it to the outskirts of Leningrad. Army Group South, Field Marshal Gerd von Rundstedt in charge, with one panzer army, three infantry armies, and a Romanian army, plus one *luftflotte*, took much of the Ukraine. Army Group Center, with two panzer armies and two infantry armies, and also a committed *luftlotte*, was driving on Moscow when it halted that summer to lend its tanks to Army Group South.

The war should have ended by then. German intelligence

identified 200 Soviet divisions when the invasion began in June. They were all destroyed, yet were replaced by another 360 divisions. They were badly led and equipped, but each one was a speed bump that would cost the Germans time and blood to remove.

Now that the Ukraine was finally taken, Hitler refocused his attention on the Soviet capital. Field Marshal Fedor von Bock's Army Group Center was reinforced with another panzer army and infantry army.

It was late September.

Just one more push and Moscow would be taken.

Stopped by Rain, Not Russians

On September 30, Army Group Center attacked. Operation Typhoon called for a pair of panzer armies to knife through the Russian line north and south of Vyazma, to surround the six Russian armies standing on the defensive. Two German infantry armies followed in the wake of the panzers, consolidating gains. Farther south, support would come from a single panzer army and infantry army surrounding Bryansk, where three more Soviet infantry armies were concentrated.

The initial gains were dizzying. Von Bock's panzers took another 600,000 Russian prisoners, 1,200 tanks, and 5,400 artillery pieces just by pocketing Vyazma and Bryansk. But by October 8, the drive on Moscow came to a halt. Rain turned the Russian steppes into seas of mud. Tanks and trucks were mired up to their axles. Troops sank to their knees. Von Bock rued the further loss of time, as he recorded in his diary: "A period of good weather similar to when we started would have enabled us to put our forces, in full strength, at the gates of Moscow. It was the weather, not the Russians, which stopped us."

Von Bock had to wait for November's frosts to freeze the ground solid. Now his infantry divisions were only operating at 65 percent strength. Panzer divisions were down to half their mechanized infantry and one-third of their tanks. German supply lines were limited, so any materiel needed to support the next attack would take the place of much needed winter clothing.

Indeed, the German supply pipeline was more like a straw. Too few trucks were available to move supplies from railheads to the front, and many were nonstandard types plundered from other conquered countries, ill-suited for service in the field. Breakdowns were common and spare parts hard to come by. Captured Russian railroads needed to be converted to the German gauge, and even then German locomotives were not up to operating in the harsh Russian winter, sometimes breaking down due to frozen water pipes. German horses also died, further limiting supply flows to the front. German steel wagons were too heavy for the smaller, hardier Russian horses to pull. Supplies still got through, but the flow was constrained by unforeseen failures.

November would find the Red Army also at the nadir of its strength. It could only field 2.25 million men after losing 3 to 5 million in the summer battles. The Russians used the rain delay to build defenses and bring in reinforcements. Marshal Georgi Zhukov now commanded West Front, covering the most critical sector west of Moscow. Transferred with him from Mongolia were twenty-one fresh Siberian divisions, some of which Zhukov had used to trash the Japanese army in Mongolia in 1939. These reserves, plus the precious few, but new, T–34 tanks becoming available, would land the counter-blow at the right time.

The T–34 proved to be Zhukov's ace in the hole. It was a modern design for its day, slated to replace the thousands of obsolescent tanks destroyed by the Germans earlier in 1941. The T–34 had wide tracks, giving it excellent traction in mud or snow. Most important, it had thicker, well-sloped armor, making it nearly impervious to German 37mm and 50mm antitank guns.

Win the War in the Next Month?

Army Group Center went back on the offensive in November, once the muddy ground froze. Starting from Vyazma, von Block planned to swing the Third and Fourth Panzer armies north of Moscow, while the Second Panzer Army would drive northward toward Moscow's southern edge from Bryansk. The two claws would drive beyond Moscow to link up to the east, thus surrounding it. An infantry army would follow each panzer army to hold ground taken by the tanks.

As the offensive began, the Russian winter was starting to bite. German equipment was never designed to operate in sub-zero temperatures. The bitter cold froze motor oil in any truck or tank after the engine was switched off, requiring crews to build small bonfires under each engine to thaw it out before starting. Gun grease congealed, freezing machine guns. Horses died, limiting the ability of troops to move supplies or artillery pieces. And German soldiers lacked winter clothing. Frostbite cases skyrocketed, further thinning the depleted ranks. With each mile gained, Army Group Center lost some of its striking power, while Russian resistance slowly stiffened. By early December, the Third and Fourth Panzer armies were now north of Moscow, while the Second Panzer was forty miles south of it. The claws were surrounding Moscow, but they could not close.

By December 1, von Bock saw his offensive spent. Army Group Center lacked reserves. He asked his superiors to allow him to pull back to more defensible lines. Four days later, as von Bock got permission to retreat, Zhukov struck hard.

The Russians Are Coming

The Red Army was still a battered bear, unequal to the Germans, but Zhukov could obtain results if he could somehow bring overwhelming force to bear on just a few points. The Soviet strength facing Army Group Center was now 1.1 million troops, while Army Group Center was fielding 1.7 million. Von Bock enjoyed a two-to-one superiority in artillery and still fielded 1,100 tanks against Zhukov's 770.

But that's on paper.

In the field, Zhukov managed to build up a two-to-one superiority of infantry to block von Bock's northern thrust against Moscow, plus greater margins in guns and mortars. The weather also helped, with snow three feet deep and temperatures reaching −15° F.

Zhukov's orders were pretty clear how it was to be done. "Pursuit must be at high speed and the enemy not allowed to break contact. Widespread use must be made of leading detachments for seizure of road junctions and bottlenecks, and for disorganizing enemy march and combat formations. . . . I categorically forbid frontal attacks against enemy fortified points. Forward echelons should bypass these without delay, and leave them to be destroyed by following echelons."

The Kalinin Front led the attack, with General Ivan Konev committing four armies to attack von Bock's northern arm from three directions. Zhukov reinforced the attack with three more armies from West Front. The cold-hardy Siberians pressed their attacks, already accustomed to the same weather that froze German machine guns, trucks, and tanks. Local German commanders quickly shuttled meager reserves from one trouble spot to another, trying to blunt breakthroughs as the Soviets were looking to surround the Ninth Army and elements of the Third and Fourth Panzer armies. Von Bock struggled to pull his units back to avoid encirclement. A more modest Russian attack tried to surround the Second Panzer Army around Tula. General Heinz Guderian pulled his units back to avoid the closing claws of the Red Army.

Moscow was saved.

But Stalin got greedy.

The Aftermath

In early January, Stalin ordered all fronts to attack.

The Red Army was not up to the task, dissipating its limited strength instead of concentrating in the few places where counterattack could make a difference. Zhukov and his generals objected, but were overruled by Stalin. The offensives petered out by spring, making inconclusive gains.

Hitler thought he saved the day by issuing his infamous "no retreat" order in mid-December, just as von Bock's armies were falling back from Moscow. All German units had to hold the line, even though pulling back one to two hundred miles would have allowed Army Group Center to fall back on its supplies. Zhukov would have advanced with ever-thinning supply lines over frozen terrain with few useful roads.

Hitler's "no retreat" order planted the seeds of Germany's defeat, only it did not seem so at first. Generals who disagreed were fired. Theater commander in chief Field Marshal von Brauchitsch was sacked, with Hitler assuming his command directly. Von Bock lost his job, along with his fellow army group commanders von Leeb and von Rundstedt, and thirty-five other generals at army, corps, and even divisional levels. Hitler's political grip on the army was now certain, having lanced its role as the governing body of occupied Russia.

While deep thrusts punched through Army Group Center's flanks, the Red Army could not close the circle and trap Army Group Center, which suffered grievous losses. From December 1941 to March 1942, 256,000 men were lost in combat and another 350,000 became casualties from sickness and frostbite. Also lost were 1,800 tanks, 55,000 other vehicles, and 140 artillery pieces.

Credit for Army Group Center's survival could not be laid to Hitler's "no retreat" order. The Red Army was not yet up to the task of destroying the German army due to its lack of tactical/ operational skill and insufficient armor forces. The Germans still fought skillfully, despite the disadvantages of weather and lack of suitable equipment.

The Germans were no longer ten feet tall.

This was good news for Stalin, Zhukov, and the Red Army.

But it was not enough, just yet, to win the war.

THE NOT-SO-MASTER RACE DECLARES WAR

Berlin, December 1941

BY PAUL A. THOMSEN

In just a few short years, Adolf Hitler had managed to rebuild the German economy, resurrect the military, and reassert the nation's lost World War I status as an empire his neighbors could fear. By pairing international outliers fascist Italy and imperial Japan to oppose his rival neighbors (Great Britain, France, and the United States), the führer hoped to gain time and resources with which he might rapidly consolidate his conquered territory, catch his breath, and then launch his next round of attacks to defeat his now weakened foes. As the self-professed master race, he thought he had chosen helpful allies and a winning strategy. Oh, was he ever wrong!

In the 1930s, Adolf Hitler managed the impossible. With intriguing prose, a keen eye for talent, and a creative, competitive management style, he completely reoriented the way Germans lived their lives and governed themselves. He transformed the most despondent people in the worst economically, politically, and militarily well-off nation into Nazi Germany—one of the most powerful players on the European continent, even in the aftermath of a destructive war (which they caused). In scapegoating the Jews, the Romany, the communists, and other minority social groups, he appeared to "clean up" city streets and actually managed to utilize their seized assets in support of industrial projects for the Reich. In violating numerous treaty stipulations, Hitler even built a large and deceptively technologically advanced army that he used to appropriate much of the territory his nation had lost to Germany's neighbors in World War I, and bullied his once and future enemies into a shaky truce that would allow him to legally keep what he had stolen. While the Nazis incredulously believed they were the "master race," most historians would concede that Hitler was, at least, a master politician. In fact, had Hitler suddenly died in early 1939 and Germany had not expanded its war, he might well have been remembered as a national hero.

Yet Hitler's plan to turn Germany into a world-spanning empire had a few minor problems. The globe was already crowded with numerous imperial powers. Few outside Germany actually supported Nazi views on race and/or Aryan supremacy (imagine that). Worse, in order to jump-start the German economy, Hitler had already spent much of his own nation's resources (largely seized from the dispossessed). Hence, if Germany wanted to maintain its current level of prosperity, it would need to continue a policy of expansion, and if it wanted to compete with the major powers, it would need a massive influx of resources. It seemed Germany was trapped inside a closed system that all but dictated the nation's return to poverty.

Had Hitler been any other German politician or a go-it-alone world leader, Germany's sudden rise would have likely been promptly followed by an equally sudden crash, but the chancellor had some very interesting ideas on how to solve his nation's problems and fulfill his own dreams of a thousand-year Reich. First, he needed to find some world leader friends like himself!

At first, the United States seemed like an ideal candidate, with riches in abundance, but there were also considerable problems with fostering a relationship with the country. While there were some supporters of Nazism in America (notably the pro-Nazi organization German American Bund) and ample resources to fight a two-front world-conquering war, President Franklin Delano Roosevelt was an Anglophile in charge of a decidedly noninterventionist nation. As a result, Hitler saw the writing on the wall and looked for more pliable candidates.

Naturally, Hitler's most likely choice for a new friend was much closer to home. Benito Mussolini of Italy had served as a model in how to create a fascist state. The two shared much in common. They were both veterans of World War I. They hated the communists. Each had a long history of assassinating and executing rivals. They had both brought together a historically fragmented and poverty-stricken region. As nationalist fascist states, their governments were ideologically compatible and backed by the popular support of the people (well, those who had not been imprisoned or shot, that is). They both had heavily militaristic cultures and geopolitical outlooks. In May 1936, Mussolini had even annexed Ethiopia by military invasion. Although each personally thought the other to be an arrogant dictator with delusions well beyond his means, the two became geopolitical friends, brokered lucrative trade agreements between their two nations, and even shared military assets. If such a thing can be said, the two leaders were as compatible star-crossed lovers without the romance.

With Italy guarding Germany's underbelly and a steady cash flow crossing their border, Hitler had found a means to stave off disaster, but in order to advance his goals, he needed a sure thing.

In 1939, he managed to broker a secret deal with Stalin for still greater trading privileges, carved up eastern Europe between the two countries, and hookwinked the Soviet leader into thinking his nation was not on Nazi Germany's dinner menu. When Hitler moved to consolidate his holdings over Poland, however, Britain and France declared war on the Nazi state, dashing any hope of creating a slow and steady buildup of resources for his imperial dreams. In response, Hitler took France in a rapid-style blitzkrieg war that he hoped would: (1) save him the monetary drain of a large conventional army, (2) acquire enough resources with which he might grow his nation, and (3) shock Britain into submission. Instead, Hitler's hopes of frugality turned into a costly army of occupation with few steady profits seized from the conquered returning to Germany as quickly as Hitler would have liked. Worse, instead of shocking Britain into submission, his efforts actually catapulted the island empire into a self-defensive posture. For Hitler, Europe was fast becoming a quagmire of his own devising, but, thankfully, the United States, the suppliers of France and Britain and next most likely contender to get involved, remained largely isolationist.

While Hitler had enlisted Japan and Italy to help advance Germany's goals, his Axis partners did not fit well within his plans. There were many ideological complications of being allied with Japan. While the Asian power had military muscle to rival Germany's and could keep the United States and the British at bay, neither the Japanese' physical appearance nor their own claims of being the world's true master race sat well with the Nazi ideology of Caucasian blood purity. Hence, as far as both German and Japanese officials were considered, there would be exchanges of technology and a sharing of some additional resources, but neither would gain the other's full confidence. They would never coordinate their strategies as closely as the United States and the British did theirs, and there would never be a meeting of the minds. Conversely, Italy shared much in common ideologically with Germany, but Germany never trusted its neighbor to the south, and Mussolini was smart enough to keep Italy out of harm unless there was a potential for substantial personal gain. Furthermore, as the war dragged on, Italy's reluctance to fight and poor resource management led the German nation to have misgivings about its closest ally, forcing the garrisoning of thousands of troops in North Africa and Italy itself to protect German interests. As a result, Hitler's allies were not only not considered friends, but were also, in many ways, considered hindrances to his master plans.

How could one get his so-called friends to help him when those same friends are reluctant to do so? The answer was simple: offer some of them a contract with a signing bonus, and then get rid of the deadbeats.

By 1940, it was way too late to ask the United States to share his world vision, but as Germany began covert planning of the invasion of Russia, Hitler coerced Italy and Japan, another country bordering Russia and at odds with Britain, to enter into a binding agreement called the Tripartite Pact in order that it might stave off disaster once more for the German nation. On September 27, 1940, the three nations agreed: (1) to work together in mutual cooperation for a period of ten years, (2) to recognize the others' "spheres of influence" as part of their new world order, and (3) that if any of these Axis powers were attacked by a party with whom it was not already at war, the others would come to its aid. While this agreement did not directly help Hitler, the German leader hoped the pact would, at least, bring new revenue to the fight, encourage the one other great power not already at war (the United States) to stay out of the battle, and, possibly, even embolden Japan to pick a fight with its old adversary Russia, in solidarity with Germany's rhetoric against Russia and its occupation of Poland. If this was the master race's masterstroke, Hitler must have been skinny-dipping at the shallow end of the Aryan gene pool!

While Hitler found his arrangement with fellow fascist Mussolini somewhat beneficial, the same could not be said for Joseph Stalin's Soviet Union. Communism had long been considered a threat to German nationalism, and Russian trade with Germany was too little to be considered meaningful. Hence, in the summer of 1941, Nazi Germany launched a surprise invasion of Russia in the hopes of achieving as quick a victory as it had attained in France and, thereby, consolidating the Asian power's resources. . . . At least that was the plan. Instead, although initially catching the Russians by surprise, the Nazi invasion quickly stalled far short of its objectives and the much coveted Russian stockpiles in the opening months. Oops!

Worse, the other Tripartite Pact signatories had failed Hitler. Instead of attacking Russia, on December 7, 1941, Japan attacked the United States, and under the treaty obligations, Germany would have to declare war against it as well. As the prospect of fighting in the legendary bitter Russian winter loomed, Germany rolled the dice one last time. In a break from *every* treaty precedent Germany had ever signed and all common sense, on December 11, 1941, Hitler upheld his nation's promised commitment to Japan in declaring war against the United States in the hope that Japan would then declare war on Russia and, to a much lesser extent, Britain. By 1941, Britain had become a manageable threat maintained in relative isolation by U-boat patrols and occupied by a destructive campaign of sustained aerial bombardment. With staggering losses in men being reported month after month with little to show besides a few meters of open icy ground, Russia, once the potential savior of Germany, was now a genuine wolf at Hitler's throat. Sadly for Germany, Japan, while thankful for the recognition, did not care about Germany's problems. After all, the Japanese did not believe in German Aryanism. Instead, they saw themselves as the true master race. Furthermore, after suffering staggering losses in the last Russo-Japanese War, Japan had learned to leave its neighbor to the north very much alone. Besides, if Germany and Russia wished to destroy each other, so much the better for the Empire of Japan.

By 1942, Hitler could no longer outpace his metaphorical creditors and his friends would not lend him the assets he needed. Germany had long wanted Japan to divide Russia's attention with a border war and Italy to play a more offensive role, allowing Hitler room to reorganize his forces, reprioritize their military objectives, and systematically deal with their enemies. Consequently, with the 1942 onset of the British- and American-led Operation Torch—the liberation of Nazi North Africa—Germany's warfighting capability began to suffer blow after blow from its new, fresh, and long-feared foe with little support from its friends. He had not wanted to declare war on the United States, but his expansive dreams and poor planning had removed from him every other option for stability. In response, the United States, which now had an unequivocal and legitimate reason to respond to the Axis powers, now delivered men, materiel, and strategic support to every anti-Axis outpost throughout the world. As German forces were now being rolled back by American resources, Mussolini's soldiers balked at their own leader's friendship with Germany. With little choice, Hitler ordered troops to protect Italy from those who would challenge Germany. In 1943, when German forces in North Africa had been defeated, Italy came under attack. After Nazi-occupied France fell to the Allies in 1944, the

Russians launched their own counteroffensive against Germany, and still, the Japanese would not lend direct military support. By 1945, Germany's friends had deserted it. Everywhere Hitler had once looked for support in fueling his vision of a stable and expansive German nation-state was now either under Allied control or soon would be.

The lessons of Adolf Hitler's disastrous wartime foreign policy was a testament to the care one should take in picking one's friends. For all of his ambition, Hitler could never seem to find the means to achieve his goals and, in attempting to reach for the world, awoke an enemy he could not afford: the United States of America.

BATTLE OF STALINGRAD

Russia, August 1942–February 1943

BY WILLIAM TERDOSLAVICH

The Battle of Stalingrad should not have been fought.

Try telling that to Adolf Hitler.

The summer of 1942 saw the German army go on the offensive again. Operation Case Blue was the grand plan to traverse the Caucasus Mountains and seize Russia's main oil fields. This would kill Russia's capacity to make war while securing new oil supplies for energy-poor Germany. To protect the rear of the main attack, the German army had to secure the narrow stretch of land between the Don and Volga rivers.

But Hitler was impulsive and could never leave a good plan well enough alone. By late July, Army Group South was split in two, the second half becoming Army Group B, still tasked with forming the Don-Volga shield. Hitler then split Army Group B, leaving the Sixth Army to advance east to the Volga while the Fourth Panzer Army reinforced Army Group A's thrust into the Caucasus. On August 1, Hitler ordered the Fourth Panzer Army to change direction, supporting the Sixth Army's attack toward the Volga. By early September, Hitler added to Army Group B's mission list, now calling for the seizure of Stalingrad, a crossing of the Volga, and an advance south to Astrakhan, where the mighty river empties into the Caspian Sea.

By doing this, Hitler changed a converging attack on one objective into a divergent attack on widely separated objectives. Instead of concentrating strength, Hitler was dispersing it. And he wanted the Sixth Army to take Stalingrad, a major industrial center, instead of bypassing it. Hitler did not give a reason for the changes, but he was confusing Soviet retreat with Soviet weakness, thus prompting him to order his armies to bite off more than they could chew.

Full-Court Press

The Russians caught on quickly and took no chances. In late July, Stalingrad's workers were drafted to dig defense lines beyond the city's outskirts. But fixed defenses alone could not stop the Sixth Army's advances. Its commander, General Friedrich von Paulus had four corps to work with, plus two panzer corps on loan from the Fourth Panzer Army, making the Sixth Army the largest operational German formation on the Eastern Front. As some units probed Stalingrad's suburban defenses in mid-August, other columns to the north and south advanced on the Volga. Reaching the river by mid-September, these columns cut off Stalingrad from the north and south. Paulus now lined up six to eight divisions to take the city itself.

General Vasily Chuikov's Sixty-second Army held the city from Mamayev Hill, its highest point northward, covering three huge factories—Red October, a steel factory; Barrikady, a gun factory; and the Dzerzhinsky Tractor Works. Word was passed through the ranks: "There is no land for us on the other side of the Volga." Retreat was out of the question. Unit commanders were told to "hug" the Germans—get in so close that German artillery or air support would risk hitting their own men. Houses and apartment buildings were turned into mini-fortresses to slow the German drive.

Stalingrad was going to be held by minimum, not maximum, effort. Units would be ferried across the Volga nightly, then drip-fed into Chuikov's line. The Sixty-second Army's attached artillery units would bombard from the Volga's east bank, looking to interdict German concentrations west of Chuikov's positions.

From mid-September to mid-November, the Germans push staggered eastward in the face of tenacious Soviet defenses. Some of this desperate resistance came from the need to fight for the homeland. Or it was "inspired" by Narodnyy Komissariat Vnutrennikh Del (NKVD) troops embedded with Red Army units, eager to shoot anyone seen retreating. But Chuikov had no choice. If the Germans reached the Volga, the Sixty-second Army would be killed off, and Stalingrad lost with it.

"Pavlov's House" is often cited as the most exceptional example of this do-or-die stance. A platoon from the Forty-second Guards Regiment seized a four-story apartment building overlooking a square, about one hundred meters from the Volga. Sergeant Jacob Pavlov took command when his commanding lieutenant was killed. Pavlov and his men beat off every German assault that came their way—*for fifty-eight days.*

Throughout the city, many Russian platoons and companies improvised similarly stubborn defenses in the ruins. It was not unusual for Germans and Russians to be separated by a street, a wall, or to be on different floors of the same building, fighting room to room. Hand grenades and submachine guns were the prime weapons, not tanks and aircraft. Most vexing of all were the Russian snipers, who excelled at picking off German artillery spotters and troops bringing hot food forward.

By mid-October, the Russians still held on. Impatient for results, Paulus lined up three infantry divisions and three hundred tanks to grind their way through the three factories in northern Stalingrad.

Dzerzhinsky fell on October 16.

Barrikady was taken by October 23.

Most of the Red October factory was captured by November 11.

Chuikov, who already had to displace his headquarters several times to avoid capture, was now holding on for dear life. Many divisions in Sixty-second Army had suffered up to 90 percent losses. This did not faze Soviet dictator Joseph Stalin and the Red Army's general staff (Stavka). According to their bloody calculus, so long as some organized resistance could be mustered, Stalingrad could be held, regardless of losses, while keeping the Germans pinned. This minimal effort would free up several hundred thousand troops to exert maximum effort elsewhere. In the meantime, Chuikov had to play the anvil to Paulus's hammer.

Only four bridgeheads were left to resupply the Sixty-second Army, which held the line just six hundred feet away from the Volga. German attacks ground on block by block, but the final push was beyond the strength of those left. Germany spent 700,000 men killed, wounded, missing, or captured to take a wrecked city from the Russians. The Sixth Army's battalions were whittled down to the size of companies. Paulus had to take the city soon, or lack the reserves to hold other parts of his line in the face of an expected Soviet counterattack.

Chuikov needed some respite immediately. The Volga was beginning to freeze. Blocks of ice flowing downstream made river crossings difficult for larger craft to deliver even minimum replenishment of ammo, supplies, and men. (The river would not freeze solid for another month, and only then could normal resupply resume.)

It was now mid-November. The two armies were like a pair of exhausted, bloodied boxers in the final round of the fight, too tired to punch, too stubborn to fall.

The Unexpected Blow

The remainder of the Sixth Army's divisions had to hold the line north and south of Stalingrad to keep the Russians from punching through and surrounding all. Some of these sectors were held by the weakly equipped and poorly motivated Romanian, Hungarian, and Italian armies attached to Army Group B. Many German generals perceived these Axis allies as weak links, as did the Russian generals.

With that weakness in mind, the Russians launched Operation Uranus on November 19, just as the Battle of Stalingrad was reaching its last bloody gasp. The Russian forces of the Southwestern Front, under General Nikolai Vatutin, blasted their way through the Eighth Italian and Third Romanian armies north of Stalingrad. The Russian Fifth and Fourth Tank armies led the assault against the hapless defenders, who lacked even basic antitank weapons. South of Stalingrad, the smaller Thirteenth Tank and Fourth Mechanized corps, spearheading two infantry armies, punched through weakened sectors of the German Fourth Panzer Army to swing northwest. The joint objective for both efforts was Kalach, a town on the Don River about thirty miles west of Stalingrad.

Lieutenant Colonel Grigor N. Fillipov led a column of five T−34 tanks and two truck-borne companies of infantry on a mad dash for the Kalach bridge. Traveling at night with headlights on, the Soviet raiding column was mistaken for a German unit. Fillipov took the bridge before the defenders were even aware of the ruse. The Sixth Army was now cut off.

On November 24, Hitler issued his "no retreat" order to the Sixth Army, even though common sense dictated that Paulus break out to the west. Instead, Army Group Don was formed, with General Erich von Manstein in command. He was ordered to take the remnants of the Fourth Panzer Army and ram a corridor into the Sixth Army's perimeter, thus restoring the supply line.

As von Manstein began planning, Reichsmarschall Herman Goering claimed the Luftwaffe could supply the Sixth Army by air. Something like this was done in the previous winter for an entire corps south of Leningrad, trapped in the "Demyansk Pocket." But this force was one-sixth the size of the force trapped at Stalingrad. The Sixth Army needed 700 tons of supplies a day just to survive. Goering figured 500 tons could be airlifted, but his air transport staff told him that 350 tons a day would be the maximum, with no margin for error, losses, or bad weather. In practice, air deliveries only averaged about 300 to 350 tons *per week*. The best single day delivery was 289 tons on December 19, not even half of the Sixth Army's daily need.

By mid-December, von Manstein attacked toward Stalingrad with two panzer corps, but had to peel off one to stop a Soviet attack threatening Rostov in his rear, a bottleneck that had to be held or else Army Group A would be lost, too. Paulus remained obedient to Hitler's "no retreat" order and did not attack toward von Manstein's thrust. By Christmas Eve, von Manstein's Fifty-seventh Panzer Corps got to within a dozen miles of Paulus's lines, only to be driven back sixty miles by a skillful Russian armored attack.

The Sixth Army was now doomed.

End Game

Von Manstein now had to worry about saving Army Group A. Rostov was held at all costs to allow for the German withdrawal from the Caucasus. The Sixth Army was now going to have to "take one for the team." By maintaining his lines, Paulus was tying down about sixty Soviet divisions. Operation Ring was the hurried Russian response. Using massive artillery barrages, the Russians wore away Paulus's defenses from without, while cold, hunger, and disease wore down the Germans from within.

In late January, the Russians renewed the attack, blasting through the Sixth Army's lines with ease, overrunning the last airfield needed to maintain contact with the outside world.

Hitler then promoted Paulus to field marshal.

No field marshal had ever been captured in German history.

Rather than oblige Hitler by killing himself, Paulus raised his hands, along with 91,000 soldiers. That was all that was left of the Sixth Army in early February, a sad fraction of the 300,000 who started the battle in late summer. Half of the captives died by the spring.

Even after the war was over, many surviving Stalingrad POWs languished in Soviet labor camps, though a few thousand were released and sent home. Early Cold War tensions and the Berlin crisis of 1949 prompted Stalin to have many of them tried and sentenced to twenty-five years' hard labor. Stalin's death in 1953 took away the main support for this policy. A state visit in 1955 by West German chancellor Konrad Adenauer thawed out German-Russian relations enough to secure the release of the remaining nine thousand German POWs, of which two thousand had fought at Stalingrad.

The blood price Russia paid was far higher. About 1.1 million casualties were suffered in the Stalingrad campaign, close to 500,000 of them killed in action. The survivors were cruelly hammered into a ruthless killing machine. At Stalingrad, they had slain the myth of German invincibility. Now they would slay Germans . . . *with a vengeance.*

MARSHAL GEORGI ZHUKOV LOSES A BATTLE AND THE SOVIETS COVER IT UP

Russia, the Rzhev Salient, November–December 1942

BY WILLIAM TERDOSLAVICH

In late November 1942, Russian forces belonging to the Western and Kalinin fronts tried to surround and crush the German Ninth Army at Rzhev. But forget you ever read this. The battle "never happened."

That's one of the oddities about history, Soviet style. The mistakes sometimes disappear from the record. Operation Uranus, which took place around this time, successfully surrounded the German Sixth Army at Stalingrad. But Operation Mars was a secret until the 1990s, found while American historians were plumbing the depths of Soviet military archives.

This was the only battle Marshal Georgi Zhukov ever lost.

At least he won all the others.

A Problem or a Threat?

Soviet high command (Stavka) was eager to kill Germans, preferably by the hundreds of thousands. That meant fighting mobile battles that encircled German armies, cutting them off from supplies, then going in for the kill once they were weakened. By focusing armor to break through the lines of the weaker Axis allies, the Russians successfully surrounded the Sixth Army and parts of the Fourth Panzer Army around Stalingrad. Defeat became final about ten weeks after that.

Stavka applied the same thinking when planning the operation against Army Group Center. The German line was irregular in many places as a result of the previous winter's "no retreat" order issued by Adolf Hitler. Germany's Ninth Army held the ground around Rzhev, roughly one hundred miles west of Moscow, with the Russians surrounding it on three sides. The Rzhev salient measured roughly ninety miles by ninety miles. It stuck out like a sore thumb from the German line, but to the generals at Stavka, it was still a dagger aimed at Russia's heart—Moscow.

Any thought about renewing the drive on Moscow was forgotten by Hitler. But General (later Field Marshal) Walter Model spent the bulk of 1942 steadily improving the Ninth Army's positions. Every division dug in. Every village was turned into a fort. Every panzer division was kept ready as a mobile reserve to rush to trouble. Successful defense relied on the Germans holding the few good roads inside their perimeter, which would allow them to shift units to trouble spots. If the Russians took any of these roads, the Ninth Army would be unable to reinforce troubled sectors and could be destroyed in detail.

Smashing a Sore Thumb with a Hammer

Russian warfare in World War II has often been mischaracterized as an unimaginative massing of hordes sent to overrun hopelessly outnumbered Germans, who would smartly parry the blows with tactical daring. Those Russian "hordes" were more like massive fists used to punch through German lines with brutal simplicity. Russian planners saw every operation as a series of battles chained together, each one setting up the next.

Zhukov looked at the Rzhev salient through this lens. Operation Mars would be the first step. Western Front, General Ivan S. Konev commanding, would attack the Rzhev salient from the east. The attack would fall just north of Sychevka, about halfway up the bulge. Kalinin Front, under General Maxim Alexeevich Purkaev, would deliver the other main attack from the west, just south of Belyi, also halfway up the bulge. Both main attacks would drive toward each other, meeting in the middle of the bulge's base to surround the Ninth Army.

That was when Operation Jupiter would begin. The Russians would pivot their forces and drive south for Vyazma, where that column would meet up with yet another attacking column driving west to encircle and destroy the Third Panzer Army. With those two strokes, the Red Army would turn the German dagger away from Moscow—and destroy two German armies.

Just remember that it is easier for a general to draw an arrow on a map than it is to drive an army down the arrow's path to make the plan real.

Going to Mars

Operation Uranus was launched on November 19, pocketing the Sixth Army in about two days. Now the Ninth Army's number came up. Zhukov had amassed 720,000 men and over 3,300 tanks and assault guns, backed by 10,000 artillery pieces and mortars, for Operation Mars. In comparison, the Soviets only deployed 890 tanks to the Stalingrad counteroffensive, but deployed 1.1 million infantry and over 13,000 artillery pieces.

On the night of November 25, all Russian forces attacked simultaneously. Large-scale artillery bombardment raked the German lines. Konev's main attack pitted 200,000 men and 500 tanks belonging to the Twentieth and Thirty-first armies against the 40,000 men of the German Thirty-ninth Panzer Corps (Fifth and Ninth Panzer divisions), northeast of the rail line at Sychevka, a much-needed supply line for the defenders.

Konev enjoyed odds of five to one on paper, which should have yielded a sure win. It didn't. Russian artillery fire was inaccurate. Red Army units had to attack across open ground, taking hits from German fire. The fortified villages broke up the Soviet thrusts into smaller columns easily blunted by mixed groups of German tanks and infantry, supported by artillery.

Soviet follow-on attacks managed to get three tank brigades and a cavalry division (yes, we are talking about horses) across the Rzhev-Sychevka Road, but German counterattacks from the north and south smashed into the flanks of the Russian advance, cutting off the horses and tanks on November 28. Zhukov wanted the cut-off units to keep moving west, but it was clear the Soviet attack was halted.

Meanwhile, Kalinin Front scored a real breakthrough.

The Forty-first Army hurled 90,000 men and 300 tanks against the German line south of Belyi, overrunning the German defenders. First Mechanized Corps, commanded by General M. D. Solomatin, was sent into battle on November 26 to attack deep into the German rear with 224 tanks. They tore out a hole measuring twenty miles deep by about twelve to thirteen miles wide out of the Ninth Army's line, reaching a vital road link that connected Belyi with the German rear—and supplies.

To the north of Belyi, the Twenty-second Army committed 50,000 men and 270 tanks to score a breakthrough following the Luchesa River valley into the German rear. The German Großdeutschland Division, an elite unit, tried to blunt the blows as the Soviets slowly advanced toward a key road that ran north from Belyi. The Germans limited the Russian breakthrough to a bulge ten miles deep by five miles wide, keeping the vital road on their side of the line.

Solomatin's successful drive needed reinforcements to keep it going, but the Forty-first Army's commander thought he could rush Belyi. Reinforcements that should have gone to Solomatin got diverted to support yet more attacks on the town, robbing the tank drive of its momentum.

By November 30, Zhukov was looking to renew his stalled attacks. He still had two hundred tanks and one more army to commit to Konev's sector. The renewed drive eastward from Sychevka bogged down again. Five days of attacks by the Twentieth and Thirty-first armies were repulsed.

With the eastern claw of Zhukov's offensive now shattered, Model focused on the western claw. His First Panzer and Twelfth Panzer divisions gripped the Belyi Road for keeps, facing the Russian Forty-first Army's northern flank. The Nineteenth and Twentieth Panzer divisions were brought across very rough terrain to face the Forty-first Army's southern flank. On December 7, they sprang the trap, driving through the Forty-first Army's lines, encircling about forty thousand men and four hundred tanks. (A week later, the remnants of the Forty-first Army broke out of its pocket. Only half the troops made it back to Soviet lines. The tanks were abandoned for lack of fuel.)

Double or Nothing

Zhukov, the general who never lost a battle, refused to admit defeat.

Drawing on deep Soviet reserves, he reinforced the secondary attacks against the northern edge of the Ninth Army's line by the Soviet Thirty-ninth Army, as well as the drive down the Luchesa River valley eastward by the Twenty-second Army. The attack along the eastern edge of the Rzhev bulge would be renewed by two fresh armies—the Twentieth and Twenty-ninth.

On December 11, Zhukov let the hammer fall again. Konev committed 20,000 men and 350 tanks to renewing the drive against the bulge's eastern edge, but the attack was a rush job; no one had time to paint the T–34 tanks white to blend in with the snowy background. They made great targets for German antitank gunners. Three hundred Russian tanks were lost in two days.

By December 15, the surrounded Forty-first Army broke out of Belyi to regain Soviet lines, at the cost of all its tanks. Zhukov kept the Thirty-ninth Army pounding away at the northern edge of the Ninth Army's perimeter. No progress was made. Losses were appalling. He might as well have been beating his own head against a rock.

Operation Mars was shut down.

Operation Jupiter was shelved.

Success was reinforced instead. Units destined for Zhukov now flowed southward to Stalingrad. Nearly 500,000 Russian killed, wounded, and missing or captured marked the butcher's bill for Mars. German defenders counted seventeen hundred wrecked Russian tanks littering their front lines.

Model's losses amounted to forty thousand killed. But the German army was already suffering losses on the Eastern Front far greater than its replacement rate. The Rzhev salient was eventually abandoned as Hitler belatedly allowed a retreat to shorten the line and free up reserves. By being steadfast in defense, patient in the accumulation of reserves, and fierce in the counterattack, Model made sure that what happened to the Sixth Army did not happen to the Ninth Army.

As for the Red Army, it was not yet strong enough to best the Germans in a direct attack. Matching strength against strength too soon was a foolish mistake made by Stalin and his generals. Their wish would come true, after the Red Army was further sharpened by more hard-won experience, and after the German army was further weakened by some more hard-won Russian victories.

BATTLE OF KASSERINE PASS

Tunisia, February 1943

BY WILLIAM TERDOSLAVICH

It was nothing more than a flat stretch of stony ground flanked by two bare hills. Were it not for an accident of history, Kasserine Pass would have remained obscure.

There in February 1943, two battalions of American troops were ill placed to stop a German tank attack. Field Marshal Erwin Rommel turned the thin green line into a bloody speed bump as he tried to reverse the Axis decline in North Africa with one bold stroke.

The scary part was that it almost worked.

A Battle Lost Before It Started

Sometimes defeat is preordained by mediocre leadership, in this case embodied by Major General Lloyd Fredendall, commander of the U.S. Second Corps. Before the war, Fredendall showed promise as a leader and trainer. This caught the eye of General George C. Marshall, who favored Fredendall for a command once war came. Marshall's favor made Lieutenant General Dwight D.

Eisenhower reluctant to relieve Fredendall, despite "danger signs." Fredendall had built a huge, underground command bunker in Tebessa, Algeria, eighty miles behind his front line. He rarely left it, often ordering his regiments hither and yon without first telling their respective division commanders.

Second Corp covered the southernmost sector of a three-corps line belonging to the British First Army. The line ran along the Western Dorsal mountain range that snaked along the Algerian-Tunisian border. Not one to read a map, Fredendall committed Combat Command A (CCA) of the First Armored Division to take Sidi Bou Zid, a key crossroad, just short of the Faïd Pass in the Eastern Dorsals. If Fredendall had seen fit to push that unit thirty miles farther from this point to reach the Mediterranean Sea, Rommel's PanzerArmee Afrika would have been cut off from Fifth Panzer Army under General Hans-Jürgen von Arnim.

Offense Is the Best Defense

Eisenhower's intelligence chief Brigadier General Eric E. Mockler-Ferryman expected the Fifth Panzer Army to attack at Fondouk, closer to the center of British First Army's line. He did not believe Rommel would launch the main attack farther south. Mockler-Ferryman was relying on Ultra intelligence, decrypts of coded German messages, which showed the Tenth Panzer Division facing the center of the British line at Fondouk. Mockler-Ferryman considered this fact the key that locked his conclusion, but he did not know that Rommel and von Arnim were bickering over plans. Von Arnim was ordered by theater commander Field Marshal Albert Kesselring to release the Tenth Panzer to Rommel, which was done with deliberate slowness, a fact not picked up by Mockler-Ferryman.

Not taking chances, Eisenhower ordered Fredendall to maintain a screen along the Eastern Dorsals, backed by the First Armored in reserve. But British First Army commander Lieutenant General Kenneth Anderson ordered Fredendall to place a combat command of the First Armored to support the British defense, as he believed Mockler-Ferryman's assessment.

On February 14, Rommel pushed the Tenth Panzer through Faïd Pass, mauling Combat Command A and the First Armored and isolating two battalions of the 168th Regimental Combat Team at Sidi Bou Zid. Remnants of CCA and First Armored fell back toward Sbeitla. This forced Anderson to pull back the southern portion of his line.

Rommel maintained a "command presence" wherever the action was, usually showing up at a divisional or regimental headquarters to see things for himself and make quick decisions on the spot, oftentimes in the middle of a changing situation. Commanding from the rear, Fredendall only had the haziest idea of what was happening in his sector. First Army's Anderson sent CCB and First Armored back to Fredendall, who in turn sent CCC and First Armored to counterattack the German thrust.

CCC and First Armored attacked on the afternoon of the fifteenth with zero reconnaissance, intelligence, air support, or artillery. A tank battalion with fifty-two Shermans clanked down the road to Sidi Bou Zid, followed by an infantry battalion mounted on trucks and half-tracks. The attacking force got to within two miles of the town when the Germans opened fire. They had ten Tiger I tanks in their gun line, each with an 88mm gun that could dispatch a Sherman at one mile. Not one American tank survived.

By now, First Armored had lost almost 100 tanks, 1,600 men, 5–7 halftracks, and 29 artillery pieces. Anderson ordered Fredendall to refrain from counterattack. Fredendall was killing First Armored one piece at a time.

Getting Kicked in the Pass

Rommel now had his falling-out with von Arnim. The Desert Fox wanted to press on to Tébessa, then northward to Bone on the coast to cut off the British First Army from its supply lines. But von Arnim wanted the Tenth Panzer to attack Fondouk and cut off a brigade or two. The generals bickered. Field Marshal Kesselring, the theater commander, intervened. He ordered von Arnim to give the Tenth Panzer back to Rommel once the detour to Fondouk was done. Kesselring then pulled the punch, ordering Rommel to thrust northward to Le Kef, well short of Tébessa.

That order forced Rommel to deal with a fork in the road—literally. Highway 71 went north to Le Kef. Highway 13 went west to Kasserine—and Tébessa. Obeying Kesselring's order, Rommel assigned the Twenty-first Panzer to attack north to Le Kef, while the Tenth Panzer's westward attack became the secondary effort. Rommel was aware that he could still hit Tébessa via Le Kef. But German strength was being thrown in two different directions instead of converging on one spot.

Fredendall confronted the threat of the Tenth Panzer in piecemeal fashion, peeling off a battalion from the First Infantry Division and attaching an engineer battalion, a battery of French 75mm guns, and a handful of tank destroyers to form a task force under the First Infantry's Colonel Alexander Stark. Order: hold Kasserine Pass.

The textbook solution was to post the bulk of the troops on the high ground flanking the valley floor and use cross fire to destroy the attackers. Stark did the opposite, posting his units to hold the mile-wide flat. A platoon from each battalion was all that held the high ground on either side.

On the morning of February 19, Rommel tried to rush Kasserine Pass with infantry backed by a few tanks. The French 75s destroyed five panzers, but the Germans gained the high ground on one side of the pass. On the morning of February 20, Rommel committed the Tenth Panzer to back up a six-battalion infantry attack on Stark's reinforced line. By noon, Rommel's tanks and infantry hit the engineer battalion from the front and from the high ground on the side, overrunning its positions. By day's end, over five hundred Americans were dead or missing.

Rommel's attack up Highway 71 failed when the Twenty-first Panzer was halted by Allied units, so the thrust through Kasserine became the main effort. Rommel hit another fork in the road—literally. He assigned the Tenth Panzer to attack north up Highway 17 to Thala. That would give Rommel another shot at Le Kef, but the rear of his attack had to be covered by a secondary effort westward toward Tébessa.

Good Ground

Still not grasping the need to fight the Second Corps in divisional strength, Fredendall ordered CCB and First Armored to hold the line at Djebel el Hamra, a significant hilltop overlooking Highway 13, along with the Sixteenth Regiment of the First Infantry Division. Finding no sign of American units east of Djebel el Hamra, Rommel rushed his forces smack into a prepared position amply backed by artillery, hitting the wall at 2 P.M., February 21.

Forty German tanks, followed by truck-borne German and Italian infantry, raced across the flat ground in full view of the American defenders. The artillery ripped up the oncoming enemy. The German task-force commander, General Karl Buelowius, lacked the artillery needed to silence the American guns. By 4 P.M., the Germans were within range of CCB and First Armor's tanks, taking more casualties. By 6 P.M., Buelowius called off the attack. It was going nowhere and getting a lot of infantry killed.

Rommel's main effort aimed at Thala fared no better. The British Twenty-sixth Armored Brigade, backed by the guns of the U.S. Ninth Division's artillery regiment, held the last piece of high ground south of Le Kef, thus halting the depleted Tenth Panzer.

Rommel took stock of the situation. His troops were running low on ammo, fuel, and food. Von Arnim wasn't sending any more tanks to reinforce the attack. It was time to turn back. Kesselring concurred.

Fixing the Blame

Rommel's command was shifted south to stop the British Eighth Army, under Field Marshal Bernard Montgomery, from entering southern Tunisia while von Arnim's Fifth Panzer Army faced Anderson's First Army in northern Tunisia. Eventually Rommel was invalided home due to poor health.

Von Arnim, who could obey orders without arguing, retained command of Fifth Panzer Army and the newly formed First Italian Army. He would launch one more attack on Anderson's line in late February, scoring feeble gains. Von Arnim would eventually surrender the whole force once the Allies took Tunis, a loss equal to Stalingrad.

Eisenhower had to clean house after nearly losing the campaign in one battle. Mockler-Ferryman was dismissed. Fredendall urged Eisenhower to sack the First Armored Division's commander, but Eisenhower sacked Fredendall instead. Eisenhower turned to Major General George S. Patton to refresh the Second Corps. Under Patton, this formation redeemed itself in a supporting attack at El Guettar and marked the beginning of Patton's ascending reputation.

The Americans made a lousy first impression. British generals underrated American potential for the rest of the war as a result. But Rommel saw the Americans in a different light. He noticed how quickly they bounced back from bad situations, rapidly reinforced and amply supplied. The Americans were bound to improve.

It was an accurate assessment that would haunt Rommel when he took command in Normandy.

THE BATTLE OF KURSK

Russia, July 1943

BY WILLIAM TERDOSLAVICH

The war on the Eastern Front was entering its second year.

It was supposed to be over and done in a six-month blitzkrieg.

Now it was a quagmire consuming four-fifths of the German army. Losses were still exceeding replacements. The manpower deficit was only growing with time. Hitler was looking for a knockout blow in a war that resisted decision in a single battle. His sense of what was possible was becoming increasingly impossible. Stalin and his generals understood the war differently. It would not be over in one battle, but many battles, each one building a foundation for the next.

As both sides struggled to master events, the Eastern Front careened chaotically after the fall of Stalingrad. Erich von Manstein's command of Army Group Don, and later Army Group South, averted disaster. But the Russians still gained ground elsewhere. North of Kharkov, an unsightly bulge in the German line took shape. Centered on Kursk, the bulge measuring 100 miles by 150 miles, thrust westward. Its north shoulder rested on Orel; its south flank brushed Belgorod.

The Russians were expected to attack in the spring. Von

Manstein offered Hitler two plans. The risky one involved giving up ground, then striking the Russian offensive from the flank to cut it off. The safer plan called for eliminating the Kursk Bulge with two attacks from north and south.

Hitler panned the riskier plan, since he did not like giving up ground already taken. He opted for attack on the bulge at Kursk. April was the best time to launch the offensive, as mud season gave way to dry ground, thus permitting mobile warfare. But Hitler delayed. He wanted the newer Panther, Ferdinand, and Tiger tanks to equip his panzer forces. Getting these new models in great numbers from Germany to the front would take time. In mid-June, an indecisive Hitler finally opted for Operation Citadel. The attack was slated for July 5.

The Russians Are Not Stupid

If German planners spotted the "weakness" of the Kursk Bulge, so did Russian generals. They used the spring to reinforce the Kursk Bulge with six layers of fortified lines, each one fronted by a mass of land mines. Within each fortified line were thousands of smaller positions—each one a cluster of bunkers and foxholes, held by an infantry platoon backed by a battery of antitank guns. German armor would have to fight through each hard layer, suffering losses with each breakthrough, only to face another tough line. Soviet armor was kept in reserve, ready to deliver the decisive counterstroke against the panzers. The Russians knew their deadline was early July, thanks to a well-placed spy ring that kept Stalin informed.

The north side of the Kursk Bulge was held by Center Front under General Konstantin K. Rokossovskiy. He was facing Field

Marshal Walter Model's Ninth Army, operating under Army Group Center. The Voronezh Front, under General Nikolai F. Vatutin, staked out the southern half of the Kursk Bulge. His forces faced General Hermann Hoth's Fourth Panzer Army, attached to von Manstein's Army Group South.

Rokossovskiy shrewdly used his time to identify likely lines of a German attack, then crafted quick response plans. Captured prisoners provided more information, allowing Rokossovskiy's intelligence department to fix the expected time of the Ninth Army's attack. Just one hour before the Germans started their attack, Rokossovksiy ordered his six hundred artillery pieces to deliver a hurricane bombardment against key road junctions where the Ninth Army's divisions were forming up. He was not going to let Model get a clean start.

Model concentrated seven infantry divisions and one panzer division along a narrow ten-mile front. His plan was simple: grind through each Russian defense line with repeated waves of tank and infantry attacks. Tigers and Ferdinands (a turretless tank also mounting the deadly 88mm gun), were organized in battalion-sized task forces, followed by infantry on foot in open order, then medium and light tanks plus more infantry mounted on trucks or half-tracks.

Overhead, the Luftwaffe sent strike groups of fifty or one hundred aircraft, looking to pound Soviet defenses. The Henschel Hs–129, designed to deliver close air support, was making its debut, while the Focke-Wulf Fw–190A fighter took to the skies to drive away Russian aircraft and achieve air superiority. These two newcomers would be backed by the war-proven workhorses of the Luftwaffe—the Bf–109 fighters, Ju–87 Stuka dive-bombers, and He–111 and Ju–88 medium bombers.

As soon as Model scored the breakthrough of the first defensive belt, Rokossovskiy knew where the Ninth Army was going—south to Ponyri, a major junction on the Kursk-Orel rail line. According to plan, Rokossovskiy flooded the zone around Ponyri with units from unthreatened sectors.

Rokossovskiy called Stalin for reinforcements.

None could be spared.

On July 6, Center Front's forces fell back to a six-mile stretch of prepared line packing three thousand guns, five thousand machine guns, and more than one thousand tanks belonging to the Second Tank Army. By July 7, Model was mustering ten infantry and four panzer divisions to crack it. Mines took out the advancing tanks. Red Army antitank brigades fought to the last gun and the last man. In desperation, teams of Russian infantry hurled Molotov cocktails and satchel charges at the enemy tanks. The battle continued like this until the next day. Ponyri changed hands several times.

Model's attacks finally bumped against high ground—the Sredne-Russki heights—after grinding through nineteen miles of Russian defenses. Blitzkrieg it was not. On July 11, the Red Army launched an attack on Orel, forcing Model to peel off units to reinforce the Second Panzer Army. Model's offensive was done.

If things were bad on the north side of the bulge, they were worse down south. Vatutin stretched his forces thin, trying to defend the whole line, but in the end defending nothing. Hoth's Fourth Panzer Army had a good day on July 5, forcing Vatutin to commit reserves earlier than he wanted to blunt the blow. Active defense robbed Hoth of over three hundred tanks and eighty aircraft, plus ten thousand Germans killed in action. Vatutin's line beat off twelve separate attacks, but Voronezh Front was being driven back.

German columns were looking to score breakthroughs at

Obayan and Prokhorovka, thence northward toward Kursk. Vatutin committed the First Tank Army and the Sixth Guards Army (infantry) to block the way. Hoth massed his tanks into wedges of sixty to one hundred, with Tigers and Ferdinands in the lead, followed by Panthers and Panzer IVs. By July 9, the drive on Obayan stalled just six miles shy of the town. The only other chance to unhinge the Soviet defense line was at Prokhorovka.

When a Small Battle Decides a Large One

Hoth now massed his armor on a four to five mile stretch of ground just west of Prokhorovka, a station town on the Belgorod-Orel rail line. Defending were the Soviet Sixty-ninth and Seventh Guards armies. Vatutin was holding back the Fifth Tank Army and Fifth Guards Army as reserves to take on the Second SS Panzer Corps, which was expected to renew the attack on Prokhorovka. Vatutin planned to hit the Fourth Panzer Army from three sides, hoping to surround and destroy it.

Stalin approved the plan. But Vatutin would not be allowed to fix the crisis he created. Stavka sent Marshals Georgi Zhukov and A. H. Konstantin Vassilevski to oversee the operation.

On July 11, Hoth renewed his drive. Second SS Panzer Corps drove for Prokhorovka, flanked on the east by the corps-sized Army Detachment Kempf (one panzer, two infantry divisions) and to the west by two panzer and one *panzergrenadier* division driving again on Obayan. Ground was gained, but no breakthrough scored.

On July 12, the Russians struck back with the Fifth Tank Army, sending 900 tanks to stop Hoth's two panzer columns—one 600 tanks strong, the other 300. One hundred of those German tanks were Tigers, each mounting a tank-killing 88mm gun that fired farther than the Russian T–34's 76mm gun. The Russians countered this German advantage by literally charging their tanks into the oncoming Tigers. At close range, the T–34's gun was able to hole any German tank, especially from flank and rear. For eighteen hours the battle went on, leaving behind the burning wreckage of 300 German and 450 Russian tanks.

For two more days, Hoth probed the Russian lines, looking for another weak point to exploit. None could be found. By July 19, Hitler called off Operation Citadel. Reinforcements were sent to Italy from the Eastern Front, now that the Americans and British had invaded Sicily.

The Blood Price of Defeat

Never again would Germany enjoy armored parity with the Red Army, let alone superiority. Germany had been losing men faster than it could replace them for two years. At Kursk, the last few full-strength armored and infantry divisions were committed—after stripping replacements expected by other divisions.

The Russians put German losses at 70,000 men killed in action, about 2,900 tanks destroyed, plus another 200 assault guns (turretless tanks), as well as 844 artillery pieces lost, about 1,400 planes shot down, and over 5,000 trucks destroyed. Panzer divisions that typically fielded 150 tanks were severely depleted, some mustering 17 tanks here, 30 tanks there.

The Germans counted 1,800 dead Russian tanks, 1,000 anti-tank guns destroyed, and over 24,000 Russians captured. Russian sources put manpower losses at close to 180,000, of which 70,000 were counted as killed or missing. But the Russians could replace these losses.

Stalin and his generals converted the defensive victory at Kursk into a southern offensive that took the Red Army to the banks of the Dnieper River. The next two years would mark nothing short of a full-court press, as anywhere from eleven to thirteen fronts would go over to the offensive simultaneously.

And it would stay that way, all the way to Berlin.

RAIDS ON PLOESTI AND SCHWEINFURT

August 1943 and October 1943

BY WILLIAM TERDOSLAVICH

World War II was not a conflict that could be ended in one stroke.

But that did not stop some leaders from trying.

For the United States, that "one-shot" thinking found fertile ground in the U.S. Army Air Force. Eager to prove that daylight strategic bombing could work, the USAAF built a mighty fleet of four-engine bombers, designed with enough defensive armament to "fight their way" to and from the target—so long as they maintained a formation that would bring all their guns to bear.

Strategic bombing could shorten a war by destroying the enemy's war industries. But there might be a quicker way: destroy a critical subcomponent of that industry that may be clustered in single locality. There were two such places. Roughly half of the Axis oil industry was centered around the refineries of Ploesti, Romania, while half of the ball bearing industry clustered around Schweinfurt, Germany.

The Americans really believed that daylight raids and precision bombing could destroy these two strategic targets. The British war planners dismissed this notion out of hand, calling the American effort "panacea targeting."

High-Level Interest in a Low-Level Raid

When USAAF chief General Henry Harley "Hap" Arnold wanted something done, he usually got his way. Arnold's headquarters in Washington, D.C., had developed a plan to execute a low-altitude bombing raid on Ploesti. It fell upon Major General Lewis Brereton, commander of the Ninth Air Force in the Mediterranean, to make it so. The IX Bomber Command's Brigadier General Uzal Ent would command the strike, comprised of five bomber groups equipped with B–24 Liberators.

The B–24 was designed as a high-altitude bomber, with single- and double-mounted machine guns placed in the nose, belly, top, tail, and waist to ward off enemy fighters. The low-level raid was supposed to increase bombing accuracies, hopefully accomplishing in one mission what a dozen high-altitude missions could do.

The B–24's biggest virtue was its long range—3,500 miles, more than adequate to cover a twenty-seven-hundred-mile round trip from Benghazi, Libya, to Ploesti. The bomb load would be a meager 2.5 tons per plane. The five-bomber groups would muster 177 planes for the mission, with each group tasked with bombing one or two refineries. Time-delay fuses on the bombs would ensure none would blow up under the planes as they let loose their loads at five hundred feet or less. Planners who crunched the numbers figured they were using twice as many planes as needed.

The five groups practiced low-level bomb runs over a full-scale outline of the Ploesti refineries placed deep in the Libyan Desert. Scale models of the actual refineries were crafted, with approaches filmed at various speeds to give a "pilot's-eye view" of the target. Pilots, navigators, and bombardiers studied the mission's details with life-or-death seriousness. Success depended upon them getting the raid right the first time.

On August 1, 1943, the B–24s took off from their respective airfields, skipping the time- and fuel-consuming task of "forming up" into a single formation. Instead, each bombardment group flew its own course, following its own schedule, to rendezvous simultaneously at the initial point (IP) over the Danube River to the west of Ploesti. Hopefully they would retain the element of surprise.

That's when things started going wrong.

Despite careful planning and flying, not all the B–24s arrived at the same place at the same time. Three of the groups circled, waiting for all squadrons to "form up." The lead plane, with General Ent and Colonel Keith Compton (commander, 376th Bombardment Group), then took a wrong turn, an easy mistake given the difficulty of low-level navigation. Three of the five bomber groups then followed the leader—all the way to the suburbs of Bucharest, Romania's capital city. Ent and Compton then turned north toward Ploesti to correct the mistake. But surprise was blown and the bombers would be making unfamiliar bombing runs from the south. Ent broke radio silence to order all bombers to seek out targets of opportunity if they could not find their targets.

Some refineries got hit twice, others hit poorly. One escaped being hit at all. Flak shredded the low-flying bombers. Planes were taking hits, burning and exploding in midair. Six B–24s from one bomber group were incinerated while making a run on a refinery already hit, time-delayed bombs going off as the planes passed low overhead.

The return trip was no picnic. German and Italian fighter planes tried to shoot down the low-flying B–24s, but a diving attack that low left no altitude for pulling up in time. Once over the Adriatic Sea, the bombers gained altitude, but their formation got sloppy, making them easy pickings for Italian fighters out of Foggia.

Of the 177 B–24s that took off, 163 made it to the target, but 54 bombers became combat losses. Allied bomb damage estimates rated the Ploesti refineries between 40 and 60 percent destroyed. In fact, damage was far lower, further reduced by Ploesti operating at 40 percent under capacity. Despite several refineries requiring up to six months of repairs, overall oil production at Ploesti remained unchanged. Repeated air raids in 1944 further mauled the facilities, but it wasn't until the Soviet Red Army overran Romania that Ploesti was permanently removed from the Third Reich's war industry.

Ball Bearing Busters

The VIII Bomber Command (later designated the Eighth Air Force) suffered setbacks in October 1943, staging three major raids mounting between 230 and 350 bombers, each effort sustaining over 10 percent losses. On October 14, VIII Bomber Command would hit Schweinfurt with a mixed force of mostly B–17 Flying Fortresses and some B–24s. The B–17 had a shorter range and lighter bomb load compared to the B–24.

Like all modern planes of the period, the B–17 was made by riveting aluminum sheets over an aluminum frame to put the "skin" on the "skeleton." Aluminum was light and strong, but could not stop bullets or metal splinters from exploding shells.

What gave the B–17 its strength was the close spacing of the spars and stringers that made up the airframe. One would have to sheer off every piece to get the plane to break in half. So long as some of the structure held, the B–17 could still fly. Thus the "forts" could absorb more damage and still make it back to base.

The weather over Britain was lousy on the day of the raid, but clear over the target. Still, three bomber divisions had to form up over eastern England or the English Channel. The 60 B–24s comprising the Second Air Division failed to form up, leaving the division leader little choice but to take his remaining 29 bombers to hit Emden, a secondary target. That left only 291 B–17s for Schweinfurt.

Escorting fighters were limited by range. The long-range P–51 Mustang was not in service yet and drop tanks were not standard on other fighters. The P–47 Thunderbolts and British Spitfires could only fly roughly 450 to 550 miles, depending on the variant. They could only escort the B–17s as far as Aachen—about 200 miles from Britain, before sparring with the first wave of Luftwaffe fighters and turning back. The B–17s were now in box formation—basically six-plane elements that were stacked and staggered to allow all planes to bring fire to bear at all points. They were on their own.

The Luftwaffe managed to get as many as three hundred fighters airborne, and they ripped into the target-bound B–17s. Attacking the B–17s head-on minimized the time spent under fire, allowing for only one brief burst of machine-gun or 20mm-cannon fire by the Fw–190 and Bf–109 fighters. Another tactic was to line up four or five fighters and make a diving/slashing attack, concentrating fire on one plane. The twin-engine Bf–110 and Ju–88s were too slow and lacked the maneuverability to engage the B–17s closely, so their preferred tactic was to "stand off" from the bombers and fire unguided rockets into their formations, hoping to score hits.

Once over Schweinfurt, the B–17s faced intense antiaircraft fire from batteries of ten to twenty guns aiming at the same point by fire control. Bombers dropped out of formation here and there, badly damaged and burning. The 228 remaining B–17s managed to place 143 of their 1,200 high-explosive bombs in the factory area. Of these, 88 were rated as direct hits.

It took six minutes each for the two divisions to fly over the target. The flight home would last several hours and was off to a rough start as about 150 German fighters pounced on the B–17s. Losses added up quickly.

Once the B–17s made it over the Low Countries, fighter escort resumed. Only 197 of the B–17s made it back, 17 of the planes too badly damaged to fly again. In all, 65 planes were lost, mostly to enemy fighters and flak, a few more to mechanical malfunctions or crashes on takeoff.

The bomb damage assessment rated the mission a success. But the Germans were the ones who knew for sure, only losing 3.5 percent production capacity. Another 6.5 percent of production was damaged. The solution was to disperse ball bearing foundries to other parts of Germany. Reichsminister for Production Albert Speer noted, however, that the bombing of Schweinfurt could have succeeded if all the factories were attacked at the same time, persistently three or four times every two weeks, with follow-up raids every eight weeks to screw up rebuilding efforts.

Getting Bombed the Right Way

The raids on Schweinfurt and Ploesti were bloody failures. To make bombing work requires persistence and maintenance of aim over time. Changing targets and delays between raids undermined these efforts.

Once the P–51D Mustang became available as a long-range bomber escort, bombing resumed in early 1944. The Mustangs would keep the German fighters at bay while the B–24s and B–17s slowly wiped out much of Germany's industrial base and rail net. By February 1945, there was nothing left to bomb.

BATTLE OF ORTONA

Italy, December 1943

BY WILLIAM TERDOSLAVICH

Nothing is nastier than house-to-house fighting in a built-up town or city. Every building becomes a fortress. Every plaza is transformed into a battlefield. Platoons and squads can only use the weapons they can carry, since air support and artillery lose their utility due to the risk of "friendly fire." The only thing separating enemies might be a wall or a doorway.

A general usually thought twice before sending his soldiers forward to take a town, the first preference being to bypass it, if possible. Sadly, Ortona wasn't a town that could be bypassed.

Montgomery's Cautious Drive

The British Eighth Army was working its way up Italy's east coast in late 1943, just as the U.S. Fifth Army was doing the same on the west coast. The Apennine Mountain Range that formed Italy's rocky spine served as the dividing line between the two forces. There were few east-west roads to exploit, with most of the progress on either side involving slogging straight north along the coastal plains, each advance being halted by another German-held hill or mountain overlooking the next river crossing. There were many rivers to cross and many hills to take, making Italy a slow, grinding killing ground.

Field Marshal Bernard Montgomery was not eager to sustain his advance at a thousand casualties per mile. Great Britain didn't have deep pools of manpower to draw from, thanks to the massive losses of World War I. Plus the army was not very able to "improvise" a plan while on the move, again the result of the war killing off many promising junior officers who would have been colonels and generals in World War II. The talent just wasn't there to "wing it."

Montgomery never asked more of his army than it could give. A successful operation was always a well-prepared, set-piece battle, fought with overwhelming force for very limited gains. All the brigade and divisions had to do was follow the plan. The Eighth Army would spend two to three weeks building strength, and after crossing the river or sweeping the next hill, halting to build up again for the next push. This kept the casualty rate down for the Eighth Army, but produced no spectacular war-winning gains. (Montgomery only threw caution to the wind once, planning Operation Market Garden. See chapter 29.)

But once in a while, Montgomery would spot an opportunity. Now it was Pescara, an Italian town that sat on a junction with an east-west over-mountain road that led straight to Rome. The Fifth Army was having no luck advancing on the west coast, so Montgomery put the spurs to the Eighth Army. In response, the Eighth Army resumed its slow crawl north, its progress stopped by the winter rains just as often as the "need" to rest, refit, reorganize, and resume.

The British Fifth Corps held the extreme right of the Eighth

Army's line. The formation paired the Eighth Indian Division with the First Canadian Division, and it was the Canadians' job to advance on Ortona to open the road to Pescara. Ortona was one of the few ports on Italy's east coast, making it prizeworthy. But Ortona was protected by a natural moat two miles to its south—the Torrente Saraceni. The Canadians simply called it "the Gully." The Torrente was anything but that, measuring three miles long, two hundred yards wide, and two hundred feet deep.

The Ninetieth Panzergrenadier Division spent the weeks during the Eighth Army's previous pause to plant landmines in the Gully and carve out firing positions to kill anyone stupid enough to try a frontal assault. Fortunately for the Germans, Major General Christopher Vokes commanded the Canadian First Division, and he was going to oblige their assumption.

On December 11, Vokes launched a single-battalion frontal attack across the Gully. It was repulsed. So he ordered a second frontal attack, again with a single battalion. It, too, was repulsed. In fact, this went on for nine days. It wasn't until the end of the week that it occurred to Vokes to try to take the other side of the Gully with a stronger three-battalion frontal attack. That failed, too.

During this pointless period, the Ninetieth Panzergrenadier pulled out and was replaced by the First Parachute Division. They held the northern edge of the Torrente with equal ease. The Canadians renamed it "Bloody Gully," as it was filling up fast with dead Canadians. At this point it was hard to say who was the bigger threat to the Canadians—Vokes or the Germans.

It was not until December 19 that Operation Morning Glory was launched, basically an attack that went around the western end of Bloody Gully. The Germans found their positions turned, so they fell back to Ortona. The price paid by the First Canadian Division to capture a ravine numbered around one thousand casualties. Two Canadian battalions had already been worn down to one-third their original size.

Welcome to Town, Boys

The next week was going to be more hellish for the First Canadian. Ortona could not be bypassed. It had to be taken.

Again, the German paratroops had plenty of time to really learn their way around town before wrecking it to raise their advantage. Rubble offered more hiding places than intact buildings. Antitank guns were hidden in alleyways, ready to take flank shots on advancing tanks. All weapons were sited to produce cross fires in the intersections and open spaces. Tunnels were hacked out to link positions. A building would be leveled here or there to become an obstacle, which was then covered by machine-gun or mortar fire. Some buildings were booby-trapped to explode, just for good measure.

Into the breach walked the battalions of the Loyal Edmontons and the Seaford Highlanders, advancing on a five-hundred-yard front down the main road leading into town. Only progress was now measured in houses gained, not blocks or miles. The Canadians had to clear each building one at a time. A platoon would start the process by setting up a perimeter around a building, with three squads laying down covering fire while the fourth squad broke in and cleared the first floor. Slowly, the soldiers would work their way up each floor, one room at a time, until reaching the top. Rather than repeat the process again, Canadian engineers would use shaped charges to blow "mouseholes" into neighboring buildings from the top floor. Then a squad or two could go through the breach as the "clearing team," working their

way downstairs through every room with grenades and submachine guns until reaching the ground floor.

The "covering team" would wait outside, using light machine
guns to provide cover fire and mortars to drop smoke rounds
where needed. Some of the mortarmen were sharp enough to
pop rounds through open windows for added support. Clean
sheets were hung out the windows to show that the building was
cleared. A few troopers were left behind to keep the Germans
from reinfiltrating. Once buildings on both sides of the street
were cleared, the tank could advance, providing more covering
fire with its machine guns and 75mm cannon.

These tactics sound bloodless on paper. In practice, no building could be taken without suffering casualties. The German
paratroops were very skillful and stubborn on defense. After a
while, the Battle for Ortona took on a bitter life of its own as
troops on both sides worked themselves up into a chaotic killing
frenzy.

This left the German generals a bit puzzled. Field Marshal Albert
Kesselring didn't want Ortona held to the last man. The German
Fourteenth Army commander Joachim von Lemelson couldn't
figure out why the Canadians were fighting for Ortona like it was
Rome. Nothing justified the losses. Kesselring shrugged. "You can
do nothing when things develop in this manner."

The Canadians ground their way toward the town center. Entire buildings were booby-trapped, they now discovered—the
hard way. The Germans exploded one as a platoon mouseholed
its way into it. Only four Canadians survived. The Germans then
fired on the rubble to keep other troops from digging their comrades out. The Canadians returned the favor by blowing up several buildings defended by German paratroops, rather than waste
time clearing them out room by room.

All I Got for Christmas Was a Wrecked Town

Ortona was finally taken a few days after Christmas. The First Parachute Division did not defend it to the last man, just the last minute. They made an overnight pullout to take up new positions in Pescara, ten miles away.

The Canadian First Division suffered twenty-three hundred casualties to raise the British flag over Ortona. Of those, five hundred were killed in action. Psychiatric casualties were also common. One battalion only had three officers left of the original forty-six who landed with the unit in Sicily the preceding July. The Loyal Edmontons could only field three companies of sixty men each by Christmas, which was less than half strength for these units.

Montgomery called a halt to his latest offensive. It took five weeks for the Eighth Army to move fourteen miles. Montgomery believed that the slow and cautious way was the best method to gain ground for the least casualties. But at this rate, taking Italy was going to be very expensive.

NOTHING GOES RIGHT IN ITALY

September 1943 and June 1944

BY WILLIAM TERDOSLAVICH

Did anything ever go right in Italy? Not really.

No matter what the Allies tried to do, it always was nearly undone by bad weather, sloppy execution, poor generalship, rough terrain, and a tenacious enemy. What difference does it make? In the end, the United States was on the winning team in World War II. Isn't that enough?

No.

Mistakes can teach more surely than victories, for the error is something that should never be repeated. And there were three in Italy that were too grave to ignore: the "victories" at Salerno, Anzio, and Rome.

Salerno: Nice Beach. Can I Borrow It?

The Fifth Army began life under the command of Lieutenant General Mark Clark, who at forty-seven was the youngest three-star general in the U.S. Army. His boss, General Dwight Eisenhower, thought Clark was the best organizer, trainer, and planner he had ever met, so Clark's appointment to command was deemed worthy.

Clark only had forty-five days to plan the Fifth Army's amphibious assault at Salerno, instead of the four to five months of planning and practice such an operation deserved. Salerno had the northernmost beach on the Italian west coast within fighter range of Sicily, and it was close to Naples, which was a port worth seizing. The invasion beach was a long crescent of sand, bisected by the Sele River and surrounded by mountains. Clark proposed landing the Tenth Corps (two British divisions) to the left of the Sele, while landing the U.S. Sixth Corps (Thirty-sixth Division) to the right of the river. Sixth Corps kept a regiment and two more battalions as a floating reserve. The two Allied formations would be landing twelve miles apart.

On September 8, this combined force of fifty-five thousand men hit the beach at daybreak, and came under fire immediately from the German Seventy-sixth Corps. Naval gunfire could have neutralized the defense prior to landing, but the Thirty-sixth Division commander Major General Fred Walker elected to do without, reasoning that the Germans were too dispersed for the shelling to be effective.

Lacking reports from the beach, Clark ordered the Sixth Corps' headquarters to be landed—thirty-six hours ahead of schedule. Major General Ernest Dawley made it to shore without his staff almost twenty-four hours later, and had to mooch radios and personnel off of the Thrity-sixth Division's headquarters. From there on out, Dawley felt incapable of changing the situation for lack of reserves.

Then there was the Sele River. With no troops covering this

corridor, the Germans had a natural avenue of attack. Clark spotted it too late and landed his last reserve of two battalions to cover the gap.

The Germans also had their problems. The German Seventy-sixth Corps did not have enough strength to drive Clark's forces into the sea. Field Marshal Albert Kesselring, who commanded German forces in the Mediterranean, requested two panzer divisions from northern Italy to aid the effort, but Hitler would not approve the request.

Clark moved his headquarters to the beach on September 12. The Fifth Army was holding on to a slice of Italy forty miles long by six miles deep. By this time, the Germans had spotted the gap at Sele River and attacked, shredding the two-battalion defense. Clark had no reserves left. To save the beachhead, naval gunfire was called in to destroy attacking German formations. A regiment from the Eighty-second Airborne was flown over from Sicily and dropped on the beach to help plug gaps in the American line. (Its previous mission to drop directly on Rome as Italy switched sides had recently been scrubbed, much to the relief of the paratroops.)

The enemy could hold but not push the Allies back. On September 18, the Germans quit the battle and retreated north. Their losses numbered only 3,500, of which about 650 were killed in action. They did not drive the Fifth Army into the sea, but came damn close. Clark's forces suffered 9,000 casualties—5,500 British, the rest American. And of the American losses, 1,200 were killed in action.

Clark fixed his problem, and now fixed blame. He relieved Dawley, who was no longer in command of the facts, let alone his troops. This made Dawley the second corps commander sacked since the U.S. Army began fighting the Germans. The first was Major General Lloyd Fredendall after the debacle at Kasserine Pass.

Rome—Why Bother?

Italy festered as a bloody stalemate. Repeated attacks by the Fifth Army against Cassino produced thousands of casualties with no gains. The beachhead at Anzio was under siege. (See chapter 23.) The war could not go on like this.

As Anzio went into its bloody lull, General Sir Harold Alexander, ground forces commander in Italy, planned to shift the Eighth Army away from Italy's east coast to focus on the Cassino sector. He would shorten the Fifth Army's front to concentrate its fighting power. A screen of several divisions would keep busy the meager German defenses in the Eighth Army's old sector. On May 11, Operation Diadem would commence with simultaneous attacks by the Fifth and Eighth armies.

The Eighth Army didn't make much progress attacking into a mountain range, but the four-division French Expeditionary Force did achieve a breakthrough east of Cassino. By taking successive peaks to the rear of the mountaintop monastery, the French forced the Germans to withdraw, lest they be surrounded and cut off. The German Tenth Army was falling back on Rome. Kesselring weakened his line at Anzio to send another division to the south, but it proved to be too little and too late to stop the Allied attack.

Alexander ordered Clark to attack out of Anzio with his Sixth Corps, take Valmonte in the east, and cut off the retreat of the German Tenth Army. On May 22, a heavily reinforced Sixth Corps busted out of its perimeter, making slow progress, but chewing up the German divisions before it. After several days, the German line crumbled. Sixth Corps lost twenty-five hundred men in the attack. But it was now fighting toward Valmonte.

Sixth Corps commander Major General Lucian Truscott Jr. then received a fateful call from Clark: pivot most of the Sixth Corps north toward Rome. (This was *not* what Alexander ordered.) The thrust toward Valmonte was now a secondary effort. German Tenth Army's escape was now guaranteed as Valmonte was left uncaptured.

But Clark did not have Rome yet. The German 362nd Division halted the Sixth Corps' drive by holding the slopes of Mount Artemisio, overlooking Velletri. Major General Fred Walker, commanding the hard-luck Thrity-sixth Division, was loath to go through a problem if he could find a way around it. The Germans didn't hold the entire mountain, so Walker got two regiments of his division into the heights and attacked the 362nd Division's flank while his third regiment attacked to pin the Germans in place. The German defense disintegrated. Clark got his open road to Rome. And Walker redeemed his division's reputation after seeing it used so badly in the past.

Operation Diadem was a success that cost the Allies 44,000 casualties, among them 18,000 Americans (of that, 3,000 killed), 12,000 British, 9,600 French, and 4,000 Poles. The Germans suffered about 50,000 casualties, among them about 6,000 dead.

Clark eventually got his victory parade through Rome on June 5, but it was upstaged by the D-day invasion in France the next day. Glory is fleeting. The Germans who got away would fight on for another year. More men would die in a campaign that might have been won sooner had Clark obeyed his orders instead of his ego.

Also ignored was the harder reality: an army doesn't win a war by taking real estate. It wins by destroying the enemy. Do that and the real estate is taken by default.

CROSSING THE RAPIDO RIVER

Italy, January 1944

BY WILLIAM TERDOSLAVICH

It starts with a general drawing an arrow on a map.

Fifth Army commander General Mark Clark spent the early months of 1944 pushing his units northward up the Italian boot, averaging about a thousand casualties per mile.

There had to be a better way.

Perhaps Clark saw it when he was studying a map. Just use the Thirty-sixth Infantry Division to secure the crossing of the Rapido River near Monte Cassino, then move the First Armored Division through to the broad plains of the Liri Valley toward Rome. With the Sixth Corps expected to land at Anzio, the two thrusts should put the German Fourteenth Army between a rock and a hard place.

There was one hitch: German possession of all the high ground surrounding the Rapido crossing. Clark ignored this since his arrow on the map outflanked the high ground. Just cross the river with the same ease as a grease pencil on paper and all will be right.

That is not how Thirty-sixth Division commander Major General Fred Walker saw it. Division cohesion was definitely weakened as total strangers filled the ranks among the few veterans who remembered working as a team. Officer and riflemen casualties were quite high.

Outwardly, Walker had to say "yes, sir" to his dear ex-friend Mark Clark. But inwardly, he knew Clark's plan would not work. Lieutenant General Geoffrey Keyes, commander of the Second Corps, also had his doubts. Both men pitched alternate plans to Clark, but he turned them down.

The crossing zone was a three-mile stretch of river, centered on the far side by the village of Santo Angelo. Walker ordered the 141st Infantry Regiment to cross north of that point, while south of it the 143rd Infantry Regiment would cross as well. To the south of the 143rd, the British Forty-sixth Infantry Division would cross the Garigliano River, covering the southern flank of the attack. The British Forty-sixth was the only one of three divisions in British Tenth Corps to fail its crossing effort on January 19 as it attacked weakly with only two battalions.

On January 20, the Americans would cross the river.

Just remember that soldiers can't walk on water. It would take a miracle to do a frontal assault combined with a river crossing before enemy-held high ground.

Sitting Ducks

At 7:30 P.M., sixteen artillery battalions opened fire on the far side of the Rapido, forcing the German defenders to hunker down while the 141st Infantry Regiment attempted its crossing.

Combat engineers had spent the previous few nights placing plywood assault boats and rubber rafts near the crossing point. They swept the approaches for landmines and marked these hazards from the covered ground of the assembly area all the way to the crossing points on the riverbank.

Things began going wrong at the start line. Replacements arrived and were unable to find their units, a task further complicated because soldiers in the attacking companies had removed their unit badges. Dead soldiers and live prisoners lacking these patches would not be able to give away their unit's identity, thus hampering enemy intelligence. But try telling that to a bunch of lost replacements trying to find their platoons and companies in the dark. In the confusion, not all newcomers joined their intended units.

Squad by squad, the men of the First Battalion, 141st Regiment, grabbed their boats and began humping their heavy loads to the riverbank. Many boats were found punctured by shrapnel from German artillery fire earlier in the day.

The engineers were supposed to use white tape to mark the paths, but switched to brown rope in some places to keep the pathways camouflaged. Not all the assaulting troops could find these dark markers in the night. Many strayed off the path into minefields, losing feet, legs, or their lives. Confusion was compounded.

Now the Germans were hearing the explosions of mines and the clattering of equipment. Enemy mortar shells began dropping in here and there, adding to the chaos. More wounded piled up. More men were killed. Still, the Americans pressed on.

At around 9 P.M., the first squads made it across the Rapido— after seeing many others in their punctured boats sink. First Battalion lost two-thirds of its men this way. The remaining third was hanging on for dear life on the farther bank, getting raked by German machine-gun fire from the higher ground. The engineers erected a flimsy footbridge, but reinforcements using this crossing were gunned down in the cross fire. Lieutenant Colonel Aaron Wyatt Jr., who commanded the 141st, held back his third battalion. The attack was not working.

The 143rd Regiment used two crossing points. A platoon made it across the northern one without getting shot. The rest of the First Battalion got raked. By 6 A.M., the 143rd had a bridgehead, but only if the surviving troops were willing to hold it to the last man. Walker denied permission for the battalion commander to withdraw. The commander pulled his unit back anyway.

A quarter mile to the south, the Third Battalion and 143rd fared worse. Not a single man made it across. Only five boats had survived the German shelling from earlier in the day. The battalion commander was relieved on the spot *for failing to find the river.* (Yes, he was that stupid.) His successor canceled the crossing by sunrise.

Try, Die Again

Contact with the shattered First Battalion/141st was nil, but Walker and his superiors assumed the battalion was clinging to the riverbank. From his headquarters deep in the rear, Clark asked if the 141st Regiment had any reserves, and if so, to use them. The arrow on the map had to move across the Rapido.

Clark knew via secret Ultra decrypts of German coded messages that the Fifth Army's cross-river attack was sucking German reserves out of Rome, uncovering the beach at Anzio, just in time for the Sixth Corps' amphibious landing. Ultra intelligence was never shared with any commanding officer below army level. Clark could not share Ultra information with Walker, but he could push Walker for results without having to explain why.

That afternoon, the 143rd Regiment managed to cross the Rapido, shrouded by a thick smoke screen. By evening, all three battalions were across, holding a position five hundred yards deep by six hundred yards wide. Farther north, the 141st Regiment's remaining two battalions crossed at 2 A.M. Saturday—almost thirty-six hours after 1st Battalion. No survivors from 1st Battalion were found. The 141st pressed on, enlarging its bridgehead.

The Germans were quick to open fire with their artillery and machine guns once the Americans had crossed the river. Neither regiment could take the first lump of high ground in the village of Santo Angelo. The drive needed reinforcement, but the division could not deliver it. The assorted engineering units by the river lacked an overall commander to coordinate the assembly of the two prefabricated Bailey bridges the tanks needed to cross. It was no surprise the bridges went un-built while the Thirty-sixth Division slowly died on the other side of the Rapido.

Now Walker got a phone call from Keyes: commit the 142nd Regiment to reinforce the two depleted regiments across the river. The commander of the 142nd told Walker it would take fifteen hours to get his regiment ready to move.

The final straw came when Keyes received a report that the 141st Regiment was wiped out. The frustrated corps commander called off all further action. By midday Sunday, the remnants of the 141st recrossed the Rapido, commanded by a single captain. The 143rd also recrossed after suffering heavy casualties.

Blame and Body Count

The next day, the remains of the 141st Regiment numbered only 200 men fit for duty. This was little bigger than an infantry company, and an infantry regiment usually has nine companies. Over in the 143rd Regiment, one company was bled from a starting strength of 187 men down to 17.

The Thirty-sixth Division entered the butcher's bill into its records: 2,019 casualties, of which 934 were wounded, the rest either killed or missing. In contrast, the defending Fifteenth Panzergrenadier Division only suffered 64 dead and 179 wounded. While Kesselring committed two divisions from his reserve to stop the British Tenth Corps, no fresh units were needed to help the Fifteenth Panzergrenadier hold the line.

Clark got down to business. He did not sack Walker, but relieved the division chief of staff, the assistant division commander, and both regimental commanders whose units made the bloody crossing. Relief meant the end of their army careers. Clark felt Walker was ill served by their "incompetence," even though the Thirty-sixth had fought well until the Rapido.

Crossing a river in the face of enemy fire is never an easy task. But the Thirty-sixth did not make it any easier on itself. Flanks were left open. High ground was not seized. Even the tanks of the First Armored Division did not lend direct fire support, and its lead units were near the river.

The failure of the Thirty-sixth Division at the Rapido generated a lot of bad feelings up and down the chain of command. A postwar hearing by a joint House-Senate committee only stirred the controversy rather than resolving it. While the division's officers blamed Clark, Clark blamed Walker for having a "defeatist attitude." The Pentagon backed Clark for having to make a much-needed attack. But Clark's less-than-stellar reputation was further tarred by the controversy.

The general who drew the arrow on the map forgot one thing: arrows are not drawn with ink, but blood.

OPERATIONS AT ANZIO

January–May 1944

BY DOUGLAS NILES

Let's Just Sit Here on the Beach and *Look* at the Objective Over There

The Allied offensive up the boot of Italy began with a crossing of the narrow Strait of Messina (from Sicily) on September 3, 1943, with the main punch being an amphibious assault by U.S. General Mark Clark's Fifth Army landing at Salerno on September 9. German reaction to the landings was swift, and over the next few days Clark's force was almost driven backward into the sea in a bloody battle. Aided by furious naval gunfire and air support, the American Sixth Corps and British Tenth Corps grimly held on to their beachheads, and slowly consolidated their positions.

By September 18, the landing area was secure, and the troops began to advance into Italy. They linked up with General Bernard Montgomery's Eighth Army later that month, and the Fifth Army took Naples at the beginning of October. However, the Germans, commanded by Field Marshal Albert Kesselring, fought savagely for every mile of ground, and progress northward up the peninsula was very slow. The steep mountains were intersected by rivers that, in autumn, swelled and raged through their valleys, and the Germans made good use of these natural barriers.

The Fifth Army fought hard to cross the Volturno River on the western side of Italy, only to quickly come up against the equally formidable Garigliano River. Meanwhile, the Eighth had an equally difficult time on the eastern side of the country, pushing forward over the Trigno and Sangro rivers only after suffering tremendous losses. Additional rain rendered the landscape into a muddy morass, and German resistance increasingly stiffened as the defenders skillfully used the ground and the weather to great effect. Both armies were under the overall command of British Field Marshal Sir Harold Alexander's Fifteenth Army Group, and on November 15 he authorized a halt so that the combat troops could rest and accept reinforcements.

Five days later the assault resumed, but now Kesselring's men had established a defensive zone some ten miles deep called the Gustav Line (or, sometimes, the "Winter Line"). Attacks into the position were exceedingly slow and terribly costly, and by the end of the year the Allies had advanced only a few more precious miles. The weather was terrible, with cold temperatures and nearly constant rain or snow. On the western side of the front, the German position was anchored at Monte Cassino, a Benedictine monastery on a mountaintop reaching nearly two thousand feet above the valley from which the Allies were forced to make their attack. It was as close to an impregnable position as anything encountered by the Allied forces in World War II, and before the Fourth Battle of Cassino (May 18, 1944) was over, American, French, New Zealand, British, and Polish units had all been chewed up badly in their attempts to capture it.

By the end of 1943, Alexander realized that something drastic would have to be done to break the stalemate and allow for an advance that would carry the Allies at least to Rome, which was another eighty miles or so up the peninsula. The result was a plan for an amphibious landing north of the Gustav Line, on a stretch of flat shoreline near the city of Anzio. Located only twenty miles from Rome, and threatening the main German lines of supply and communication, it was thought that Allied possession of Anzio, and an aggressive breakout toward the road, would force the defenders to pull out of the Gustav Line and retreat to a new position north of Rome.

The plan was called Operation Shingle, and it (the plan itself, that is) was for the most part quite sound. In fact, it mimicked a tactic that the Americans under General Douglas MacArthur were using with great success along the coast of New Guinea, in the Pacific—MacArthur was avoiding attacks against strong defensive positions by leapfrogging past them with landings that had the effect of cutting the Japanese bases off from support and letting them "wither on the vine." It made sense to exploit the Allied command of the sea to enhance mobility, and a steadily growing mastery of the air gave the landing and subsequent offensive a good chance of success. The Germans' attention was to be diverted by a renewed offensive in the Cassino area, hopefully drawing away any potential reinforcements that could otherwise be sent to the Anzio area.

However, Alexander was hampered by the fact that many of his amphibious forces—ships and landing craft—were being stripped away from him for use in the upcoming Operation Overlord, the Invasion of Normandy scheduled for the late spring of 1944. This meant that, after the initial forces landed, a secondary wave would have to be loaded and delivered a few days later. Alexander enhanced this weakness by assigning too much of his available force to the frontal attack against Cassino, which was really intended to be a diversion against the Anzio flanking attack.

The landings went in on January 22, 1944. The attacking force was the Allied Sixth Corps, commanded by Major General John P. Lucas, which was under the overall command of General Clark's Fifth Army. The initial forces included about fifty thousand British and American troops, with more than five thousand vehicles. The British First and U.S. Third Infantry divisions were the largest formations of the corps, which were augmented by airborne, commando, and tank units. Over January 22–23, the entire initial wave was landed on the beaches, going ashore against no opposition as the Germans were completely surprised. General Clark landed with the attacking troops of General Lucas's corps so that he could keep his finger on the pulse of the operation.

Lucas was faced with a tremendous opportunity. From the beachhead he could see the Alban Hills, an elevation of rolling terrain only about twelve miles away that was the only geographical obstacle between his force (which, as noted, was equipped with a great many vehicles) and the prize of Rome. Incidentally, the old saying "All roads lead to Rome" is not just an idle aphorism; possession of that city would block every major supply route leading to the Gustav Line, with the exception of a single narrow highway along the Adriatic coast of Italy.

But Lucas, with the full concurrence of General Clark, decided that it was more important to consolidate his position on the beach than to move out and seize the undefended high ground that was less than an hour's drive away. He didn't even send out reconnaissance forces to study the terrain, preferring instead to dig artillery emplacements, organize a perimeter around the beachhead—which extended as much as seven miles inland—and to wait for additional reinforcements, including tanks, heavy artillery, and additional supplies.

The Germans were delayed by no such overabundance of caution. By the end of the day on January 23, Kesselring had cobbled together troops from northern Italy and from some quiet sections of the Gustav Line to create an entire, if extemporaneous, army (the Fourteenth) blocking Lucas's corps at Anzio. These troops would steadily flow into the Alban Hills and the other heights around Anzio over the next week.

Lucas wasn't ready to move until January 30, when he ordered a two-pronged assault from the beachhead, one driving toward Campoleone and Rome, the other through Cisterna toward the Rome/Cassino highway. The Alban Hills stood firmly between these two routes, and General Eberhard von Mackensen, commanding the Fourteenth Army, had had plenty of time to prepare his defense, which included plenty of German tanks firmly entrenched in well-screened positions. Both of the Allied prongs were hurled back with heavy losses, and the fighting raged continuously as February progressed.

On February 16, the Germans hurled a massive offensive of their own at the Sixth Corps. Charging tank units, supported by artillery batteries emplaced on the heights, pounded the beachhead, finally driving a wedge right through the Allied position and separating the British and American divisions from each other. Only a massive barrage of naval gunnery and some ferocious counterattacks allowed the Allies to reunite their position and reestablish the perimeter that Lucas had so meticulously created.

On February 23, General Clark fired Lucas and promoted General Lucian Truscott Jr. (formerly commanding officer of Third Division) to command of Sixth Corps. Certainly Lucas had displayed a singular lack of aggressiveness and initiative, but there must be a certain sense that he was used as a scapegoat, since his superior had been at his side the whole time. As Lucas failed to capitalize on his opportunity, Clark had made no effort to provoke him into motion—indeed, he had gone on the record as agreeing with his corps commander's careful approach.

In any event, there was not much that Truscott or anyone else could do to change the situation in the months ahead. His troops were pinned down on a beachhead that was exposed to enemy artillery fire along its entire breadth and depth. The Germans would wryly refer to Anzio as their largest prisoner-of-war camp, and the grim humor was very close to the truth, for the men of Sixth Corps were not going anywhere for quite some time. Over the four months that the corps was trapped on its beach, some twenty-four thousand American and nine thousand British casualties were evacuated from the bloody sand.

In the meantime, Alexander launched several major offensives against Monte Cassino. Convinced that the Germans were using the Benedictine monastery as an observation post, he ordered the destruction of the monastery by aerial bombing preparatory to the Second Battle of Cassino (February 15). For once, however, the Germans had actually been following the quaint notions of the Geneva Convention, and had refrained from using the religious facility for military purposes. After the Allies bombed it to rubble, of course, the Germans moved in, making excellent use of the rubble and ruin to carve fortified defensive positions. As a result it proved exceptionally difficult and costly to dislodge them. The mountaintop was finally captured on May 18, after five days of bitter fighting (the Fourth Battle of Cassino) by two divisions of Polish troops.

Finally the Gustav Line was cracking, and on May 23 a reinforced Sixth Corps began to push its way out of the Anzio position. German troops were retreating northward in great numbers along the Rome/Cassino road, but Clark ignored the chance to capture tens of thousands of prisoners, instead pushing along the coast. The Fifth Army took Rome after the Germans had passed through, on June 4. But even then these hard-fighting men of the Italian Campaign were denied no more than the briefest taste of publicity and glory—for on June 6, 1944, the Normandy landings occurred on D-day, and the attention of all the Western Allied nations turned to northern France.

THE BOMBER WILL SCREW UP . . . MOST OF THE TIME

Strategic Bombers Do Tactical Air Strikes: Operation Avenger, Operation Goodwood, and Operation Cobra

February 1944 and July 1944

BY WILLIAM TERDOSLAVICH

Pity the poor four-engine bomber, for so long misunderstood by the generals. This fine machine was built to carry a few tons of explosives through skies of burning blue or blackest night to destroy Germany's factories and cities. This strategy was supposed to win the war on the cheap, without the need to fight major battles. So why did the heavy bombers get used over battlefields, where their "talent" was wasted?

To the general fighting the ground war, a B–17 was just a bomb truck. Ditto for the B–24, the Avro Lancaster, and the Handley-Page Halifax. They were able to put more bombs on target than the average fighter plane. Whenever a general found himself sty-mied by an impossible situation on the ground, he would take out his frustration by blowing it to bits with a few hundred heavy bombers. Today's warplane can accurately put a single bomb on target, thanks to bomb guidance systems that rely on laser illumi-nation or the global positioning system. Boom. Problem solved. But the same problem was rarely fixed by the same technique in World War II. "Precision" bombing was not always that precise, requiring hundreds of planes per target to score the few critical hits that would make the difference.

Trying to Hit the Jackpot at Cassino

February 1944 found the Allies stalled before the commanding heights of Monte Cassino. There, German paratroops dug into the slopes, able to see anything moving on the valley floor below. If an artillery spotter can see it, he can kill it. German artillery made it so.

The direct approach called for capturing Cassino. That would take massive prep fire, followed by a ground assault up the heights. The Fourth Indian Division was given the job, and division intel-ligence concluded erroneously that German paratroops held the monastery at the mountain's top.

Italian civilians claimed the monastery was bristling with en-emy machine guns. A German POW claimed that his comrades based a command post and aid station in its buildings. Previous recon flights allegedly spotted antennae on the monastery's roof-tops and machine-gun nests guarding its approaches. Lieutenant General Geoffrey Keyes, commander of U.S. Second Corps, did his own flyover and saw nothing.

The Fourth Indian reported to the New Zealand Corps commander Lieutenant General Bernard Freyberg, who favored the
aerial bombardment, figuring it would save him some casualties.
If the Americans did not bomb, Freyberg would hold the Fifth
Army commander General Mark Clark responsible for the higher
casualties, a notion that went down poorly with New Zealand's
prime minister.

At that point, the squabble became political. The New Zealand
government was not eager to see its soldiers used as cannon fod-
der to capture yet another Italian rock pile. Clark was pressured
to say yes. Operation Avenger was on.

Good weather finally arrived on February 15, allowing 140
B–17s to fly over Monte Cassino, dumping 350 tons of bombs
on the Abbey. They were followed by 100 twin-engine medium
bombers dropping another 300 tons of bombs to make the rubble
bounce higher. The buildings, walls, chapel, and cloisters took
about 1,500 bomb hits, killing an unknown number of refugees
taking shelter there.

The solution created two problems for the Allies. First, the
Germans were now free to enter and fortify the wrecked monastery, turning it into a superb impromptu fortress. Second, no-
body told the Fourth Indian Division that the aerial bombardment was set for that day. The division was expecting to launch
its attack the next day. Now the Indians and New Zealanders
had to launch the attack in a hurry. The Germans fought until
evening to defend their heights, leaving six hundred dead from
the Fourth Indian and another two hundred dead from the New
Zealand Division, which supported the attack. In the end, all this
effort produced was another deadlock.

Bomb Harder!

On July 18, 1944, the British would try to use the same technique to crack German positions in Normandy's hedgerow country. German panzer divisions had bottled up British forces around Caen. Field Marshal Bernard Montgomery had to find a way to break out, seize Bourguébus Ridge to his south, and exit onto the Falaise plain, where his tanks would have enough open space to move and fight effectively.

To get that breakthrough, Montgomery was willing to blast the Germans to smithereens. Literally. RAF Bomber Command was willing to work the day shift, loaning 1,056 Lancaster and Halifax heavy bombers to drop five thousand tons of bombs on German forward positions. Another 1,021 heavy and medium bombers of the U.S. Eighth and Ninth Air Forces would bomb German positions farther to their rear. Once the blasting was done, the Seventh Armored, Guards, and Eleventh Armored divisions would charge through the gap, attain the Bourguébus Ridge, and zip into the green fields and beyond. The plan was christened Operation Goodwood.

That was all well and jolly good, but there was only one problem. The massive bombardment didn't kill enough Germans. The Sixteenth Luftwaffe Field Division, a piece of garbage even in the best of times, and the understrength 346th Infantry Division were mauled and offered little resistance. But the remnants of the much more potent Twenty-first Panzer Division managed to ride out the storm of steel. One battle group that was located outside of the bomb path launched a flank attack on the advancing British columns, disrupting their assault. The scant remnants of a panzer regiment and a Tiger tank battalion halted the British spearhead. Time gained by delaying the British was put to good use bringing in reinforcements. German antitank guns and tanks worked as a team; the gun line flamed British formations to a halt, then the panzers delivered the knockout punches. Operation Goodwood did not get Montgomery his breakthrough, although enough advantageous ground was gained for a second try.

Blast It!

The Americans did not have to face as much German armor in the First Army's sector at St.-Lô as the British Second Army around Caen. General Omar Bradley added three divisions to Lieutenant General Joseph "Lightning Joe" Collins's Seventh Corps, turning it into a mini-army of six divisions. Operation Cobra would blow a hole in the German lines, allowing the Seventh Corps to rush south. Passing through in second echelon would be the lead elements of Patton's Third Army, which would pivot east and follow the Loire River Valley across France.

Blowing the hole in the German line was a job given to 350 fighter-bombers of the Ninth Tactical Air Command and the 1,800 B–17s and B–24s of the Eighth Air Force, followed by another 400 medium bombers of Ninth Air Force. The start line was a four-mile stretch of the St.-Lô–Periers Road. The trick was trying to match the start line with the bomb line without threatening American troops with "friendly bombing."

Bradley thought that keeping the Seventh Corps about a half mile back was enough. Once the bombing was done, he wanted that unit to rush the Germans, giving them no time to shake off the blow and restore their defenses. But the air generals wanted Bradley to keep his troops about two miles back to zero the risk of bombs falling wide of their aim points. Many Seventh Corps generals and field officers balked at this. Why give back ground that Americans paid for with their lives? Air and ground generals eventually compromised on keeping the Seventh Corps about three-fourths of a mile behind the St.-Lô–Periers Road.

Roughly ninety minutes before the attack on July 24, the massive air armada arrived. The B–17s and B–24s were expected to drop thirty-three hundred tons of bombs alone. But the plan did not come off without problems. Several bombardment divisions found clouds over the target area and did not drop. Some found breaks in the clouds and let go. The Thirtieth Division was beneath the break in the clouds. Bombs slammed into the troops, killing 25 and wounding 131.

Worse, the whole effort would be repeated the next day. Now the Ninth Division took the hit from "short bombing," losing 111 dead and 490 wounded. Among the dead was Lieutenant General Leslie J. McNair, the architect of U.S. Army training and division organization, who had strayed forward to observe the breakthrough.

Gambling that another day of bombardment wouldn't help much, Seventh Corps' Collins committed his divisions to the attack. Progress was slow on the first day as the troops had to pick their way through the many bomb craters. Once past the moonscape, they were able to hit open road and make some progress.

The bombing was credited with playing a substantive role in the breakout at St.-Lô. The Americans only got nicked compared to the Panzer Lehr Division, which took the brunt of the bombs. Tanks were destroyed only by the occasional direct hit, but soft-skinned vehicles were shredded into flaming scrap metal. Any infantry that survived was left stunned. Panzer Lehr Division commander General Fritz Bayerlein estimated that the bombing knocked out about 70 percent of his front-line troops. But

Supreme Commander General Dwight D. Eisenhower was disappointed by the gains made on the first day of the breakout, as well as by the losses suffered from short bombing.

Strategic bombers were made for bombing cities from high altitudes. Fighters and twin-engine bombers were better suited for the low-altitude work of destroying enemy infantry and tanks. The ground generals would still tap the heavy bombers in the future, with mixed results. But the tactical use of heavy bombers in France left Eisenhower jaded. "I gave them the green light this time," he said. "But I promise you, it's the last."

THE BATTLE OF THE D-DAY BEACHES

Normandy, France, June 1944

BY WILLIAM TERDOSLAVICH

The Desert Fox had nowhere to run.

Field Marshal Erwin Rommel made his name as a master of maneuver warfare in North Africa. Now he had to figure out how to use fixed defenses to protect Normandy from invasion. The German army had no doctrine for defense against amphibious landings. Past practice at Dieppe, Sicily, Salerno, and Anzio was to "flood the zone"—scrounge up any units handy and counterattack the invaders as close to the beach as possible. The key was to reinforce faster than the attackers could.

Except for Dieppe, the Germans lost every beach battle. Rommel had to find a way to win.

Time and Place

Adolf Hitler was convinced that the invasion could fall anywhere along the coast of Norway, Denmark, the Low Countries, or France. Building a coastal Maginot Line was beyond the resources of the Third Reich. Defenses had to be concentrated in the areas most likely to see action. That narrowed it down to two areas: Calais and Normandy. Calais had the advantage of closeness. It was only about twenty miles away from Dover in southeast England, located at the English Channel's narrowest stretch. Normandy was farther away, about one hundred miles from England's south coast, but still within fighter range. Normandy was also near Cherbourg, a vital port whose capture would enable supplies to be landed and forwarded to the invading armies.

To invade Europe, the Allies had fifty-two divisions to work with. Field Marshal Gerd von Rundstedt, as Commander in Chief West, had fifty-eight, including ten panzer or *panzergrenadier* divisions. On paper, von Rundstedt had the upper hand, but the count was deceiving. Many German infantry divisions were "static"— once placed, they did not move.

As soon as he received command of Army Group B, Rommel had the Fifteenth Army covering the Calais area all the way to the Belgian border; the Seventh Army covered Normandy, Brittany, and Bay of Biscay Coast down to the Loire River. Both armies had twelve to fifteen infantry divisions. But the Fifteenth Army only had to defend fifty miles of shore. Seventh Army had over two hundred miles of coastline to worry about. German army rule of thumb dictated that a division could defend a six-mile front. By this measure, Seventh Army clearly had a problem, with division frontages averaging eighteen miles.

Rommel was aware that defending everything meant defending nothing, so he sought to use fortifications and obstacles to make up for the lack of manpower. Concentrating on Normandy, Rommel envisioned a defensive zone roughly six miles deep. Starting at the beach, defenses were constructed with an invasion expected at high tide. Iron girders welded into X shapes and upright wooden logs topped with waterproof mines were implanted

below the high water mark to impale or destroy incoming landing craft. Going inland, open fields ideal for glider landing were
well planted with landmines or mounted posts topped with
landmines. Low-lying ground would be flooded, denying cross-
country access to mechanized forces, thus limiting them to roads
that could be covered by small units at intersections and villages.
Minefields could also accomplish the same task where flooding
was not option. The goal was to use obstacles to channel attackers toward strong points held by German troops.

But this defense was incomplete without tanks. Here Rommel clashed with von Rundstedt. The old-school field marshal
doubted the coast could be defended in depth, so the panzer
divisions should be kept to the rear as a mobile reserve until the
Allies invaded. Having suffered the wrath of the RAF in North
Africa, Rommel understood that enemy airpower could stop any
reinforcement. Put the panzers close to the beach and drive the
enemy into the sea right away, Rommel reasoned.

The bickering finally reached Hitler's desk, and in typical führer
fashion, he assigned only three armored divisions each to Rommel
and von Rundstedt, keeping the rest in reserve. If anyone wanted
panzers, they would have to say, "Please, Führer, may I?"

Two more factors clouded Rommel's setup.

First U.S. Army Group (FUSAG), under the command of General
George S. Patton, was one worry that could not be ignored. FUSAG
threatened to put twenty to twenty-five divisions on the beach at
Calais as the main effort, with a secondary effort likely at Normandy. This "truth" proved false, as FUSAG was part of an Allied deception effort that had turned Germany's spy network in Britain into a
conduit feeding bogus, but plausible, information to German intelligence. FUSAG kept von Rundstedt's attention fixed on Calais, and
in turn kept divisions there that could have been used elsewhere.

Rommel's second problem was lack of unity of command. He had no call on Luftwaffe assets (about nine hundred aircraft) or navy assets (about a half dozen U-boats plus several gaggles of mini-subs and E-boats). Allied Supreme Commander General Dwight Eisenhower had command of American and British naval and air assets to do what was needed for the D-day invasion.

During the months leading up to D-day, Rommel and Army Group B's staff consulted tide charts and identified suitable beaches worth defending. German troops kept laying down landmines and erecting obstacles according to Rommel's plan. Over 6 million mines were laid in by the spring, but Rommel needed another 194 million to perfect his defense. "I have only one real enemy now, and that is time," mused Rommel.

Invasion of the Nazi Bashers

Rommel's staff got a lot of practice looking for warning signs of the invasion throughout 1944. The weather was lousy on June 5, so the attack was considered unlikely. German intelligence successfully noted the invasion messages to the French Resistance broadcast over the BBC. Warnings were passed on to Rommel's and von Rundstedt's headquarters. But word was not passed on to the Seventh Army, which covered Normandy. A previous false alarm robbed this red flag of its urgency. Bad weather only fed German complacency. Rommel used the downtime to drive home and surprise his wife for her birthday on June 6.

That night, paratroops of the 101st Airborne, Eighty-second Airborne, and British Sixth Airborne dropped out of the skies to secure the east and west flanks of the invasion beaches in Normandy, which stretched along fifty miles of coastline. The five invasion divisions were brought to shore by sixty-five hundred ships, with air superiority guaranteed by twelve thousand aircraft.

The Luftwaffe only managed to send two fighters to strafe Omaha Beach. The Kriegsmarine used its tiny fleet of U-boats and E-boats to sink one destroyer and six ships, while mines scored hits on forty-three more. That still left over sixty-four hundred ships in the invasion fleet.

Now it was up to the German army.

How well did it do? The U.S. Fourth Infantry Division made it to Utah Beach unscathed. British and Canadian forces hit Gold, Juno, and Sword beaches with some resistance, but pushed inland nonetheless. At Omaha Beach, the First and Twenty-ninth divisions hit defenses manned by eight German battalions, not four as expected, due to the German 352nd Division's untimely arrival. This American landing was made more difficult by mishaps. Close to forty amphibious tanks were lost offshore. The Americans lacked engineering vehicles to clear beach obstacles and minefields. Naval prep fire was lacking. Yet despite these drawbacks, the 352nd was picked out of its positions by nightfall, even after inflicting a near defeat on the Americans.

The situation was more chaotic on the German right flank. The Twenty-first Panzer Division was deployed just east of the Orne River. British paratroops belonging to the Sixth Parachute Division, which had airdropped in the night before, held the Pegasus Bridge over the Dives River near Bénouville. This forced the Twenty-first Panzer to take a lengthy detour via Caen, then north again to attack on Sword Beach. One battalion of Twenty-first Panzer made it to shore, threatening to split the British position. A counterattack supported by naval gunfire drove the German tanks away. (The Sixth Parachute was relieved by the end of June 6 by British infantry.)

By nightfall, von Rundstedt got Hitler's approval to move the

Twelfth SS Panzer Division to Caen and to activate the Panzer Lehr Division for movement to the coast. But it was too late. The Allies managed to land 130,000 troops on the Normandy beaches.

The Score

When the invasion came, five Allied divisions from three different corps overwhelmed a German corps fielding two divisions that covered a fifty-mile front. Despite Allied mistakes, it was no contest.

In World War II, the amphibious landing was usually a frontal assault. If the defender was based on the mainland, he could commit reserves via the road and rail network to build up strength faster than the attacker could bring troops to bear. Allied lessons learned, however imperfectly, contributed to the plan's success. Rommel was cognizant of Army Group B's weaknesses, but his deployments could not bring greater strength to battle.

The great "what if" of Normandy is Rommel's preferred plan. Had that two-division corps been backed by two to three armored divisions, there would have been a more robust counterattack that might have won the battle.

The consequences would likely have been devastating. Eisenhower's relief would have been certain, ending his military career. Britain, already war-weary after being booted off of Europe four times, would have struggled to carry on under a tired Prime Minister Churchill. German units committed to the defense of France, especially those ten armored and mechanized divisions, would have been freed for deployment on the crumbling Eastern Front.

Instead, the invasion succeeded. The Allies would go on to make many mistakes while liberating France and conquering Germany. But they prevailed through strength and mostly competent, unspectacular generalship.

BATTLE OF NORMANDY

France, June–July 1944

BY WILLIAM TERDOSLAVICH

The D-day invasion was a triumph of planning and a master-piece of execution. Four of the five invasion beaches in Normandy saw successful landings of division-sized units; the fifth (Omaha Beach) was bloody touch-and-go but successful in the end.

But the liberation of France didn't get far past the beach before being halted by hedgerows. Since the Middle Ages, the peasants of Normandy delineated their fields with walls of earth topped by hedges. Almost a thousand years later, these hedgerows were pretty thick, topped by trees and bushes, and laced with nettles. This made the Norman countryside a series of mini-fortresses.

Allied generals found themselves being stymied by terrain they never took into account. Yes, generals know how to read maps, but when it came to reading ground, they seemed illiterate.

Scottish Pride, German Stubbornness

First to break their tactical teeth on the hedgerow country was the Fifteenth Scottish Division, which moved out on June 26 from the Caen-Bayeux area southward toward the Odon River, the prime objective the line of the Orne River five miles beyond. The division advanced with two infantry brigades forward, each brigade with two battalions forward, one in reserve. A rolling artillery barrage masked the advance, but the prep fire had little effect beyond stunning the defenders.

The Germans had used the previous three weeks to turn the hedgerows around Odon into a defense belt five miles thick. Had the Fifteenth Division advanced through wide-open fields, it would have been free to concentrate its infantry and tanks in any strength to overwhelm or outflank the defenders at any point. But this was not open country. The ditches, sunken roads, berm-bound fields, and villages forced many units of the Fifteenth to fight on narrow fronts. The constricted landscape forced the Scots to fight in platoons and companies, not as more powerful battalions and brigades. No overwhelming strength could be brought to bear against the Germans. Just two battalions of the Twelfth SS Panzer Division held off the nine battalions attacking them.

The Germans fought flexibly. They would hold fire until point-blank range, then get the sure kill. The defending squad or platoon then shifted to a new firing position, quickly getting another shot in. This would often mislead the attacking infantry into thinking they were being fired on from different directions by several enemy squads. Artillery fire would then be called in, only to slam into a vacant German firing position as the defending squad shifted to new foxholes elsewhere.

Ground to a halt in a countryside with a few narrow roads, the Fifteenth Division suffered a six-mile traffic jam as its lead battalions picked their way through the tricky terrain. Committing the Eleventh Armored Division to help only worsened the jam.

By June 29, the "Scottish Corridor" was cleared of the enemy, but not before the Second SS Panzer Corps was brought on to counterattack the Scots. The tactical roles reversed; the SS troopers could not make headway, again due to the terrain.

Yankee-Doodle Can Do

As the Americans built up their strength to the south and west of Utah and Omaha beaches, they ran into the same constricted terrain. The key toward breaking out into more open country was the town of St.-Lô, a regional road junction about fifteen miles south of the invasion beaches. The town was the highest point in the river-laced and swampy Norman lowlands.

So far, the Germans concentrated seven panzer divisions against the British Second Army around Caen. The U.S. First Army had it easier, fielding fourteen divisions to face six German divisions, three of which were either panzer or *panzergrenadier* divisions. On paper, it looked as if General Omar Bradley could crush the opposition. Again, terrain favored the defenders, with no open dry ground that could permit an outflanking move. Bradley lined up three corps and began grinding his way south in early July.

The defenders suffered horrendous attrition. The German Eighty-fourth Corps clocked its loss rate at one to two battalions per day. But it wasn't much better for the Americans. Each infantry division, while over twelve thousand strong, only had a frontline strength of fifty-two hundred infantrymen spread among its twenty-seven companies (three companies per battalion, three battalions per regiment). The rifle companies suffered 90 percent of a division's losses, and it was not unusual for Bradley's infantry divisions to replace 100 percent of their infantrymen in the few weeks it to took to pick their way through the hedgerows.

The Americans tried to bring technology to bear in any way to lessen casualties. Here artillery was quite potent, using the Time on Target (TOT) doctrine. Batteries were on call. When a front-line unit needed fire support, an artillery forward observer would call in the job and any available batteries would reply, usually in about two minutes. Sometimes these fires could be massed to drop a freight train's worth of woe and hot metal on the German defenders.

Other solutions came from the bottom. Sergeant Curtis G. Culin of the Second Armored Division used scrap steel scrounged from the invasion beaches to fashion blades that would be welded on the front of Sherman tanks. The blades would catch and up-root the hedges by simply driving the tank through. American troops could then bypass the sunken roads, but still had to fight the Germans for each field.

It was not uncommon for the defending Germans to post machine guns on the two far corners of each field. This would bring the open ground under their cross fire, backed by preregistered mortars or artillery to hit the middle of the field as the Americans crossed.

The Americans would respond by sending a single Sherman through the hedge. It would then fire white phosphorus rounds at either corner to burn out the machine gunners. A squad of riflemen, backed by a machine gun and a 60mm mortar, would follow the tank. The Sherman would rake the tree line with more machine-gun fire. The mortar team would drop rounds behind the tree line to nail any Germans hiding behind the hedges. The infantry squad would deploy behind the tank and follow it forward across the field.

The tank would have to keep its hatches shut, protecting the commander and crew from German fire. But this cut down visibility, so the tank crew could not spot targets as effectively. To compensate, a telephone was mounted on the back of the tank, so the squad leader could talk to the tank commander, spotting the targets the tankers could not see and guiding the tank's supporting fire where it counted.

Still, this tactical system could not take the next hedgerow without casualties. A few men always got hit in every fight. The attacking Americans would paste their targets with artillery, pause, probe, pop off a few rounds, then pour it on, pause, fire, rush, pause again, then advance. Once the farther hedgerow was taken, the fight repeated itself, acre by bloody acre. There were thousands of acres between the beaches and St.-Lô.

The Price of Winning

By July 15, the Twenty-ninth Infantry Division was making its final push for St.-Lô. The division was running close to 100 percent replacement of its front-line riflemen. Major General Charles H. Gerhardt of the Twenty-ninth opted for an all-out assault, with no reserves handy. The second Battalion of the 116th Regiment was within a mile of the town when the German defenders managed to cut it off from the Twenty-ninth Division. The battalion hung on for two days, awaiting relief while getting pounded, but the Germans lacked enough strength to destroy the unit.

Gerhardt ordered the Third Battalion, 116th Regiment, to relieve the Second Battalion and take St.-Lô. Third Battalion commander Major Thomas D. Howie responded with a laconic "will do," and ordered a predawn attack on July 17. Howie told his company commanders to limit rifle fire to two men per platoon, otherwise sticking to bayonets and grenades, and above all, *keep moving!*

Surprise paid off handsomely as Howie's companies quickly broke through the German lines and seized Hill 122. Possession of the local high ground allowed the 116th to provide support for the 115th Regiment and Task Force C to take St.-Lô on July 18.

But the rush came at a cost for the Twenty-ninth Division— three thousand casualties, mostly concentrated among the five thousand riflemen who did the bulk of the fighting. Among them was Major Howie, who was killed by a mortar shell fragment that entered his back, shortly after taking Hill 122. Howie's flag-draped body was laid to rest outside the wrecked St. Croix church in St.-Lô. The media picked up on the story of "the Major of St.-Lô," making Howie's story symbolic of the human cost of Bradley's offensive.

St.-Lô was the local high ground that would serve as the gateway for Bradley's breakout offensive. Operation Cobra would get the Americans out of the Norman hedgerow country and into the open fields of the Loire Valley, where mobile warfare would once again become possible.

But every victory has its blood price. The divisions of First Army suffered forty thousand killed and wounded, plus another ten to fifteen thousand psychological casualties from constant, bitter combat. One oft-quoted remark came from a regimental historian in the Eighty-third Division: "We won the Battle of Normandy, [but] considering the high price in American lives, we lost."

THE GAP AT FALAISE

France, August 1944

BY WILLIAM TERDOSLAVICH

Breakthrough!

The U.S. Seventh Corps slogged its way through heavy resistance south of St.-Lô. An early commitment of two armored divisions crushed the brittle shell that was once the Panzer Lehr Division.

France was finally opening up for the Americans. Patton's Third Army finally became operational. Despite the side trip to Brittany by one of its corps, the rest of the formation passed through, reached the Loire River Valley, and made a left, heading east, full speed ahead, flanks be damned.

Patton was never shortsighted about war. As his peers pondered reaching the next phase line ten miles away, Patton was eager to reach the French-German border. As soon as Patton got the Twelfth Corps, he ordered its commander to capture a town fifty miles away—a town that wasn't even on the map being used. Once Twelfth Corps captured the town, Patton simply ordered it to "keep moving."

That phrase might as well have been the Third Army's motto. Patton had an instinctive feel for mobile warfare, even if the real estate where he practiced it was not as broad as the Russian steppe or the North African desert. If any unit of the Third Army penetrated the enemy line somewhere, the enemy had to counterattack to contain the breakthrough or fall back to avoid being cut off and surrounded. Pursuing the Germans in retreat was a cheaper way of winning a battle, compared to liberating France at one thousand casualties per mile, as the First Army did in the hedgerow country in Normandy.

Patton's Third Army had a good start line, bounding southward forty-five miles from Avranches, which was about forty miles south of St.-Lô. By going south, Patton skipped around the left flank of the German Seventh Army, then made a wide, looping left turn to outflank it. The move was turning into a huge wheeling left hook.

Hitler made Patton's job a little easier by ordering an attack on Mortain, about halfway between St.-Lô and the Loire River. If successful, this attack would cut off Patton's Third Army in the south from the First Army in the north. But a rock-hard stand by the U.S. Thirtieth Division stopped the German blade from cutting the American advance in half.

Patton now drove several corps hell-for-leather eighty miles down the Loire River Valley toward Le Mans, making another left turn to head fifty miles northward toward Argentan. This would form the southern claw of a huge encirclement. The British to the north also scored their breakthrough near Caen and were driving south toward Falaise. If these two claws closed, the German Seventh Army and Fifth Panzer Army would be surrounded, leaving little to stop the Allies from reaching the French-German border.

Filling a Hole

The Fifteenth Corps was making its objectives in good time, capturing Alençon on August 12. Patton ordered it to push farther north to Argentan, just eighteen miles south of Falaise, the Canadian objective. But the Canadians were not on schedule. German resistance had stiffened tremendously, knowing that the Allied claws had to be kept apart.

The ever-impatient Patton called the Twelfth Army Group commander General Omar Bradley for permission to advance north from Argentan to close the gap. In jest, Patton added that maybe the Third Army could keep going north and give the British another Dunkirk. This went over badly with the humorless Bradley. The order was to hold at Argentan.

On August 12, the Canadian Third Infantry and Fourth Armored divisions launched Operation Tractable, blowing through the Twelfth SS Panzer Division and reaching Falaise two days later. The attack was greatly aided by "Kangaroos"—Sherman tank chassis refashioned as impromptu armored personnel carriers that could keep up with the Canadian armor.

Army Group B's commander, Field Marshal Günther von Kluge, was forced to commit the First and Second SS Panzer and the 116th Panzer divisions to hold the Falaise gap open. The units were worn down to just a fighting tenth of their tanks and men. Had Fifteenth Corps pressed its four divisions to close the gap, it would have blocked the escape of the retreating Germans, but only by spreading itself thin by holding forty to fifty miles of frontage.

"I'd rather have a solid shoulder at Argentan than a broken neck at Falaise" was Bradley's oft-quoted reasoning for halting the Fifteenth Corps. Bradley spotted risk where Patton saw opportunity. On August 17, the northward attack resumed slowly as the Fifth Corps was brought up to drive northward toward Trun and Chambois on a narrower front.

Poles Apart

Spearheading the Canadian offensive was the Polish First Armored Division. Manning this unit was returning Poles who were living abroad at war's start and any survivors of the 1939 invasion who had made their way to France, thence to Britain.

By August 16, the Canadians had captured Falaise and sent the Polish First Armored southward toward Trun and Chambois to finally close the gap. If they could cover the last six miles, the Poles would trap 100,000 Germans, comprising the remnants of close to twenty divisions.

Major General Stanislaw Maczek, commander of the Polish First Armored, had to fight shrewdly. While the Poles could replace any equipment or tanks lost in a fight, replacing manpower was difficult. There were only so many of his countrymen living outside of Nazi-occupied Poland. Any attack had to produce a gain that far outweighed losses.

Upon reaching the Chambois area on August 18, Maczek dispatched the division's antitank guns and two battalions of infantry in their half-tracks to take the hill near town. The ridgeline east of the town became the objective for the division's two tank regiments and three battalions of infantry, also mounted on half-tracks. Once the high ground was taken, the Poles would go over to defense. The next day, recon patrols of U.S. Nintieth Division (Fifth Corps) advanced northward and made contact. The Falaise pocket was closed.

Or was it?

Taking command of Army Group B from von Kluge, Field Marshal Walter Model engineered an attack to blow the closure wide open. Second SS and Ninth SS Panzer divisions would attack the Trun-Chambois sector from outside the pocket, while remaining elements inside the pocket would stage a breakthrough toward the two SS divisions. The Poles on the ridge east of Chambois took the blow.

This attack cut off the Polish task force of eighty tanks and fifteen hundred men from the remainder of Polish First Armored and its parent formation, Canadian Second Corps. The American main force was held up while advancing on Chambois, so no support could be expected. The Poles could not attack for lack of supply, but could call in artillery fire from their hilltop, now nicknamed "the Mace." Incoming rounds crashed into the retreating columns of Germans below, turning trucks into wrecks and men into dead bodies.

Task-force commander Colonel Stanislaw Koszutski tried to improve his position by using a tank-infantry team to cut off the road that ran along the edge of the Mace on the morning of August 20. Second SS Panzer preempted the attack by hitting the Mace from the north, forcing the team to reinforce the perimeter and beat back the attack.

Things stayed hot for the Poles as German spotters from a nearby hill called down their artillery to hammer the Mace. Again, Koszutski formed a tank-infantry team to seize the nearby hilltop, but the force was beaten back, with the loss of five Shermans. Constant German artillery fire whittled down the Polish defenders. The Germans tried to drive the blade home at 7 P.M. with an assault by tanks and infantry. The Polish task force's mortar platoon, now out of shells, picked up rifles and rushed to meet the crisis, driving the attackers away. At day's end, losses were running as high as 30 percent among the Polish infantry battalions still holding the Mace.

Was It Victory or Defeat?

On August 21, the Poles had to repel one more attack from the south. The heavy German infantry assault forced Koszutski to commit his last reserve—a small group of machine-gun equipped antiaircraft tanks. Guns leveled, they hosed the attacking German infantry. The Poles expected to lose the Mace if the Germans attacked again. But the low rumble of tank engines in the distance heralded the arrival of the Canadian Grenadier Guards.

The Poles lost a fifth of their men holding the Mace, but prevented about 50,000 men of the German Seventh Army from slipping the noose. Another 10,000 Germans were killed in action. Found inside the Falaise pocket was another 220 tanks, 160 assault guns, 700 artillery pieces, 130 antiaircraft guns, 130 half-tracks, 5,000 trucks and other vehicles, 2,000 wagons, and 1,800 dead horses. But closing the Falaise Gap five days earlier would have netted the Allies a far bigger haul: nine of eleven panzer divisions stationed in the west, and probably double the haul in prisoners.

A third of the German Seventh Army got away. Among the escapees were elements of Third Parachute; 84th, 276th, 277th, 326th, 353rd, and 363rd Infantry divisions; First, Tenth, and Twelfth SS Panzer divisions; and Second and 116th Panzer divisions. The survivors were like the heads of a hydra—each stump of a division became the experienced foundation for the incoming recruits. Lost equipment was replaced.

Many of these escaped divisions would later attack the Americans again in the Ardennes. Only the Americans called that fight the Battle of the Bulge.

THE BATTLE OF ARNHEM
Netherlands, September 1944

BY WILLIAM TERDOSLAVICH

This is the tale of how a small battle can screw up a larger war.

It was a sunny Sunday afternoon. The C–47s were droning in the clear blue sky. The German flak batteries were blasting away at them. Here and there a flaming plane or a burning glider crashed to earth. The sky was full of parachutes gently descending to earth.

The British First Airborne division landed around 2:30 P.M. on September 17, 1944. The paratroops had some bridges to seize. Third prize was a railway bridge between Oosterbeek and Arnhem. Second prize was a pontoon bridge in Arnhem. First prize was the highway bridge just one mile farther to the east.

Possession of any bridge would allow the British Thirtieth Corps to cross the Rhine, outflanking Germany's Siegfried Line (also known as the West Wall), Germany's network of bunkers and obstacles that ran from the south bank of the lower Rhine to the Swiss border. Thirtieth Corps could then blast across the North German Plain to Berlin—followed by the Twenty-first Army Group, of course. That was how Field Marshal Bernard Montgomery envisioned the outcome of Operation Market Garden, an uncharacteristically daring operation for such a deliberate, cautious man.

But there were a few catches. Two American airborne divisions dropping to the south of Arnhem had to capture four other crossings or the Thirtieth Corps would not be able to relieve the First Airborne. The plan required holding a sixty-mile-long corridor against German attacks. And it violated another axiom of airborne operations: never drop paratroops deep behind enemy lines. Airdrops only work when ground forces can quickly relieve the paratroops.

The whole operation had to be done in forty-eight hours.

If anything went wrong, all would be for naught.

Terra Firma, Terror Firmer

Airborne rookie Major General Robert Urquhart didn't have much choice of drop zones. Known German antiaircraft positions forced Urquhart to settle for a drop zone northwest of Arnhem, eight miles away from First Airborne's prime objectives. This violated another airborne rule of thumb: always drop as close to the objective as possible.

Owing to a shortage of transport aircraft, only two brigades could be dropped on the first day. First Air Landing Brigade, commanded by Brigadier General Philip Hicks, had to protect the drop zone while First Parachute Brigade, under Brigadier General Gerald Lathbury, would seize the bridges right away.

Allied intelligence ignored the presence of German tanks around Arnhem, so Urquhart and Lathbury were unaware that they had just dropped into the midst of the Second SS Panzer Corps. Lieutenant General Wilhelm Bittrich commanded this formation, comprised of the understrength Ninth and Tenth SS Panzer divisions. Bittrich quickly realized that the capture of the Arnhem Bridge would give the British a springboard to invade Germany. He committed the Ninth SS Panzer to defend Arnhem and secure the bridge, sending the division's recon battalion south to look for more paratroops.

Not long after the SS recon battalion motored over the Arnhem Bridge, the Second Battalion of Lathbury's brigade, Lieutenant Colonel John Frost commanding, made it to the prime objective. The railway bridge to the west had been blown. The pontoon bridge had its center section removed. First prize it would have to be.

Frost's paratroopers rushed the bridge, killing off the few defenders. The paratroops fanned out, securing eighteen buildings surrounding the bridge's north approach. Two buildings with river views were most vital to the defense. Frost placed his headquarters in the building on the west of the bridge, while one platoon held the building on the east. Thus the bridge was partially secured just seven hours after landing. Frost sent a platoon across to capture the south end, only to be twice repulsed by the Germans.

Unknown to Frost, his accomplishment was about to be badly compromised by breakdowns in communications and command. Most of First Airborne's Type 22 radios failed shortly after landing, able to do no more than produce garbled squawks at short range. Without a decent radio net, First Airborne could not coordinate combat by its subunits or report to higher command. The Type 22 normally had a range of about five to eight miles in open country, but the clutter of villages and woods cut down that performance to half its range, if it was working at all. The Type 22 was the most commonly used radio set in the division.

This led to the command failure. Urquhart left division head-quarters on foot to look for his recon commander in Arnhem. While in town, he and Lathbury got lost and separated from the First Parachute Brigade. Lathbury was badly wounded after taking a bullet in his back. The two generals spent the next twenty-four hours hiding from the Germans. Hicks assumed command of the First Airborne, but the First Parachute Brigade was leaderless.

The Ninth SS Panzer flanked the approaches to Arnhem and held the intersections. Paratroop companies and platoons groped to-ward the bridge, hitting roadblocks or blundering into ambushes. A few managed to run the gauntlet to join up with the Second Bat-talion, bringing its strength up to about five hundred men.

All Frost had to do was hold for the next forty-eight hours until the Thirtieth Corps showed up. But that meant holding the bridge with a single battalion, not a brigade as was planned.

Monday Was Bad. Tuesday Was Worse.

The SS recon battalion that crossed the bridge the day before now came back at high speed, trying to rush the crossing. Here Frost got lucky. Lathbury's brigade headquarters managed to join the Second Battalion. It had a working radio—not a Type 22! A fire mission was called in to First Airborne's light artillery. High-explosive rounds blasted the trucks and half-tracks while antitank fire from the PIATs (a man-portable antitank weapon) killed the armored cars. The roadway was covered with burning wrecks and dead bodies.

Frost was gamely holding his ground, but his position was slowly being pressed by the Ninth SS Panzer. Every firefight drove away the enemy, but cost the Second Battalion a few more men and some ammo, neither of which could be replaced.

Unknown to Frost, Hicks sent two companies toward the bridge the day before and sent another battalion from the Fourth Parachute Brigade after it landed on Monday. These units made no more headway than their predecessors. By Tuesday, September 19, things were getting desperate for Frost's battalion. Food and ammo were running low. The wounded were piling up in the basements. Medical supplies were scant.

Where was the Thirtieth Corps? It was supposed to be arriving by now.

The Ninth SS Panzer was making concerted attacks to retake the bridge. Its tanks were firing shells into the buildings to flush out the paratroop. Frost pulled his perimeter in. Word went out: no firing unless targets were close and certain. Make every bullet count.

Urquhart finally made it back to division headquartes after spending the previous twenty-four hours eluding capture in Arnhem. (Lathbury was too badly wounded to move and was left behind, later being captured by the Germans.) Four battalions were struggling to reach the bridge, but they could not coordinate their attacks. Urquhart tapped Hick's deputy, Colonel Hilary Barlow, to rush into Arnhem and take over Lathbury's brigade.

Barlow never made it.

His body was never found, either.

So Close, Yet So Far

For two more days, Frost hung on to the bridge. German tanks were now firing into the buildings at point-blank range, demolishing them floor by floor. Over the single decent radio link, Urquhart told Frost that he could expect no reinforcements. To save First Airborne, Urquhart pulled back the remnants of First Parachute Brigade to help form a perimeter around Oosterbeek and a ferry landing at Driel.

Holding the Arnhem Bridge became pointless. Frost, now wounded, ordered his surviving troops to drop their guns and raise their hands. He had no way of knowing that relief was only ten miles away.

The delays were cumulative. The 101st Airborne saw two bridges blown before they could secure them, requiring British combat engineers to put in a Bailey bridge. That stymied the advance for twelve hours. The Eighty-second Airborne began its operation with seventy-four hundred men landing on the first day, but this was not enough to seize the Nijmegen Bridge over the Waal River and defend the drop zone, which sucked in men as it faced constant attack. The Eighty-second eventually seized the Nijmegen Bridge by crossing the Waal in small boats, supported by gunfire from the tanks of Thirtieth Corps' Guards Armored Division. The next problem was the raised highway between Arnhem and Nijmegen, flanked by soft, muddy ground, which made the tanks road-bound. German-held villages blocked the road until infantry could be brought up. The Thirtieth Corps had little infantry to spare as other brigades and the American paratroops fought hard to keep the corridor open in the face of persistent German attacks.

It Only Takes a Week to Destroy a Division

Urquhart bravely and desperately hung on for a few more days. Efforts to resupply the First Airborne failed. Amphibious DUKW trucks belonging to the Thirtieth Corps could not find a viable crossing point. Uncoordinated airdrops of supplies fell within the German lines. The Polish Airborne Brigade, which dropped south of the Rhine, tried to improvise a ferry to shuttle reinforcements, but its few rafts were raked by German machine gunners holding the north riverbank. By September 25, First Airborne was evacuated at night by a hodgepodge flotilla of rafts and canvas boats crossing the Rhine. Some paratroops even swam across.

Losses were nasty on both sides. Of the 10,005 paratroops belonging to British First Airborne, 7,578 were killed, wounded, missing, or captured. German losses around Arnhem were approximately 1,300 killed and another 2,000 wounded or missing.

As for the Dutch civilians around Arnhem and Oosterbeek, no accurate figures on losses are available. Author Cornelius Ryan, who penned the classic *A Bridge Too Far*, heard estimates ranging from five hundred to ten thousand, including many who died from cold or lack of food after Arnhem was forcibly evacuated by the Germans.

Since Operation Market Garden failed, many tens of thousands fell in combat until May 1945. But had it succeeded, these men would have lived to tell their grandchildren about how they saw the end of World War II—in the fall of 1944.

BATTLE OF HUERTGEN FOREST

September–November 1944

BY WILLIAM TERDOSLAVICH

There were times when World War II resembled World War I, only without the trenches. The Battle of Huertgen Forest was like that. Once again, the generals would try to go through a problem instead of around it. And once again, the infantry would pay the price for the folly of their leaders.

The Huertgen Forest could have easily been bypassed by advancing through the open ground to the south, focusing on the town of Monschau. Capturing this objective would have placed units of the U.S. Army upstream from the Roer River dams, a feature that would later complicate this battle. This outflanking move would also have rendered moot any German defense of the Huertgen Forest, forcing units there either to fall back or risk being surrounded.

On a map, the Huertgen Forest is a blob of green ink lying south of Aachen, astride the Belgian-German border. It measures roughly 25 miles by 10 miles. Two gray bands run through it—the prepared fortifications of the Siegfried Line. This was a series of steel-reinforced concrete pillboxes with interlocking fields of fire that ran thick and thin along a 375-mile line, which also used local terrain like forests and rivers to increase defensive strength. The line was never designed to be impregnable, but to slow down an attacker long enough for mobile units to concentrate and counterattack the enemy. The town of Schmidt, in the forest's southeastern corner, became a principal objective given its proximity to the Roer River dams.

To the U.S. First Army, the Huertgen Forest might as well have been the deep, dark woods found in a German fairy tale. Closely spaced tall pines robbed the troops of any visibility, obstructing clear fields of fire. Roads were few, muddy, well mined, and easily covered by German machine-gun cross fire or preregistered artillery. In short, it was a natural fortress for the defending Germans. Allied airpower, artillery, and armor were all useless, and the constant autumn rains made it a perfectly miserable place.

Green Hell

In mid-September, First Army began its approach toward Aachen. Its commander, General Courtney Hodges, planned to surround the city with two corps then clear it out. It took two weeks to accomplish this, at the cost of five thousand casualties. One corps commander was sacked for not going fast enough.

With Aachen in hand, Hodges looked at his uncovered right flank. Securing it meant taking the Huertgen Forest. Two ridges ran diagonally through the thick woods, with a deep ravine between them marking the path of the Kall River. Defending the thicket was the lackluster 275th Division, rated by U.S. intelligence as just another understrength infantry unit. But its fighting prowess would be much improved by the forest itself, which would break any divisional attack into a bunch of smaller company- and platoon-sized actions where the Germans could hold their own.

The U.S. Ninth Division began its attack into the Huertgen with two of its three regiments. The objective was Schmidt, as the village held one of the highest points in the forest and was a natural springboard for taking Monschau to the south, or the Roer River dams to the east. That looked easy on paper. By October 6, the Ninth Division was averaging four to five days just to advance one mile. Roads were really muddy trails or firebreaks, usually mined and blocked by felled trees, and well covered by machine guns. Eventually Ninth Division managed to push another two miles, losing forty-five hundred men before halting on October 16.

Hodges now gave the task of taking Schmidt to Fifth Corps, which led with the Twenty-eighth Infantry Division on November 1. All three regiments would go into the attack, each supported by an engineer battalion. While the hard-luck Twenty-eighth hit resistance in many places, the Third Battalion and 112th Regiment got lucky, advancing into Schmidt unopposed on November 3. But the unit could only be reinforced via a single muddy track leading down to the Kall River. Despite the terrain, three Shermans managed to reinforce 3rd Battalion. The next day, a joint counterattack by units of the 116th Panzer and the Eighty-ninth Infantry Division broke the American battalion. About two hundred troops ran away in the wrong direction, deeper into German-held territory, while remnants of the battalion joined up with its sister formation, First Battalion/112th Regiment, holding the nearby village of Kommerscheidt.

The overextended Twenty-eighth Division had no reserves left to reinforce Schmidt when needed. For the next few days, the

112th Regiment would hang on to the Kall gorge and Kommerscheidt village, pulling back when its 2nd Battalion was overrun.

Hodges was eager to sack Major General Norman Cota, the Twenty-eighth Division's commander. In a November 9 meeting between Hodges and Cota, with Eisenhower and Bradley in attendance, Hodges relented. But he ordered Cota to maintain the attack on Schmidt with his depleted division, also ordering Cota to support two separate attacks by other divisions on the town of Huertgen to the north and Monschau to the south. Instead of concentrating the remains of Twenty-eighth Division's strength on attaining one objective, Hodges was ordering Cota to advance in three different directions, dissipating what was left of the Twenty-eighth's combat power.

Now the Twelfth Regiment of the Fourth Infantry Division pressed the attack, supported by the Twenty-eighth Division. In five days, the regiment would suffer 500 casualties for minimal gains. Cota tried to support the attack with three companies that had already suffered over 50 percent losses, to no avail. By November 13, the Twenty-eighth Division exchanged places with the Eighth Division of Eighth Corps. Losses for the Twenty-eighth totaled 6,184 casualties—well over the division's "rifle strength" of 5,000.

For the First Army, the Huertgen Forest was turning into a bloody stupid battle.

First Army Grinds On

By mid-November, the Allies were going to resume their drive on the Rhine. The First Army's attack would be the main effort. The German 275th Division was badly battered after mauling two American divisions, but grimly held its ground.

As the Seventh Corps tried to take the high ground east of Aachen, the Fourth Infantry Division would relieve the Twenty-eighth Division and attack into the Huertgen Forest from Sch-evenhutte to take Huertgen village. There was no artillery prep fire. Upon sensing the changeover, the German 275th Division pounced. Now the 112th Regiment, Fourth Division, was driv-en back, losing contact on its left with its sister regiment, the Twenty-second.

The Twenty-second was having no better luck attacking a Ger-man outpost line known as "the Raven's Hedge." After three days, the Twenty-second attained its objective, but then risked being cut off from its division when a key road intersection in its rear area came under German artillery fire, a hazard the regiment could not eliminate.

Hodges expected the Fourth Division to cover more ground than it was able, so the unit never could concentrate its strength to get anything done. Hodges shortened Fourth Division's sector. He then threw in the Eighth Division of Fifth Corps to take the southern half of the forest, aided by CCR, Fifth Armored Divi-sion. At least the Eighth Division got a heavy prep bombardment before launching its attack.

The four-day drive was costly for the Eighth Division's 121st Reg-iment, which lost six hundred men. The commander of the 121st, Colonel John Jeter, sacked two battalion commanders and three company commanders for failure to make gains. Likewise, divi-sion commander Major General Donald A. Stroh was feeling the heat from Hodges's headquarters asking "Where's the progress?"

Stroh backed the 121st Regiment's attack with tanks from CCR/Fifth Armored, with orders to take Huertgen village. The attack began on November 25, but CCR/Fifth Armored just could not get off the start line. A tank got stuck in a crater, blocking the advance. By noon, engineers had removed the tank and bridged the crater. The next tank hit a landmine. The tank retriever sent to clear the stricken tank got hit by a shell. All this happened while CCR/Fifth Armored was peppered with small arms fire and artillery.

Stroh's solution was to fire Jeter.

Fourth Division's advance to the left drew Germans away from Eighth Division's front. Stroh reinforced the 121st Regiment with a battalion from another regiment. After two days of fighting, aided by a platoon of Sherman tanks, the 121st finally captured Huertgen village.

That's when Hodges sacked Stroh.

Brigadier General William G. Weaver, the deputy commanding officer of Ninetieth Division, got Stroh's job. Weaver was luckier. A break in the bad weather permitted air support. CCR/Fifth Armored attacked through a clearing, finally having some space to maneuver. Eighth Division quickly captured the next village in its path.

Now Eighth Division had to attack southeast along the spine of high ground toward two villages. The Germans controlled the woods to either side of the road and brought the advancing troops under cross fire. Weaver supported 121st Regiment with the Twenty-eighth Regiment to pry the Germans out of the woods. That took three days.

Weaver's division finally captured the objective villages of Brandenburg and Bergstein, but that triggered the arrival of German reinforcements to keep the Americans from reaching the Roer River. Weaver still needed to gain Castle Hill to the east of Bergstein. He had no divisional reserves left, but received the Second Ranger Battalion from Fifth Corps headquarters. The Rangers used two companies (over one hundred men each) to capture the hilltop and hold it for a miserable twenty-four hours as an artillery observer called in fire to beat back the Germans. Once the Rangers were relieved, only twenty-five of their men walked off the hill.

Dam It!

First Army captured a worthless forest in three months at the cost of twenty-four thousand casualties, plus another nine thousand noncombat and psychiatric casualties. It now had a nice view of the Roer River plain to the east. But it was open ground not ripe for the taking. The Roer River dams upstream were still in German hands. If First Army tried to cross, the Germans would open the floodgates to inundate the valley floor.

So why bother with the Huertgen Forest? Why go through a problem instead of around it? Unimaginative generalship plagued the Allies for much of the war. This "straight ahead" thinking was more likely to cause the leaders to worry about uncovered flanks rather than outflanking the enemy. It did not occur to Hodges to threaten the enemy with encirclement by going *around* the forest.

Open ground to the south at Monschau would have enabled the move. But the attack up this corridor only got under way in mid-December. It became moot on December 16, when the Germans struck out of the Ardennes in force. The failure of the Battle of Huertgen Forest was replaced by a bigger problem—the Battle of the Bulge.

CAUGHT NAPPING, OR HITLER'S GREATEST GAMBLE

Allied and Axis Intelligence Failures at the Battle of the Bulge, 1944

BY JOHN HELFERS

By the fall of 1944, the Third Reich was reeling from the Allied offensives advancing on its beleaguered nation from both sides. Caught between the implacable anvil of Stalin's massive, revenge-hungry army to the east, and the advancing hammer of the combined American and British forces that had swept into France on D-day to the west, German troops had spent the summer and early fall retreating to their homeland's borders. The Allies' confidence was so high about the war's end that General Dwight D. Eisenhower bet Field Marshal Bernard Montgomery five pounds that the fighting would be over by Christmas.

Yet by mid-December, Germany had amassed a twenty-division force—almost 410,000 men, more than 2,600 artillery pieces and multiple-rocket launchers, and approximately 1,400 tanks and assault guns—on a 110-kilometer front along the lightly defended Ardennes Forest, practically under the nose of the Allies. Against the advice of his senior military officers, Adolf Hitler prepared his most audacious gamble yet—a strike toward the heart of the Allies' logistical nexus of Antwerp, Belgium, hoping to drive an exploitable wedge into the enemy army. And, despite Allied warnings of a major German offensive, he almost got away with it.

By late 1944, Hitler was anything but sane. Severely demoralized by the failed assassination attempt against him by several high-ranking Nazi officers, and unwilling to accept the major defeats the powerful Allied forces kept dealing his once vaunted army and Luftwaffe, Hitler thought outside (way outside) the box. When the Allied advance ground to a halt because their front-line army units had advanced beyond their supply lines, he formulated a last-chance plan to save the Reich and bring the Allies to the negotiating table. His army would strike through the Ardennes (as he had done successfully in 1940) and recapture the port city of Antwerp. At the very least, the assault would distract the Allies from their relentless drive toward Berlin and give the rest of the German army three or four months to regroup. At best, Hitler felt a successful surprise attack could demoralize the Allies' unity enough that the Americans and British would fall apart, and might even sue for peace, leaving only the Russians to contend with.

Named Operation Wacht am Rhein ("Watch on the Rhein") to disguise its true purpose, the plan was given no chance of success by Hitler's military commanders. This was Hitler's first (and very common) mistake: not listening to his senior officers, all of whom had a much better command of the German military's operational status—undermanned, under equipped, and exhausted. Hitler, of course, came up with immediate solutions to these problems. He bolstered troop numbers by lowering the minimum and raising the maximum age of recruitment, sending inexperienced teenagers and old men to the front lines. As for supplies, he expected his troops to capture enemy equipment, particularly gasoline (keep in mind that the lack of resources was why the Allies couldn't advance, so how were the Germans going to use equipment and fuel that didn't exist?), to continue their offensive. And as for exhaustion, Hitler simply used the freshest troops he could find to spearhead the attack.

As for where the assault would happen, while the Ardennes Forest would hide troop, truck, and tank movements, the land itself—turned to treacherous mud by the winter snows—was, in the opinion of SS Colonel General Josef "Sepp" Dietrich, "the worst terrain imaginable for a thousand tanks." Nevertheless, Hitler gave his orders, and his men carried them out as best as they could.

Furthermore, Hitler probably made his greatest mistake in severely underestimating the Allied response to his undeniably bold attack. Although the Allied forces far outmatched his German army, he still held an unshakable belief in his own ability as a tactical genius, and of his commanders and his men to defeat their enemy. He demanded that his officers adhere to his plan, even when practically all of them expressed doubt about achieving his objectives. In particular, Hitler wanted to attack the Americans because he felt they were inferior soldiers compared to the British. What he hadn't considered was the two-year blooding the U.S. troops had taken during the North African and Italian campaigns. The fierce American resistance at the key town of Bastogne during the operation would prove just how wrong Hitler was about the quality of American soldiers. His wildly optimistic assumptions about how the operation would progress, combined with his unwillingness to see the deficiencies of the proposed offensive, all but guaranteed its failure.

And yet, he succeeded in amassing his more than 400,000-

man army, complete with tanks and artillery, right in front of the Allies with no reaction on their part until the operation began. How was this possible?

Well, Hitler certainly had one thing on his side—the almost total element of surprise. Although certain Allied officers, notably the American chief of intelligence Colonel Benjamin "Monk" Dickson, Major General Kenneth Strong (a British intelligence officer on Eisenhower's staff), and U.S. Army Colonel Oscar W. Koch, all saw signs of a troop buildup on the German-Belgian border and warned about a possible enemy offensive, their cries fell on mostly deaf ears. General Koch even scheduled a private briefing with General George S. Patton to emphasize the potential danger. His concerns prompted Patton to order a contingency plan drawn up in the event of an attack on the Eighth Corps, stationed near the Ardennes Forest. But these alerts, and even Patton's plans, were made and executed too late. With the momentum firmly on the Allies' side, the idea of a mass assault by the battered German army was apparently too unrealistic to contemplate.

There were other reasons why the Allies didn't take the idea of a German offensive seriously. Despite his failings, Hitler's paranoia and desire for secrecy served him well in the abbreviated run-up to Operation Wacht am Rhein. All officers involved had to sign a pledge that if they revealed details of the plan to anyone who didn't need to know, their lives and that of their families were forfeit. Fearing that the German radio network had been compromised (which it was), Hitler ordered all communications about the operation to be done over telephone and telegraph lines, stymieing the Allied eavesdropping network. German forces assigned to the attack were given fictitious names that implied they were administrative units. Last, the German troop buildup began on the Roer River, to further mislead the Allies into thinking the initial assault would happen there, rather than through the Ardennes.

The decreased flow of German radio signals lulled the Allies into a false sense of security. Concentrating solely on decoding radio message traffic from Germany (as older methods were deemed less reliable), the Allies grew complacent when the stream of usable information slowed to a trickle in early December, figuring the weak, demoralized enemy army was unable to mount a large-scale offensive. In fact, the Germans were about to show the Allies just how determined they could be.

All of the misinformation and deception proved surprisingly effective. Even the one thing the Allied forces knew for a fact—that many German motor vehicles were moving into the Ardennes, as reported by the 106th and 28th Infantry divisions—was dismissed by higher-echelon officers. One officer's reply even suggested the Germans were playing phonograph records of truck engines to demoralize the men stationed there.

Another key failure on the Allies' part, particularly the Americans, was the failure to perform efficient front-line patrolling. This lack of security allowed the Germans to concentrate their forces without fear of discovery, as well as prevented early warning about the offensive once it had begun. Also, due to inclement weather and overtaxed squadrons, Allied air reconnaissance on the front lines was essentially nil in the weeks leading up to the operation. The Germans skillfully exploited this weakness, making most of their troop and vehicle movements under cover of night and foul weather.

The last reason for the Allies' unpreparedness for a massive German offensive was their incorrect assumptions about Hitler's intentions, rather than basing their analysis on what they knew about the enemy's strengths and capabilities. Even in the face of a growing buildup of German men and armor on the Western Front, Allied intelligence officers (with the exception of those mentioned previously) felt that while there might be small-scale counterattacks, they simply didn't believe Germany was capable of executing a large-scale, all-or-nothing offensive. The fact that the Eighth Corps on the Ardennes was not reinforced in the late months of 1944 shows that despite multiple warnings, Allied leaders had no real knowledge or expectation that the massed German units would spearhead a huge assault on the thinly spread forces near Belgium (again, despite the fact that Hitler had executed the exact same maneuver back in 1940). The Allied leaders and officers simply couldn't grasp the idea that a military leader in command of an exhausted and under-equipped army that was surrounded on all sides would charge into the very teeth of his enemy.

But by the time the scattered pieces of Allied intelligence pointing at a larger military operation could be pieced together, it was too late. The Third Reich's soldiers, tanks, and artillery were already rumbling through the Ardennes Forest, overwhelming the scant units stationed there, and heralding the defiant last charge of the German army.

THE WEHRMACHT'S LAST GASP

Belgium, December 1944–January 1945

BY DOUGLAS NILES

As the last month of 1944 chilled its way across the European continent, Germany was on the defensive on every frontier. To the east, the Soviets had pushed the Nazi front back into the middle of Poland. Bulgaria, Romania, Hungary, Greece, and most of Yugoslavia had been reclaimed from the invaders. A combined American/British force was forcing its way into the northern part of the Italian peninsula, while France and Belgium had also been liberated. It seemed obvious to every rational observer that the Third Reich was doomed.

But Adolf Hitler was not a rational observer. If he ever had been, he had lost that grasp of reality in July 1944, when some of his most trusted officers had tried to assassinate him with a bomb. Always skeptical, he now no longer accepted *any* advice from his senior commanders and issued wild orders with unattainable objectives, expecting them to be obeyed.

Even a basic assessment of the true dangers to German survival would seem to have suggested that the Russian Bear, encroaching as it was on the very borders of Germany proper, presented the greatest menace. Stalin had hundreds of divisions, many thousands of tanks, and a thirst for revenge that boded very ill indeed for any Germans who fell into his clutches. Yet Hitler still clung to the maniacal belief that he might be able to knock England out of the war and carry on against the greater forces of the USSR and the United States.

The way to accomplish this, he believed, was to stage a repeat of his army's dramatic breakthrough in 1940. He even chose the same locale, the Ardennes, for this stroke, and dared to envision the same result: his armies would cut off the British forces to the north of the attack by driving to the Channel coast and forcing the encircled Allied armies to be evacuated in an even more disastrous version of the Dunkirk escape.

In making this his goal, and in fact planning the operation himself, he was ignoring many key facts that rendered it essentially a pipe dream. For one thing, even as he concentrated his best armored formations against the Ardennes and massed two huge armies for the attack, he was now fighting an experienced, well-equipped, and mobile enemy whose strength far outweighed his own. The air superiority that had aided the Germans so much in the attacks of 1940 was long a thing of the past—indeed, now they had to pray for bad weather so that the Allies' five thousand tactical aircraft would remain on the sidelines. The German infantry in 1944 was a mere shadow of the vibrant, powerful arm it had been in 1940—now some units consisted of old men, the sick, and the very young. And finally, the army lacked the supplies to even carry it halfway to its objective, so much so that a key feature of the plan involved capturing Allied supply depots and using their fuel to keep the tanks rolling.

But this was Hitler's plan, and no one in the German army

dared to tell him no. Field Marshal von Rundstedt was nominally in charge of the theater, but he had enough courage to refuse to take part—in effect, his headquarters simply served as a conduit for Hitler's orders to be passed directly to the operational units. Hitler accepted this passivity on the part of a major commander, perhaps because he himself was so determined to micromanage the operation.

And despite the limitations imposed by Germany's strategic situation, these were some formidable units indeed. The main thrust was to be delivered by SS General Sepp Dietrich's Sixth Panzer Army. Dietrich was an old Nazi Party crony of Hitler's, and one of the men the führer still trusted. South of this formation was the Fifth Panzer Army, under General Hasso von Manteuffel. At only forty-seven years of age, Manteuffel had been personally promoted by Hitler after some spectacular, albeit limited, battlefield successes on the Russian front, and had displayed courage and an inventive command of tactics that also placed him on the short list of those who were actually allowed to discuss important matters with the Nazi dictator. Finally, General Erich Brandenberger of the Seventh Army was charged with guarding the southern flank of the assault. Together these armies included nearly 300,000 men and 1,000 armored vehicles.

Although almost to a man the German senior commanders gave the offensive no chance of success, the Allies seemed ready to do their best to give them a chance. Several factors contributed to a sense of complacency that allowed the attackers to achieve a rather frightening level of initial success. For one thing, the Americans and British had been attacking for so long that they seemed to have discounted the chance that the enemy might somehow seize the initiative. Also, knowing that the seventy-year-old von Rundstedt was in command of the Western Front, they expected the Germans to follow a conservative strategy. And they seemed to have completely forgotten the historical lesson of just four years earlier, when German tanks had broken through a weak section of the Allied line in a completely unexpected fashion—the success that led to the fall of France in June 1940.

The American front in the center was held by General Omar Bradley's Twelfth Army Group, with General Courtney Hodges's First Army to the north of General George Patton's Third. The Ardennes fell into Hodges's sector, but was considered by almost all to be a secondary front. Thus, facing the twenty divisions assigned to Operation Wacht am Rhein were only four divisions of American troops. Some of the men were newly arrived to war, while others were assigned to the Ardennes sector as a breather from fierce fighting they'd experienced elsewhere. All seemed to assume that this quiet part of the front was certain to remain quiet.

The Germans moved into position with exceptional secrecy. Radio silence was paramount, so even the Allied code breakers of the Ultra project had access to no messages that would have given any indication of the attack. General von Manteuffel himself was only given four days to prepare, while the division and other lower-level commanders had even less notice. Von Manteuffel was able to persuade Hitler to make some changes in the führer's precisely detailed plan, such as launching the attack with only a minimal artillery bombardment to add to the surprise, and moving forward in the dark. The latter tactic would be enhanced by a unique innovation: von Manteuffel suggested that German searchlight units play their beams up to the constant layer of stratus cloud, and that the reflected illumination would provide enough light for night operations.

Under the glare of this eerie "artificial moonlight," the attack commenced on December 16 and achieved complete tactical and strategic surprise. One of the new U.S. infantry divisions, the 106th, and another battle-weary unit, the Twenty-eighth Infantry Division, were overrun and virtually obliterated in the first day of the attack. This opened a wide breach in the American lines, and the German armor started to pour through. But Dietrich's army, in the north, quickly ran into problems as the U.S. Second and Ninety-ninth Infantry bent but didn't break. They fell back to a rugged promontory, Elsenborn Ridge, and here they held, essentially blocking what was to be the leading army of the breakout.

To the south, Fifth Panzer Army had better fortune, as von Manteuffel's tanks drove toward Houffalize, St. Vith, and the key road junction of Bastogne. General Eisenhower, the supreme commander, Allied Expeditionary Forces (SHAEF), was meeting with General Bradley, and when they first heard about German offensive activity on the afternoon of December 16, they were both inclined to dismiss the reports as exaggerated. It wasn't until the next day that Eisenhower finally ordered his strategic reserve, telling the Eighty-second and 101st Airborne divisions to make ready to move.

By the third day of the battle, Sixth Panzer remained tied down by the stubborn defenders on the north flank of what had come to be called "the Bulge." Hitler had one chance to make a decisive move and augment the chances of his colossal gamble: he could transfer some of the reserve panzer formations from Dietrich to von Manteuffel's Fifth Panzer Army, which continued to plunge deep into the salient. Several of his senior generals, including Army Group B's Field Marshal Model, urged him to take this step—but the führer was adamant that his favorite SS general could handle the objective, and obstinately refused to display any flexibility.

By December 19, SHAEF's reserve formations were moving into position to block the spearhead of the Fifth Panzer Army. Traveling by truck, the 101st Airborne Division, under Brigadier General Anthony McAuliffe, arrived at Bastogne, which would soon be surrounded. The Eighty-second, with Major General Matthew Ridgway in command, was placed farther north, in the vicinity of St. Vith. Both of these veteran, well-trained formations would play a key role in halting the German breakthrough.

Eisenhower changed his command structure on December 20, transferring command of all divisions north of the Bulge from Bradley to British field marshal Bernard Montgomery, thus allowing each army group commander to deal with but a single side of the Nazi salient. Montgomery began bringing British divisions down to screen the Meuse River, in case the Germans reached that barrier, but by now the attack was far behind its intended timetable.

At St. Vith, on the north flank, the U.S. Seventh Armored Division fought a brutal defensive fight, delaying the Sixth Panzer Army for three days before it was finally forced to withdraw. South of St. Vith, at the most important road network in the entire Ardennes area, General McAullife's 101st Airborne Division joined the garrison already holding out there. Some eighteen thousand men held on for days, delaying the Fifth Panzer Army's advance even as the city was gradually surrounded. When von Manteuffel's spearheads finally moved on, they were forced to bypass the besieged city, and thus were denied the use of the critical road junction.

In the meantime Patton's Third Army, south of the Bulge, disengaged from the enemy in front of it, turned ninety degrees, and started driving toward the relief of Bastogne on a frontage two corps wide. They reached the city on December 26, and the next day the skies cleared and the Allied air forces went to work. The most advanced of the German spearheads ran out of gas just about six miles short of Dinant—which, ironically enough, was where Rommel's Seventh Panzer Division had made its important crossing in 1940.

But that campaign, though only four years past, might as well have been in a different era. The two panzer armies were now pressed from the north and south by powerful American armies, and the December 26 marked the high waterline of the attack. The battle would continue until the middle of January before the Allies restored the previous line of the front, but by that time the inevitable end result of the war was clear to just about everyone but Hitler.

The Battle of the Bulge was the largest battle ever fought by the U.S. Army, and the cost—7,000 killed, 33,000 wounded, and 21,000 captured, as well as some 750 tanks lost—proved it. Hitler's Ardennes gamble had also delayed the Western Allies' timetable by about a month, but it had cost him 120,000 men and 600 precious tanks.

And by the time it was over, Stalin's Red Army was ready to resume the advance, and the Soviets had Berlin squarely in their sites.

THE HAND OF GOD PROTECTS THE FÜHRER
Germany, 1933–1945

BY PAUL A. THOMSEN

When the first Nazi war crimes trials began in November 1945 in the bombed-out city of Nuremberg, neither the Allied prosecutors nor much of the world could understand how badly mistaken the German people were to follow a man as destructive and self-serving as Adolf Hitler straight to their own ruin. Acting against sound military strategy and conventional wisdom, they had fought a world war on multiple fronts against overwhelming odds without blinking. Contrary to period air-war doctrine and liberal expectations, they had also not only endured a sustained campaign of heavy bombing that degraded their ability to make war and their quality of life, but somehow managed to grow socially stronger, more inventive, and even more audacious with each new air raid. Fantastically, even with their cities in ruins and their enemies at their gates, in the spring of 1945, most Germans refused to believe that Hitler was not touched by god or destiny and that, in following him, they were not committing suicide.

The German people embraced Hitler at their lowest point (up

to that time) in history. The events of the World War I had demoralized the people and nearly destroyed the entire German
state. The economy was in shambles. With sanctions against governance and a standing military, and a massive war debt, the Allied surrender terms and the ensuing Great Depression seemed
to take everything else. Worse still, every attempt to reverse or
manage the crisis by the German government (called the Weimar
Republic) died a slow death in the chaos of multipartisan legisla-
tive bickering. Having suffered so many blows in such a short duration, most Germans thought their lives had, indeed, become a
cruel joke. In time, the Germans took notice of a young war veteran named Adolf Hitler who gave compelling speeches on German pride to packed crowds, offering listeners a path that would
take them away from their present troubles. Before long, this nationalist attitude spread like an infection. As a result, when the
economy did rebound (for reasons unrelated to the Nazi spokes-
man), Hitler proved to be Germany's good fortune (that is, if you
weren't Jewish, Romany, homosexual, or any one of a number of
social groups deemed undesirable by the Nazis).

This leap of logic associating Hitler with success would be a
mistake many Germans would not live to regret.

Unlike his contemporaries, Hitler, a frustrated artist and
wounded-veteran-turned-politician, shied away from the squabbles of common political leaders to showcase a grand vision of
a new Germany made possible by his Nazi Party. Well organized
and brimming with talent, Hitler's speeches and choreographed
uniformed parades gave supporters a strong sense of nationalism, zeal, strength, and, above all, hope for the German people.
Without naming individuals and engaging in personal campaigns
of negativity, Hitler blamed the nation's decline on the cowardice and corruption of a fatally flawed political leadership. When

asked about present crises, he invoked the ephemeral boogey-
men of modern communism, evil nation-states, and age-old anti-
Semitic conspiracy theories as the drains on their good society.
For a rudderless people, Hitler's answers for everything served as
a lifeline.

Sadly, the German people believed him.

The people just might have forgotten Hitler as another mediocre politician with lots of promises, but when the world powers recalled their German loans in the late 1920s, Hitler's words
proved an even greater enticing elixir in tough times. In rallies,
he told the people they needed neither the outsiders' money nor
the dysfunctional government with which they had saddled Germany. In their place, he argued, people could rely on the strength
of their Aryan blood, their personal convictions, and the help of
the now-national grassroots efforts of the Nazi Party movement
to provide organization, structure, and resources to aid the German people in their time of need. After all, with a pitch like that,
who could say no to the man?

Initially, a few people did openly disagree with Hitler, but
they were swimming against the current in a river filled with
sharp-toothed predators. Naysayers and competitors alike were
quickly silenced by their poorer constituents, publicly humiliated by those who wished to gain Hitler's favor, intimidated by
Nazi Party muscle, or even fingered as an agent of corruption and
summarily eliminated. After the first few competitors were neutralized and Hitler managed to gain a sizable national following,
most anti-Nazis figured their best course of action would be to
keep quiet, bide their time, and wait for Hitler's popularity with
the people to decline.

Ironically, Hitler's more intelligent detractors never got the
chance to upstage him, because Hitler was just that smart. He was

a consummate public relations expert. While mobilizing popular support on a national level was a feat worthy of record, Hitler kept the masses inspired and, more important, solidly behind him throughout a radical transformation of the beleaguered nation, leading them into war in territories previously undreamt of.

This was his plan:

First, Hitler spread responsibility for his initiatives among trustworthy local leaders and Nazi Party officials, with at least two levels of redundant bureaucracy to give everyone the appearance of personal involvement in governance, to minimize his own risk of being blamed and to retain his control as the final arbitrator of disputes (which he almost never did). It was a win-win situation. Everyone had something to do, and Hitler's series of checks-and-balances almost ensured that he would never get the blame when something went wrong.

Second, Hitler projected an image of Nazi involvement in local decisions across the entire nation through the almost overnight appearances of Nazi symbols, flags, and uniforms, as well as portraits of himself and Germanic iconography in local party members' offices and leisurely retreats. If people chose not to display their colors, they would be branded as unpatriotic by party members and either intimidated into compliance or removed from business by a series of ad hoc boycotts and public demonstrations against these alleged underminers of Germany's destiny. As a result, Hitler and the swastika served as brands that connoted trustworthiness and German reliability.

Third, Hitler made regular use of new passenger airplanes to hop from one town or city to another for meetings and rallies, offering locals the appearance that Hitler was not only a man of the people, but also deeply concerned about local issues (an images which stood in stark contrast to the motions of Weimar Republicans). Like old St. Nicholas, he appeared to be everywhere at once, bringing gifts of money and support to needy causes. Likewise, by inference, his vision for Germany was as modern as the vehicles that carried him.

Fourth, the Nazis created a massive propaganda machine like no other. Led by a prize-winning author and Nazi Party member, Joseph Goebbels, the organization published reams of fliers, pamphlets, and books about their beliefs for distribution throughout the nation. Likewise, as a supplement to Hitler's personal appearances, Nazi officials would frequently utilize the radio to reach into the homes of beleaguered Germans with their message of hope, strength, and determination to make their nation whole once more. If one didn't believe the message the first time, repetition would either help eventually win the day or drum the opposition into silence.

Fifth, the Nazi Party eliminated the ability of the press to criticize party programs and leaders through the use of intimidation, vandalism, physical violence, and, eventually, through censorship laws. There's nothing like breaking a few windows, burning a few stores, smashing some presses, or busting someone's kneecaps to show the unconvinced who was really in charge.

Sixth, when a wellspring of support was needed to change national policy in its favor or boost morale in wartime, the Nazi Party made widespread use of the cinema, releasing inspiring documentaries about Hitler on the campaign trail, about his vision for a new Germany, and about the effects his programs were having on average Germans. In equal measure, they also released pseudo-documentaries allegedly proving their theories on racial inferiors and communist insurgents, and touting the evil deeds of their former international oppressors. After all, he who looks the best and shouts the loudest makes the deepest impression, no?

Finally, by the mid–1930s, Hitler and his people managed to covertly undermine the already hobbled national government and, when it fell, rapidly replace Weimar with their own working Nazi Party structure. When you're the only game in town, with whom else can you do business? One either shuts up and takes what is offered or one leaves. Hero or villain was just a matter of arranging the details.

When the war came in 1939, it seemed to the German people that there was nothing Adolf Hitler could not do. Hitler's few surviving military detractors (distinguished veterans of World War I and consummate military strategists who had forecasted doom if Germany even tried Hitler's battle plans) suddenly fell silent when, once more, against convention and sound military reason, Hitler repeatedly accomplished the impossible. First, in clear violation of the Treaty of Versailles, he rebuilt the German military and reannexed the territory his nation had lost in the last war. Undeterred, his forces next successfully invaded Poland, occupied France, defeated the fielded British army, and made rapid advances against Russia, using novel tactics and new technology.

After their defeat in World War I, the people saw this newfound change in fortune, just as Hitler had promised, a welcome respite from their seemingly entropic past existence. Some might even have said that Hitler was touched by the divine. With Germany's new resources, low unemployment, and propaganda-inspired high morale, in less than twenty years, few could argue that Hitler had accomplished more than any other person for Germany in the region's history, or at least since Frederick the Great. Likewise, after surviving approximately forty-one separate assassination attempts, Hitler was seen by his admirers as invincible (and his silent detractors as an incredibly lucky man). It seemed the hand of God itself was protecting their leader. By all accounts, this was the quintessential everyman hero for whom the German people had long been yearning.

Investment is also a powerful motivator behind denial.

Better still, even when the country suffered shortfalls or mistakes were made over the course of the war, Hitler's past work was popularly supported without question and repeatedly mobilized the German populace as a single unit. As in the case of the Jewish fugitive family of Anne Frank and numerous others deemed undesirable by Nazi policies, when the governmental agencies, such as the Gestapo, suffered a shortfall in security, German citizens readily volunteered the locations of fugitives and traitors. When blind eyes needed to be turned away from delicate matters or a helping hand was needed with dirty deeds, such as the Holocaust, they became, to quote historian Daniel Goldhagen, "Hitler's willing executioner." Even when the blunders were large, such as the stalled invasion of Russia, the Nazi public relations machine hid the failure or minimized the damage with tales of grand heroics and high enemy kill ratios.

Likewise, when the Allies invaded the continent of Europe, Hitler and his adjutants were able to stir the masses to support the nation's efforts by (1) calling on past victories against equally improbable odds, (2) once more appealing to their Aryan strength, and (3) calling on the people to fight for their very lives and homes against invaders depicted as hordes of racial inferiors and ideological savages. By drawing on these emotional resources, the German people gave their enemies pause against sustained strategic bombing campaigns, in the Ardennes Forest counteroffensive of December 1944, and in the sacrificial acts on the entire German Eastern Front against the vengeful Soviets. Finally, when Hitler's war efforts deteriorated to the point of enlisting children and the elderly to defend their homes and families against the onrushing Allies (who, as both Nazi propaganda claimed and historical fact would bear out, did not discriminate between combatants and noncombatants), there was neither the time nor the luxury of questioning their leader. The wolf was at the door ready to devour their kin. Deserters and soldiers in dereliction of their duties were being shot. With their leader's past track record of attaining victory in the face of overwhelming odds and his own almost divine invulnerability from personal harm, German defenders could at least take hope in the chance that once again the world might turn and his words would again lead them out of the darkness and toward that thousand-year Reich.

The German people failed to see Adolf Hitler as he truly was, because he projected an enticing image of the future for Germany. The German citizenry, previously beaten almost to the breaking point, wanted to avoid a return to that state at any cost. They ignored the facts in favor of blessed illusions. Ironically, when the war turned against Germany, the few surviving detractors of the Nazi regime also found themselves fighting for their very lives beside the only game in town: Hitler. Time was fleeting, fear was a grand motivator, and there was always the possibility that Hitler's almost divinely inspired touch would once again save the day, or so many thought. Surely God would not now abandon their leader and their homeland, right? It was their destiny, right?

The German people mistakenly believed the hype and paid the price.

WHO IS WAITING IN THE FBI HEADQUARTERS' LOBBY?

Washington, D.C., December 1941

BY PAUL A. THOMSEN

In the months before the December 7, 1941, Pearl Harbor attack, President Franklin Delano Roosevelt directed Federal Bureau of Investigations (FBI) Director J. Edgar Hoover, leader of America's premier law-enforcement community, to investigate potential threats to American domestic stability and arrest the perpetrators. The nation was preparing to engage in a war against the Axis powers that had already repeatedly proven in several other nations that they would utilize any means at their disposal to attain their goals. As the primary supplier of the Allied war effort, the nation could little afford the loss of time, lives, materiel, and morale enemy operatives might steal. In turn, the FBI shuttered several Axis covert operations and even managed to turn a few enemy agents against their German masters. Hence, by the end of 1941, Hoover was convinced that the FBI could solve any problem the Axis could devise for the United States. In early 1942 and again in 1945, the Nazis repeatedly proved that he had been gravely mistaken.

Throughout the nineteenth century, many Americans were convinced that this lack of imminent danger afforded the nation the luxury of maintaining a small, cost-effective peacetime militia system with wartime volunteers over the more expensive outfitting of standing armies and large navies other nations fielded in peacetime to ward off rivals. After all, militias were good for the taxpayers and good for morale and, if the enemy came, the nation's farmers would spot and stop the invader before they could do harm. Similarly, the American Revolution had been fought in opposition to a perceived tyrant and his grand red-clad army. In the years after the war, the states feared one another and their own residents as much as they feared international predation. A large organized peacetime military (or intelligence service) was the last thing their shattered nerves needed.

Until the dawn of the twentieth century, the United States held a unique security position in the history of the world. Bordered by two great oceans and two grossly underutilized European colonies, the eighteenth-century patriots of the American Revolution had simply outlasted their colonial master's resolve and gained their freedom. Thereafter, world leaders generally considered the country far too remote or too costly to be worth acquiring. Even when the United States tried to seize others' territory (most notably the attempted War of 1812 acquisition of Canada), the injured or offended nations frequently chose more judicious responses (including the 1814 hit and fade raid, which burned Washington City to the ground) over the more cumbersome and time-consuming course of conquest and occupation as a means of teaching America a lesson. In fact, most nations considered the United States to be far better producers of refined goods than as a ruined colonial dominion. Consequently, by the end of the nineteenth century, the great powers allowed the United States to keep Texas, the Philippines, and even exert some influence throughout Asia with minimal punishment and a fair share of the traded goods.

As the United States developed, the advent of oil-fueled ship engines and the burgeoning national economy encouraged both the United States and its competitors to engage in acts of spying and counterespionage to protect their interests abroad. While the coast guard made the coastlines safe for civilian watercraft, the militia system began to fail in light of rising organized crime, counterfeiters, anarchists, mafiosi, and foreign espionage/sabotage networks. In response to these emerging threats to national security, in 1908, the Bureau of Investigation (BOI) was created, filling these gaps between the nation's federal and state security interests. This new intelligence organ, born of the militia tradition of civilian-run operations and later renamed the Federal Bureau of Investigations, eagerly followed the investigative whims of Congress and the president (including hunting suspected communists and tracking the extent of Caucasian prostitution throughout the United States).

Still, the new intelligence service had only a limited budget and, if it was to be effective in its job, the bureau needed to grow. Over the next several decades, the FBI found great success in publicizing the crimes of "public enemies," and capturing or killing bank robbers, but there was more to national security than projecting an image of security. Most Americans considered Director J. Edgar Hoover and his agents to be well equipped to handle any contingency, but when Europe devolved into World War II, wartime demands forced Hoover to become highly creative with his meager budget. Utilizing decrypted messages intercepted from communications signals running between Germany and Japanese consulates and their respective homelands (and provided to Hoover in a sanitized form—"scrubbed" clean of references that might give away the message's origin), the FBI staged a series of sensational public arrests and, as in its bank robber days, took all the credit for ending the underworld activities (without once mentioning the military origins of the intelligence, which had made the busts possible). After the attack on Pearl Harbor, Hoover also ensured that most enemy spies and spymasters were secretly captured and kept out of the public eye to fool Germany and Japan into believing their spies were still active and continuing to transmit legitimate intelligence via wireless radio, which really sent disinformation packets compiled by the intelligence community. As a result, the FBI gained new public appreciation, greater funding for an expanded bureaucracy (but not agents), and acceptance of the bureau as the ubiquitous protector of the nation.

Too bad the FBI's image was entirely misleading. Their prewar success and Hoover's celebrity as a semi-omniscient federal agent had come with a series of steep management problems in World War II. First, while presenting an image of omniscience and omnipresence, the FBI actually saw little and could do even less. In fact, there weren't enough special agents to deal with the volume of every major city post. Second, while administrative efficiency had become a goal for the agency, its public image had generated a veritable deluge of tips from concerned citizens, prank callers, mischievous children, vengeful-minded workers, and paranoid housewives that required investigative reports to prove the FBI had followed each and every lead. Hence, instead of chasing criminals, most period agents were forced to chase papers in the order they arrived. Third, there was very little coordination between field offices. Fourth, the bureau may have had broad mandate, but Hoover cared little about the affairs of nations outside the Americas. Hence, as the war developed, the FBI had no measuring stick with which they might gauge potential Axis actions. Fifth, the FBI director could not turn down a direct order from the president to make the home front safe from Axis predation. At the same time, his bureau was equally incapable of enforcing the peace, because it was so poorly understaffed and grossly ill equipped to handle the demands of a wartime domestic intelligence organ. Finally, the FBI was already heavily engaged in the prosecution of criminals. Consequently, a single failure to catch a spy or prevent sabotage, if disclosed, could ruin the fear and respect Hoover had worked for decades to achieve. As a result, by December 1941, the FBI was ill equipped to spot, let alone stop, enemy agents from infiltrating the United States.

While the FBI had a lot of weaknesses, one thing saved Hoover, his agents, and the nation from two Axis sabotage teams in 1942: luck! In the summer of 1942, two Nazi Abwehr agents, recently dropped on Long Island's shoreline by a Nazi U-boat with several accomplices, panicked about their mission (designated as Operation Pastorius) to bring the Axis war to America and ditched the rest of their group. After much discussion, the two men attempted to alert the U.S. government of Abwehr's plot to sabotage war industrial sites in New York, New Jersey, and Illinois. Try as they might, the two turncoats, however, couldn't get themselves arrested. The FBI didn't take the German defectors' calls seriously. In a last-ditch attempt to surrender to the Americans, several days after they had landed, one of the Germans spent his allotment of travel money on a train ride to Washington, D.C., a hotel room, and a cold call to the FBI headquarters. When the German turncoat was finally escorted through the FBI headquarters lobby and granted access to a special agent, he immediately started pulling maps and other pieces of German intelligence tradecraft from his pocket as proof that he was a Nazi saboteur of dubious loyalty to Hitler who had been sent across the ocean to destroy America.

Over the next several hours, the German relayed the tale of his recruitment, his mission, and the team he had led across the ocean and abandoned in New York. Later, when his accomplice was picked up by the New York FBI, the turncoats gave the bureau the names of previously unknown sleeper agents and the known locations of their in-country weapons caches. The special agent in charge of the debriefing, his boss, and Hoover were speechless. Not only had the FBI failed to detect the infiltrators, but, according to the Nazi turncoats and their own field office records, the bureau had failed to follow up on a passersby report, claiming to have actually talked with the team as they crossed Jones Beach on their way to New York City.

After paddling ashore on June 13, 1942, the two turncoats claimed, the team buried the explosives for their operation in the open sand, dropped the shovel on top of the pile, and proceeded inland. When briefly challenged by coast guardsman John Cullen walking on beach patrol, the Nazis replied that they had been out fishing and were allowed to pass without further challenge. Later, realizing that the men had not been carrying fishing poles, the coast guardsman ran to the nearest coastal post where he reported the incident to his superiors, who, in turn, alerted the FBI of the encounter, but, as the infiltrators managed to blend in with the New York City nightlife, law enforcement failed to pursue its targets. Rather than rouse the office staff from their beds with Cullen's news and canvas the area for the suspected infiltrators, the bureau agent assigned to office night duty carefully recorded the incident, filed the report with the other unsolicited nightly messages, and waited for the morning staff to visit the crime scene before alerting the intelligence community that suspected Nazi infiltrators had penetrated the United States.

Yet there was still more to the Nazi turncoats' story. On June 17, 1942, the second Abwehr team, which included Herbert Haupt, Edward Kerling, Hermann Neubauer, and Werner Thiel, quietly landed at Ponte Vedra Beach, Florida, by U–584 without incident. Like their New York counterparts, they too disappeared in-country and headed for their targets. Whereas the people of the United States had come to believe their nation was safe from Axis predation, in actuality, these two teams had placed Hoover, the FBI, and the entire national security of the United States on shaky ground as the incident threatened to expose the Bureau's heavy reliance on smoke, mirrors, good intentions, and wishful thinking.

According to investigative records, as the more committed Abwehr agents were hunted down and apprehended, Hoover realized there was only one way for the FBI to save the day and its public image. For the sake of the country, the entire fiasco would be classified, the turncoats would be tried alongside their comrades in a carefully choreographed display of the FBI's alleged watchfulness, and although the turncoats would be sentenced to life in solitary for their moral virtue, their colleagues would be executed. Dead men, after all, told no tales.

Having caught the two teams, many Americans also mistakenly believed the threat of future espionage teams had been curtailed. In 1945, the Germans sent one of their best available assets, Agent 146: Erich Gimpel, and American-born defector, William Colepaugh, to complete the mission of the other two teams. While the operation may seem absurd today, Gimpel (who couldn't speak a word of English) and his companion (a depressive alcoholic) did manage to land undetected on the shores of Frenchman Bay, proceed inland, and make contact with still other undetected Nazi sleeper cells under the noses of the now more vigilant FBI.

Amazingly, the FBI received another lucky break. One day, Colepaugh slipped away from Gimpel, and began wandering from bar to bar for the next several days, downing drinks and telling his drinking buddies of his present mission as a German spy. While most dismissed the story as the ramblings of a drunkard, one bar attendee took Colepaugh seriously and alerted law enforcement, who dispatched a unit of FBI agents to arrest the spy. With one team member several sheets to the wind and singing like a canary, one might imagine FBI agents rapidly picking up his companion. They did not. After a while, the FBI located Gimpel with a tip, but the agents were sloppy and the spy easily gave them the slip. In fact, it took the FBI more than a day to reacquire the now notorious Agent 146. The FBI cornered and arrested the enemy spy in the process of buying a newspaper from a vendor in Times Square.

Where the FBI would have been without the assistance of America's suspicious citizenry, Hoover did not wish to contemplate. Unlike the previous case, the arrest of Agent 146 and his rather soused associate were played down by the FBI. Instead, the men were quietly tried, convicted of espionage, and the entire fiasco swept under the rug. To cover their misdeeds, the FBI fell back on past glories by helping Hollywood studios produce fictional accounts of its prewar anti-Nazi success stories (for example, *The House on 92nd Street*). Shortly before Gimpel was to be hanged, the war ended. He was pardoned by President Harry Truman and quietly slipped onto one of the first ships back to Germany where everyone knew he wouldn't dare talk about his wartime activities. The reputation of the FBI and its dismal role in wartime homeland security remained sealed away in the recesses of the FBI headquarters until the records were finally declassified approximately fifty years later.

While FBI Director Hoover would later discredit himself in the hunting down of alleged communists and attacking the civil rights movement in later decades, this mistake, born of arrogance and poor foresight, continued to haunt the man. Considered untrustworthy by the president, in 1942, Roosevelt quickly filled this now glaring hole in American national security by creating a wartime foreign military intelligence service, called the Office of Strategic Service. After the war, Truman transformed the organization into the civilian Central Intelligence Agency as much to keep Hoover on his toes as to keep America secure from future foreign-born attackers.

ARYAN COMPETITION BREEDS NAZI CONTEMPT

Germany, 1939–1945

BY PAUL A. THOMSEN

In the aftermath of World War I, Germany was a socially, politically, and economically shattered nation. Within just a few short years, Adolf Hitler and his Nazi Party managed to regain Germany's former glory by plying an ideology of Aryan supremacy and integrating multiple grassroots cells into an organized political insurgency.

Still, the real fuel for the Nazi's success was a policy of unceasing competition. Each German institution, each government department, and each individual was effectively pitted against one another, providing the propulsion necessary to return the state to glory. By applying the strongest results from these socially engineered conflicts, most Germans rapidly came to believe the Nazi's accomplishments were proof that they were the master race. Almost overnight, the Nazis managed to achieve incredible results. They raised the German economy from the depths of the Great Depression. They significantly cut unemployment. They even returned Germany to its place as a key player in the great game of geopolitics. Ironically, while the nation marched to glory under the Nazi Party, hubris had so blinded the leadership that the very system they used to achieve success in peacetime germinated the seeds of their own annihilation in war.

At the end of World War I, the shining light of German nationalism was almost extinguished by a host of problems. In the 1919 Treaty of Versailles, France and Britain made Germany pay severely for the war through a series of humiliating concessions. In effect, with a few strokes of a pen, Germany lost access to industrial resources, territory, the ability to defend itself, and its own choice of governance. Similarly, although the Allied powers did allow Germany to retain portions of its prewar geographic boundaries, the selected territories were little help to the Germany people. Their lands held limited resource value. Their economy was in ruins. Their new government, the Weimar Republic, was similarly factionalized, and their economic system deeply dependent on foreign loans for the nation's very survival. Moreover, now unable to effectively provide for themselves in this weakened state, the German populace became socially demoralized, politically divided, and deeply mired in inefficient parliamentary procedures. Consequently, while other nations were celebrating the postwar boom, Germany sputtered, stuttered, and stammered through the otherwise positive economic conditions of the 1920s and nearly imploded with the onset of the Great Depression.

Although the future looked bleak for the former empire, a few Germans, most notably the National Socialist/Nazi Party and their occasional orator Adolf Hitler, were able to use the postwar entropy to draw recruits from the disaffected masses by appealing to the dwindling pride in Germany's now largely out of work veterans. Originating as the German Workers' Party under Anton Drexler, the Nazis' special brand of socialist economic beliefs wrapped around ultranationalist and antidemocratic rhetoric were initially attractive to German veterans, most notably Hermann Goering and Rudolf Hess.

With the acceptance into their ranks of a Viennese-painter-turned-German-war-veteran-and-orator named Adolf Hitler, the National Socialist/Nazi Party of the mid–1920s began to branch out beyond its worker and veteran origins.

Not content with playing a minor role in the Weimar Republic, Hitler cultivated in the contentious band of low-level German military veterans a social Darwinian sense of strength and ancestral pride in themselves and their national potential. The German people, he asserted, were unlike any other populace. They were Aryans, an ancient genetic stock of pure blood, pure heart, and grand strength capable of turning adversity into prosperity and, through hard work, returning Germany to international glory. For a poverty-stricken populace, his ideas were attractive. Eventually, his brand of National Socialism rapidly became a cultural virus, infecting the diminishing post–World War I nation one person at a time.

Over the next several years, Hitler took control of the party, defeating a number of potential challengers for the party leadership (now renamed the National Socialist Party), and set his sights on Germany leadership. He wanted to remake the country, removing it from perceived foreign control, reunifying the German-speaking countries and regions under one banner, and addressing past errors visited upon the people by their ancestral enemies, competing nations, and the Weimar Republic. Through creative competition and Hitler's leadership, the Nazis surmounted every new obstacle placed before them and claimed to have attained a far superior position than Germany had ever reached as far back as Frederick the Great . . . or so they said.

By taking advantage of the political dysfunction of the Weimar government, the Nazis easily supplanted national competition with party competition. In the years following the Treaty of Versailles, the starkly polarized political landscape had made a quorum an improbability and political consolidation a near impossible task. Instead of attacking competitors head on, the Nazis sought to create a unified right-wing front by absorbing their rivals through the forging of alliances and co-opting of competitors' positions. They also incorporated a grand pageantry style of uniforms and militia aesthetics, attracting otherwise apolitical citizens with theatrics, parades, and public relations campaigns. Finally, Hitler reorganized the Nazi Party from a centrally located political social group into a large nationwide collection of semi-independent cellular groups, which worked on a two-tier system of political rhetoric and local-level strong-armed enforcement (often involving physical intimidation, vandalism, and leg-breaking), encouraging the strong to join their side, the weak to flee, and the indifferent to remain indifferent. As a result, before long, the Nazis had broken and absorbed the competitors on the right.

By the end of the 1920s, the Nazis had become a national phenomenon. With alternative national political choices now effectively sidelined by the Nazi's competitive drive, Adolf Hitler restructured the party to ensure that the party's now diverse collection of farmers, veterans, and laborers competitiveness worked for him. His solution was as elegant as it was simple: bring these groups together under one organization, set between them a conflict, and have them compete for the best solution. Hitler's structure provided a political mechanism for a seemingly endless generator of innovative ideas for, first, the Nazi Party, then the affected economic sector, and, finally, the nation. In this system, everyone, he believed, would work for the greater good of Germany. When enough people were drawn into the system to fight for their own interests, the Nazis would then create new departments within the organization to deal with dedicated problems on a regional level, fostering simultaneously closer and more contentious relations between geographically and, often, socially distant groups of citizens. On local, state, and now national levels, these groups, he theorized, would fight bitterly over the virtues of their designs over their neighbors' until only one choice survived for Hitler to anoint as the national standard, ensuring in perpetuity a boundless creativity and progress . . . or so he thought.

Adolf Hitler's infectious competitiveness did, in effect, breed a new Germany, but this socially engineered system also had some nasty side effects, including the human failings of greed and lust to be the grand architect. In the 1920s, Hitler had come to lead the party through perseverance and brutal competitive cunning, networking with the more popular members and insulating himself from threats through the deployment of personal guardsmen. Once he reached the level of party leader, however, Hitler realized that the guards who had once protected him would likely eventually turn, completing the cycle of competition over the party leader's dead body.

As one can imagine, this idea did not sit well with Hitler. Taking a lesson from the flawed political structure of Weimar, the Nazi leader rapidly removed himself from the firing line and created additional groups to foster completion against established groups, thereby creating a stabilized level of antagonism for his guards and his political adjutants. For example, Hitler engineered an ongoing rivalry between the brown-shirted Sturmabteilung (SA) and the black-uniformed Schutzstaffel (SS) over who would act as his private security force. Just when SA leader Ernst Röhm and his staff seemed poised to consolidate power and overthrow their own leader, Hitler had both Röhm and his SA loyalists eliminated in the June 1934 "Blood Purge." With Röhm gone, Hitler elevated a number of previously apolitical SA officers into the vacant positions. Simultaneously, Hitler also transferred the control of his inner-circle security to the SS and created an ever increasing hierarchy of concentric rings of power and responsibility, limiting the possibility of the SA rising against him and saddling Himmler (who also had his eye on Hitler's position) with an unwieldy bureaucracy of busy work. As long as everyone played by the rules, the system worked as an ideal solution for keeping everyone in check and their leader reasonably safe from betrayal. Thereafter, all Hitler needed to do was sit back, watch everyone vie for his favor, and reap the fruits of their frustrated labors.

As designed, Nazi competition did generate a plethora of novel (and amoral) ideas and a host of devoted followers willing to engineer their success. The dispossession and removal of the Nazi-viewed socially undesirable (including Jews, communists, homosexuals, and the Romany) freed up much capital for the Reich. The development of blitzkrieg warfare likewise solved the strategic problem of static defenses and trench works. Upon assuming the national governance, the Nazi Party similarly consolidated the German political landscape. By utilizing the new media of radio and cinema, they resurrected people's morale from the pit of despair with rhetoric, parades, and technological innovations, reaching more people in a far more profound way through more skilled technicians and theatrical personnel than anyone had ever used before. Similarly, with this newfound drive, former military personnel found new hope in finding social, technical, and strategic solutions to the nation's failures in the last war for their own sake, for the party, and now for the approval of the führer.

With a modest section of the German populace now behind them, the Nazis next grafted their infectious competitiveness onto German national politics and governance. First, they offered Germans their Aryan vision as the strong, proud, and brilliant architects of their own destiny. Second, they divided the nation by re-forming Germany into party districts, enabling Hitler to circumvent established state governments. Third, they encouraged the people to compete for the accepted supremacy of their own ideas over their rivals, and when the groups inevitably deadlocked, the Nazis restructured the antagonism by consolidating the public and private services, forcing the rivals to fight anew. Finally, the Nazis engineered the production and literally fruits of these labors to be returned to the system (minus a small handling fee) and sent abroad, building political and rewarded competition, and revitalizing the German nation. As a result, by the mid–1930s, Germans had even begun producing material beyond their own consumption needs.

In a sense, the Nazi competitive system was also brilliant for stifling dissent. The people who might have otherwise complained about offensive racial or militarily aggressive Nazi policies were often either misdirected by competing with others for their place at the table of prosperity or had essentially self-selected their removal from Germany society by not competing. For example, when Hitler rebuilt and field-tested a new army in clear violation of the Versailles treaty, questions of legality or use failed to surface. Instead, the Nazis competed to improve the size, strength, and versatility of the force, effectively endorsing

the German army's "secret" rise in the east and the military replacement of attrition with rapid dominance. Once their armies
were showcased to the world, German citizens focused on the
newfound prosperity brought from annexed territories. In fact,
even the most anti-Nazi political leaders and military officers
gave Hitler credit for revitalizing the economy, reinvigorating national pride, and succeeding where everyone else had failed. If
you didn't compete, you didn't succeed. If you didn't succeed,
you weren't rewarded. If you weren't rewarded, you were ostra-
cized, jailed, and/or starved . . . and no one wanted to return to
the era of Weimar stagnation and starvation. Enlightened self-
interest on a level playing field kept everything in balance. It was
just that simple.

With an ideology based on strength through competition, the
remilitarization of Germany and its use of force became the singular unifying element of this drive. Germany's new productivity
gave most Germans a newfound sense of purpose, which encouraged many to defy the disarmament strictures of Versailles in
favor of military enlistment or actively engage in the business
of defense production. The sponsorship of new production ideas
and strategic thinking broke with traditional military technology and battlefield doctrine, including the adoption of blitzkrieg
warfare to overwhelm neighbors' fixed line defenses. As a result,
by 1938, Germany had amassed a military force that rivaled its
neighbors in strength, size, and boldness.

On an international level, the Nazis' equation of strength
through competition also dominated their international policies
and, in fact, spelled the downfall for the German nation. Like
every other empire in history, Nazi Germany's national development required an expansion of the nation to fuel their next stage
of growth. As peaceful international trade was against their ideo-

logical nature, the Nazis' aggressiveness led to acts of belligerency. In 1938, they reannexed the Sudetenland by political fiat. In 1939, they took Poland by force. As German business production accelerated to previously undreamt levels, in 1941, the Germans felt ready to test their mettle simultaneously against France, England, and Russia. For most Germans at the time, this groundswell of unity and productivity could only be seen as the acme of their competitive achievement. Moreover, with every nation now recoiling at Germany's advance, for the Nazis, it seemed as if there was nothing Germany could not do. When the United States brought its might to bear in Africa, the Nazis realized too late that their striving for competitive perfection had lead them to seize more than they could manage and bred in them a level of bureaucratic greed, which limited their ability to counter the Allies advances and led to a deeply flawed defense of their Aryan fatherland.

As the stakes for the nation's survival grew steadily higher, internal competition, which had once fueled the peacetime boom, now backfired, replacing Nazi competition with bitter avarice and personal contempt. With the early–1940s seizure of its neighbor's resources, the once resource-poor nation ballooned with the avaricious desire to grab as much territory, assets, and governmental power as the Nazi departments could find to effectively compete against their internal and now international rivals. This infusion of riches also fostered the creation of even more parallel departments with overlapping duties and parallel running chains of command. For example, matters relating to who could gather intelligence for Germany grew from the simple SA intelligence division of the prewar era to include elements of the SS, Luftwaffe, Gestapo, and others, with still more divisions for French, Polish, and Russian offices. Hence, no one group had a clear and comprehensive picture of the Allied war plan until everyone met, and even then, the desire to maintain one's own fiefdom precluded much sharing of relevant material. As a result, the Nazi's symbolic pinnacle of national strength, the German high command, was crippled by Balkanization, departmental functions were diluted in red tape, and Germany once more began to sigh, shudder, and rapidly decline.

When the Allies returned to the European continent in 1944, these different chains of command and overlapping departments made defense highly problematic and a successful counteroffensive almost impossible. For example, a longstanding feud between Abwehr leader Wilhelm Canaris and Reinhard Heydrich resulted in the destruction of one Nazi intelligence organ and the hobbling of the other. While SS units reported to Himmler, SA units (because of several intractable intra-army squabbles between generals that no one wanted to touch) reported directly to the reluctant and unschooled strategic command of Adolf Hitler. Similarly, while the Luftwaffe units reported to Goering, these wonder weapons driven by knights of the air regularly required heavy industry and fuel demands from other commands. As a result, when the Allies pushed inland, the now self-paralyzed German state was unable to stop them.

By mid-1944, the Nazi Party policies of Aryan pride and competition had begat Nazi contempt, cannibalism, and still worse. The complete failure of the Nazi management system forced Hitler to take an active decision-making role across nearly the entire spectrum of foreign and domestic affairs. Where Hitler hadn't been a good decision maker at the start of the war, his military actions at the end of the war did not show much improvement. He grasped at wonder weapons to solve Germany's problems. He threw lives away like confetti in the hopes of buying time for the competitive process, which had once raised them from misery, to now save the nation in its new darkest hour. German soldiers were being overrun by the enemy. People were starving. German industry, spread thin filling mounting orders for essential supplies, was sidetracked and mired in the development process for weapons systems (such as the Me–262 jet fighter and the Vengeance rocket systems) whose deployment had come too late to turn the tide of battle.

By 1944, Nazi competition had sewed the seeds of Germany's destruction. Six months after the invasion of the continent of Europe, Hitler finally took an active strategic role in the war's prosecution, devising a massive do-or-die counteroffensive with the deployment of every asset at his disposal against the Allies in the worst winter Europe had seen in several hundred years. It failed miserably, but still worse, he refused to even consider a negotiated peace. Next, when Hitler finally took an active role in fighting the Allied forces, his own people, bereft of the means to defeat their enemies or blame their boss, started open war amongst themselves. Some Nazis openly fingered others as traitors. Others plotted to kill Hitler. Still others stole and hid everything of value they could find in the hopes of buying their freedom from their enemies. By the spring of 1945, chaos reigned supreme inside what was left of Germany.

The Nazi management system and the Aryan ideology of a pure race had become a master mistake. They appeared to be the means of returning Germany to unity and prosperity; in the early years, Nazi competition gave the people hope and purpose. But contrary to Nazi claims of unity, German businesses, military services, and the citizenry worked in parallel. Over the years, the Nazi system taught the virtues of greed, cunning, and contempt wrapped in the guise of nationalism and the guiding principle of self-reliance. Prior to 1940, limited resources and enlightened self-interest maximized the nation's potential in a controlled environment, but once the nation went to war, those controls fell by the wayside as the lure of untapped power and riches fueled people's baser motives and the system indirectly encouraged them to do their neighbors harm. As reward for their vices, in 1945, the German state was reduced to ashes as its enemies closed in around them.

On April 30, 1945, the great drive to revitalize Germany through Nazi competition ended with Germany's master race relegated to the loser's circle. As Nazi officers and industrialists attempted to make off with as many valuables as they could carry away from the ruined state, Adolf Hitler was left to die in his bunker with his manservant, secretary, a few loyal staff members, his new wife, and his dog. During his final days in April 1945, eyewitness accounts report that Hitler recognized the depravity of his Nazi Party membership as Himmler and others attempted to declare themselves the true leader of Germany. The Nazis were looking out only for themselves and he now damned them for it.

In peace, they were unstoppable. In war, the Nazi Party could not break from its competitive ways to forge a united bureaucracy to mirror its national dream. The Nazi system of competition may have given Germany Aryan pride and a new order in a time of crisis, but the Nazis mistakenly believed that order, like themselves, to be perfect. So much for the master race. . . .

UNITED STATES
INTELLIGENCE FAILURES
Europe, 1941–1944

BY ROBERT GREENBERGER

It is intelligence that provides the foresight that gives the captains their vision. If the captain is provided with complete and accurate intelligence on the enemy and uses it properly, it can lead to victory. If the captain is not given adequate intelligence on the enemy or disregards what intelligence is provided, it can lead to disaster," wrote Lyman B. Kirkpatrick Jr., who served as General Omar Bradley's intelligence briefing officer from 1944–1945 and authored *Captains Without Eyes: Intelligence Failures in World War II.*

Going into World War II, American intelligence was a hodge-podge of offices and agencies spread throughout the government. Unlike its European counterparts, America didn't place great emphasis on intelligence gathering, especially with the isolationist mood in the days following the Great War.

There were intelligence offices located in various departments, including the State, Treasury, Navy, and War departments. As it was, the army had the Signals Intelligence Service while the navy had its OP–20-G code-breaking department, but there was a coordinated effort to share their findings. Then there was the infamous 1929 statement made by Secretary of State Henry Stimson as he shut down Herbert Yardley's MI–8 operation in the State Department: "Gentlemen don't read each other's mail."

Little changed until a global conflict seemed inevitable. President Franklin D. Roosevelt recognized the deficiencies in his own government and sought counsel from William Stephenson, head of the United Kingdom's Western Hemisphere intelligence. The time had come for America to have its own centralized intelligence, and Stephenson recommended General William J. Donovan, a Medal of Honor recipient, as an ideal candidate to prepare a report. By then, Donovan, a fellow classmate of Roosevelt's at Columbia University, had traveled extensively throughout Europe, and the president liked his pragmatic views. After several months, Donovan delivered his "Memorandum of Establishment of Service of Strategic Information" to the president. In July 1941, Donovan was appointed as the co-coordinator of information, which led to the formation of the Office of Strategic Services on June 13, 1942.

As the OSS got organized, conflicting agendas led the Americans to totally miss the Japanese preparing for an attack. Much as modern-day intelligence didn't share information and failed to reach consensus leading to the 9/11 attack, uncoordinated intelligence allowed the sneak attack to occur at Pearl Harbor and points throughout the Pacific, including Siam, Hong Kong, Burma, North Borneo, the Dutch West Indies, the Philippines, and the Pacific Islands.

While this was the most glaring intelligence error, it was not the only one made by the United States during World War II.

There were many gaps of intelligence as the global apparatus was put into place. The OSS was extremely successful in recruiting German-speaking Europeans to work with it, but it could never stay on top of the global requirements of an intelligence agency while other intelligence arms continued to obfuscate vital data. While the OSS supplied information and analysis to the Joint Chiefs of Staff, the army and navy maintained their own intelligence branches, which still didn't share information with each other let alone the OSS.

A classic example of intelligence failing the commanders was the Battle of the Kasserine Pass, fought from February 19–25, 1943, in Tunisia. The objective was to secure the pass, a two-mile-wide access point in the Grand Dorsal chain of the Atlas Mountains.

The battle pitted the U.S. Second Corps, led by Major General Lloyd Fredendall, against the Axis forces commanded by Field Marshal Erwin Rommel and the Fifth Panzer Army led by General Hans-Jürgen von Arnim. Fredendall, whose command style did not inspire confidence, lost the support of Omar Bradley and General Dwight D. Eisenhower. While Fredendall was on the field, the deployment orders came from Eisenhower, who was stationed four hundred miles away and working from incomplete information. In turn, his appointed commander for the mission, Major General Lucian Truscott Jr., chose to stay two hundred miles away from the pass and also counted on the same faulty data. As a result, the commander of the First British Army, Lieutenant General Sir Kenneth Anderson, was given day-to-day operational command with Fredendall leading the raw American troops.

This was the first significant battle between American soldiers and Nazi troops, and rather than take control of the pass, the Allied forces were shoved back some fifty miles and had their collective noses bloodied thanks to inadequate information.

Although America entered the European conflict by declaring war in December 1941, it was months later before the first American forces arrived to bolster the Allies. That entire first year was spent building an army from troop training to converting factories to a wartime footing. That also included gathering useful intelligence to provide to the commanders.

The Allies were at a disadvantage from the beginning by the commanders relying on information from a remove. The information received was scattershot, and reliable lines of information were never properly established. As a result, a series of tactical errors were executed, resulting in the humiliating defeat.

The American troops were positioned too far apart in addition to them being improperly prepared for the terrain; they didn't know to dig proper foxholes for protection.

In the weeks leading up to the battle, Allied intelligence told Anderson that the Germans were planning a massive assault on the French troops. This meant they were ordered to abandon their position, something the French objected to but Anderson insisted upon.

Ten days later the fighting broke out with the Germans launching their strike in the midst of a sandstorm. The battle was brief, with forty-four American tanks, twenty-six artillery guns, and twenty-two trucks destroyed in just the first day of the fight. Rommel began moving his men toward the pass, attempting to take it en route to his real goal some sixty miles away. Anderson, sensing chaos, ordered everyone to hold his position. This left the land once protected by the French troops exposed.

By February 22, Rommel gave up trying to take the pass given his own supply issues. There was no intelligence providing useful information as to the enemy's moves, and as a result, Anderson did not order a pursuit and press his sudden advantage.

Lack of proper military intelligence also meant the First Armored Division was ill prepared to withstand the German armored tactics. After advancing, the German tanks fell back to their original positions, luring in the First Armored, which was caught by hidden antitank fire. Additionally, it ceded the air space to German forces, which were free to attack the Allied forces.

Of course, the Americans learned quickly from this. Fredendall was relieved of his role and shipped stateside to conduct training. He was replaced with the newly formed Eighteenth Army Group, commanded by General Sir Harold Alexander.

Similar lessons were learned in other battles, and just weeks later, a smarter, battle-hardened American army once more faced Rommel. This time, it was victorious.

Through the war, intelligence often made the difference between success and defeat. The European Theater of conflict's final act, the Battle of the Bulge, is another excellent example of this maxim.

Adolf Hitler announced to his generals on September 19, 1944, his desire to move through the Ardennes in eastern Belgium to Antwerp, crushing the Allies along the way despite Allied numeric superiority of nearly two to one. He had already determined that the rainy months of November and December would blunt any aerial support his enemies could rely on, and the muddier terrain would slow down the ground forces.

Hitler also swore a tight-knit group of leaders to keep these plans top secret. Any leak, he warned, would lead to execution. The field leaders were not to be fully briefed of their mission objective until just hours before beginning the assault.

While the fighting took place in France, the French Resistance offered frequent and invaluable information that the Allied forces used. As the battle crossed into Germany, the information spigot dried up. This included the Allies' transcribing radioed German orders, having already cracked the Enigma machine's secrets. In Germany itself, though, security was far tighter by 1944 with orders now issued via telephone and teleprinter, which couldn't be intercepted by the Allies. Also, Allied intelligence didn't know that radio silence had been ordered as the Nazi forces readied for the battle of the Ardennes.

Without that accustomed level of information, the Allies were lulled into believing that the Ardennes, a hilly, heavily wooded region, was not a staging area. Intelligence had been saying for weeks that the Germans were on the ropes and defeat was imminent, so they doubted the Axis could mount any sizable operation.

As Hitler had begun moving his pieces into position, the American intelligence concluded that fall, "The enemy's effort to build up a strong Panzer force as a strategic reserve is indicative of the use the enemy makes of the time granted him by inevitable Allied delay."

A subsequent analysis reported, "The enemy's most likely and serious capability would now appear to be a counterattack with strong forces of Panzer reserves against any Allied breakthrough in the Ninth or First Army sectors which threatens to opus out advance to the Rhine. . . ."

By November 18, the Germans had moved man and equipment through the region, leading American intelligence to advise, "The most important enemy capability relates to the employment of Sixth Panzer Army particularly as it may be supported by a large fighter force. German fighters have not put in a large-scale appearance since the Merseberg raid by the Eighth Air Force and their recent inactivity may perhaps be explained by preparation for support of ground forces. . . ." All theorizing of a counteroffensive was dropped by the December 12 weekly report.

That final report from intelligence sources before the Ardennes battle began, "It is now certain that attrition is steadily sapping the strength of German forces on the Western Front and that the crust of defenses is thinner, more brittle and more vulnerable than it appears on our G–2 maps or to the troops in the line."

That failed assessment led to a bloody, prolonged fight.

The Germans successfully lulled their enemies into believing that their activities were purely defensive, forming an army around Düsseldorf in the northern Rhine while a major offensive strike was really being readied. False radio transmissions in that region fooled the scant intelligence forces.

When Germany attacked on December 16, the Allies were caught off guard and ill prepared for a fighting force of that size. It took Allied command until the seventeenth to determine that this was the counteroffensive that had been theorized during the previous months.

While the intelligence reports properly reflected where troops had been moved, the clampdown of information from Germany meant intelligence operatives had to make educated guesses, which in turn lulled the Allies into complacency. While the guesses were fairly accurate from a field perspective, there was no knowing the men were being moved from Berlin, under Hitler's exact command, with an entirely different endgame in mind.

The German-ordered lockdown on information also led to increased security to prevent desertions, which led to a paucity of prisoner-of-war intelligence, depriving Americans of any crumb of useful information.

There was also a lack of captured documents during this time, another tool that had proven useful earlier in the war. Had any of the human messengers Hitler used in lieu of electronic methods been captured, their instructions would have proven insightful. Instead, they all managed to carry their missions to completion.

The OSS and other intelligence arms of the United States all lacked having properly trained field agents, relying instead on capturing documents or tapping electronic lines of communication. When prisoners of war failed to convey knowledge, the agencies couldn't properly forewarn the armed forces. There was little time to properly train such human intelligence sources and embed them in Axis-held lands, but those spies later proved informative as America entered the Cold War. Still, the OSS, working from flawed data, wound up making a series of incorrect assumptions that ill prepared Eisenhower's Allied troops for the coming fight.

As a result, the battle dragged into the New Year, ending on January 25, 1945. By the time the gunfire ended, the Americans had 89,500 dead, wounded, or captured, while the British lost 1,408. Germany lost 100,000 men in comparison. The Axis also lost eight hundred tanks and one thousand aircraft. Hitler had once again underestimated the Allied fighters and his objective was not met. The loss of men and equipment hastened Germany's fall just months later.

LUFTWAFFE PILOT TRAINING

Germany, 1939–1945

BY ROBERT GREENBERGER

In direct violation of the Treaty of Versailles, the German government secretly began building an air force of its own. According to a 1970 U.S. Air Force study, the plans began as early as 1920, less than a year after the accord was signed. By March 1, the Germans began building the foundations of their air force, including training programs and manufacturing facilities. The rest of Europe wasn't paying attention, so by 1925 training manuals were already emphasizing the importance of air strikes and bombing from high altitude, well before there was a plan for such missions.

Over the remainder of the decade, planes were designed, built, and tested, and industrial capacity increased to give the demoralized country aerial superiority. "German air leaders from 1928 on had excessively optimistic estimates of the Reich's industrial capacity. This led to an almost pathological belief that German industry was capable of doing 'the impossible.' Only late in World War II was there an effort to put industry completely upon a war footing, but, by that time it was too late to offset years of poor direction," the report stated.

There was such tremendous pressure brought to bear on the notion of air superiority that the early pilots were the equivalent of rock stars, given lavish treatment compared with foot soldiers or those assigned to naval vessels. That continued in the wake of Hitler's ascension to power in 1933. As Hitler took control of Berlin, he brought Hermann Goering into the picture. Named the Reich's minister of aviation and commander in chief of the Luftwaffe, Hitler's confidant was also a World War I ace who celebrated the concept of the Luftwaffe leading the new Nazi Party. As a result, Goering saw to it his branch of the military received favorable allocations of raw materials. This actually proved to hinder the army and navy's development, but no one in command realized this until postwar analysis.

Goering actually wanted to convert Lufthansa's commercial air fleet into the core of a new air force, but once his technicians realized how dated the craft actually were, the plan was scrapped.

That same year, he established the Flying School Command to prepare pilots and crew. Over the next two years, the training, which was already good, was increased in duration, coupled with accelerated airplane construction. The Luftwaffe was publicly announced on March 10, 1935, sending a chill across a Europe that had been turning a blind eye to Germany's reconstruction. European countries, of course, were still coping with the Great Depression that had them looking inward, not daring to start a conflict they could ill afford at that time.

Hitler took advantage of the Continent's complacency and pushed his plans forward, counting heavily on Goering to deliver a decisive edge when the time was right. Goering, in turn, ordered that the training calendar be organized with one-third of the time devoted to understanding ground and naval strategies so the pilots could better support those forces on missions. Such integrated efforts were unique and would certainly given the Nazis an early edge until the other countries could catch up.

An anxious Hitler further taxed resources when Goering relayed the führer's order, on December 5, 1938, that the Luftwaffe be enlarged fivefold. This was Germany's response to Britain's rearmament in the wake of the Munich conference. Such an order was impossible to fulfill given scant resources and raw materials already dedicated to all other military orders. In fact, securing raw materials and trained factory employees to manufacture munitions would become a recurring problem for the Axis almost from the beginning of hostilities.

Similarly, while Hitler kept asking for more planes, his staff never saw to it that a parallel order for enlarging the pilot pool be issued. Although Goering had a highly trained class of pilots ready to enter a war, the next classes were fewer in number. Developing manpower would also prove to be an ongoing problem—one Germany never solved as World War II also became a war of attrition.

The Office of the Chief of Military History, Special Staff, U.S. Army, prepared an appraisal called *Airborne Operation: A German Appraisal* and devoted an entire chapter entitled "Reasons for Success and Failure." Lack of sufficient resources and training were repeated phrases throughout the document.

The Luftwaffe was considered the strongest air force when hostilities began in 1939. Without control of air space, Hitler's plan for a blitzkrieg could not have worked as well. The steady march of aircraft rattled Britain to its core in the fall of 1940, and the Luftwaffe was recognized as the world's best air force.

The rush to build airplanes, stock them, and have pilots ready to fly the craft continued as Hitler's early successes spread his forces very thin across Europe. The haste to get men in the air led to the death of 997 personnel, with another 700 wounded, and the loss of 946 airplanes. Hitler and Goering acted as if there was an endless supply of trained personnel to take the planes into battle.

After all, when the war broke out in earnest in 1939, Goering's Luftwaffe could count 2.2 million personnel (3,941 of them rated to fly planes). The planes continued to be improved with new models, contributing to the sense of invincibility within the Axis. While the Royal Air Force bloodied their noses time and again, they were no match in terms of numbers or reach.

What changed, though, was a resurgent Allied effort once America entered the conflict. As America retooled its factories to churn out airplanes by the dozen, Germany was beginning to struggle to keep pace in restocking its planes and its pilots. Those who were flying found themselves spread too thin as the Luftwaffe was called upon to defend Germany. Additionally, Goering did not count on Russia also being able to churn out as many airplanes and pilots as it did, effectively stalling the Axis's aerial advance during the harsh Russian winter of 1942–1943.

Lieutenant General Walter Krupinski recounted what his training was like: "I started flight training in September 1939 at the Officers Cadet School at Berlin-Gatow, later transferring to Vienna-Schwechat, which was the Fighter Weapons School. It started with classroom instruction, aerodynamics—the basics really. Then after a couple of months we were introduced to the [Heinkel] He–51 biplane trainer, in which we learned the basics of takeoffs and landings, or touch-and-goes, as well as proper aerial maneuvers with an instructor. When we were considered competent we soloed, and I just took to it quickly. It was after six months or so that we actually trained on the Messerschmitt 109, which as you know was the primary fighter throughout the

war. Then we trained on instrument flying, enemy aircraft identi-
fication, emergency procedures, formation flying, gunnery skills
such as deflection shooting, and learned about our particular aircraft, including minor maintenance."

Having survived the war, he looked back and noted, "All I can
tell you is that the Germans had to pretty much stay in combat
throughout the whole war. They didn't have limited ops like the
British did. So they would almost always rack up huge amounts of
kills if they survived long enough. It must have been an annoying
sight for a 109 pilot in 1944 to see the Spitfire since he could never
retire and that the 109 pilot would probably have encountered
Spits since the beginning of the war, but of course it bought you
experience. . . .

"At the latter stages of the War, most of the seasoned vets
knew that going on a fighter-bomber sweep meant a few guys
not coming home, as the odds were so lopsided that it wasn't
uncommon to have 10 Mustangs/Tempests/Spitfires on the ass of
one single 109/190. . . ."

When the war broke out, the average German pilot was receiving 240 hours of flying time before entering combat. In comparison, British pilots were trained for just 200 hours. Germany ruled
the skies.

At much the same time, though, the British were sending their
students to Canada for more extensive training, which would pay
dividends in the coming years.

As the war progressed, not only were raw materials harder to
come by, but so was fuel. The lack of long-range planning would
continually haunt Hitler and his commanders, but by the time
it became apparent, it was too late to successfully make adjust-
ments. As a result, beginning in 1942 pilot training suffered, which
correlated with an increased number of planes being shot down.

Starting in the 1930s through 1942, pilots were treated well under Goering's watch. They were taught not only flying but also social dance during the day, and they were taken on ski vacations, all indicative of an air force comfortable in its superiority.

That all changed as the Allied forces began to cohesively work together, challenging the Axis on land, on sea, and, finally, in the air. To combat the sudden increase in aerial competition, German crews were prematurely taken from training programs and put into combat situations as early as January 1942.

A month later, the Luftwaffe could no longer receive proper details on the manufacturing rate of new craft given the recurring supply shortages and bombing attacks. With every passing month, increasingly raw recruits were taken earlier and earlier from their training and sent into the skies.

The lack of training and flight hours, coupled with the consistent loss of craft, began eroding the Luftwaffe's sky superiority.

At the same time, as demands in Russia increased, not only were students pressed into early service, but experienced-flyers-turned-instructors found themselves back in the skies, leaving students without qualified teachers, creating a downward spiral that Hitler didn't realize and Goering couldn't solve.

The issue of an adequate fuel supply remained an erratic one, resulting in altered flight schedules month to month. In September 1942, for example, the flight schools received fourteen thousand tons of fuel, while that October saw the number increase to twenty thousand, with twenty-two thousand tons received in November.

That same November, Goering ordered training aircraft diverted from schools to the Russian front, which further eroded the ability to prepare pilots. The losses that cruel winter meant fewer craft to work with in addition to the loss of pilots prepared to fly multiengine planes. The consequences on future flight crews was devastating, with just 1,662 pilots graduated that year compared with 1,093 pilots lost that year.

Fuel continued to be a recurring issue in early 1943, so that February, the training program was cut back from seventy-two to fifty-two weeks, another step down the slippery slope.

Goering continued to push for more planes (which were getting harder to manufacture) and more pilots (which were getting harder to find) despite a consistent lack of fuel. In 1943, he actually stated, "I am of the opinion that further building of our aircraft should not depend on in any way on the fuel program. I would rather have a mass of aircraft standing around unable to fly owing to a lack of petrol than not have any at all."

General Werner Kreipe, head of the training program in 1943, was quoted as saying at the time, "The needs of the front had been met." Clearly, he was misinformed.

In late 1943, with available aircraft at a premium, it was suggested crews be trained on aircraft salvaged from Italy after Germany's ally surrendered. With greater supplies of fuel available that year, some 3,276 pilots were pushed through the accelerated system, but even they were inadequate to match the country's needs on multiple fronts, from Africa to Europe. Measures showed that the graduating pilots that year barely outpaced those killed in combat.

Once fuel grew short again, Nazi Germany cut back training hours to just 205. On the other hand, the rebuilt Royal Air Force was in a far better position and increased its training hours by over 50 percent, rising from 200 to 340. American fighter training was in between, at 270 hours.

A year later, Germany once more reduced training hours to 170 while American fighter training increased to 370. After all, they had a far larger pool of men to pick from, giving them the luxury of taking their time to do the job properly. In 1944, a frantic Germany once more trimmed training, so the pilots received a mere 110 hours, more than half of that time in class, not the air. No doubt, this trend weakened the overall Luftwaffe efficiency and contributed to the Third Reich's defeat.

From January through May that year, more planes and pilots were lost through poor training and related causes than losses from actual combat.

The irony is that by late 1944, the Me–262 and other innovative airplanes were ready for use, but fuel was in short supply after a devastating Allied bombing run on German depots in May, curtailing proper training to use these superior fighters. When nine Me–262s were dispatched to France in July, only four pilots were qualified to fly them.

Luftlotte Three, one of the fighter groups, discovered in July 1944 that the majority of its pilots had between eight and thirty days' combat experience.

During this same period, the much needed and late in arriving long-range bombers were finally built in sufficient numbers. Hitler insisted that the top-rated pilots be assigned to helm these new airships, and as they got shot down, the ranks of superior pilots was dramatically reduced.

Also contributing to this was the decision not to emphasize fighter pilot training at the Luftwaffe schools. This put inexperienced pilots into combat situations, and their inexperience further reduced the ranks. The teaching did not reflect reality until late in 1943, but by then, the skies had effectively been ceded to the Allied forces.

By the time Germany surrendered, its stealth planning and construction had virtually ground to a halt. What it spent over a decade building fueled the belief that it could blitz across the Continent and seize control of the sleepy countries. Hitler may have proclaimed a thousand-year Reich, but never planned for one.

As a result, he placed his countrymen into untenable positions, facing better-trained pilots in greater numbers. There were never enough pilots, enough air-worthy equipment, and enough fuel in the same place at the same time at any point after 1942 to give Germany a fighting chance to maintain its aerial superiority.

Instead, England, America, and Russia called upon a great reservoir of materiel and personnel to take back the skies and keep them clear. The vaunted Luftwaffe crashed and burned.

TANKS FOR THE MEMORIES

World War II's Best and Worst Tanks

BY ROLAND GREEN

The perfect tank is like the cure for the common cold—it hasn't been made yet. But in World War II they certainly tried hard, giving birth to the modern tank.

We'll look at the efforts in Britain, the United States, Germany, and the Soviet Union. The French lost their armored forces (and practically everything else) in 1940, and neither Italy nor Japan gave tanks a high priority because of their weak industrial bases.

Britain, or Tanks in Two Kinds

The British not only invented the tank, but worked on them steadily between the wars. Unfortunately, they also believed that tanks should be divided into infantry and cruiser tanks.

The first, as the name implies, was for supporting the infantry in breaking through enemy defenses, especially machine guns and barbed wire. So they wound up with heavier armor, light guns, low speeds, and roomy interiors.

The cruiser tank was to be the new cavalry, roaming through breaches in the enemy's lines and deep into his territory, destroying supplies, communications, and command posts. This meant higher speed, lighter armor, and (to save weight) the same light guns as their infantry counterparts.

Add to this that at exactly in the middle of their rearmament in the late 1930s, the British War Office abolished their central tank-design committee. Most of the contractors flocking forward had to start nearly from scratch, and for nearly four years the results were not often felicitous.

But in 1943–1944, the British finally got it almost right. The last and best mass-produced infantry tank was their Churchill. Weighing in at a hefty forty-three tons, it began with the classic armament of a two-pounder antitank gun in a turret and a three-inch howitzer firing forward from the hull. It was slow (15 mph max), but from first to last the most heavily armored tank of the Western Allies.

An unreliable transmission nearly killed the Churchill before it saw combat, but in the rugged terrain of North Africa, it lumbered where no other tank could go. So it was up-gunned, first with an armor-piercing six-pounder and then with a longer-range 75mm, which let it suppress enemy antitank guns and infantry at reasonable ranges. It also acquired a reputation for being very slow to catch fire, and easy to get out of if it did. Finally, its hull was basically an armored box on tracks, making it easy to convert for a host of other battlefield tasks: laying bridges, clearing mines, demolishing fortifications, and even flame-throwing and bulldozing.

If you went to war in one of the five thousand Churchills built, you might be the last to arrive, but you could do good work when you did.

Men in one of the four thousand Cromwells in service from 1944 might arrive sooner but might not do as much or last as long. The Cromwell was the last classic cruiser—fast (up to 40 mph), agile, and lightly armored (at least when it came to facing the lethal 75- and 88mm guns the Germans mounted in their tanks starting in 1943). It was the first cruiser tank built around a 75mm gun whose real (if inadequate, against the German heavies) performance the British had learned from Lend-Lease American tanks in North Africa.

Though it could fight many early-model German tanks and tank destroyers on equal terms, against the Wehermacht's heavy iron of 1944 (Tiger and Panther), it was often a deathtrap. Cromwell crews required sneakiness or the nerve to close to suicidally short ranges to get in a killing shot from the flank or rear.

The United States,
or Shermans Everywhere

As war approached, the United States had few tanks, most of these obsolete, and fewer still heavy equipment (locomotives and construction vehicles), and little experience to make more. However, the War Department, with the usual American talent for logistics, made two sound decisions that went a long way to make up for lost ground.

One was to combine the tanks of the infantry and the "combat cars" of the cavalry into a new branch—armor. This meant only one user of tanks and only one set of designs.

The other was to expand tank production to the incomparable and un-bombed American automobile industry. Dozens of converted or custom-built plants allowed the American automobile industry to turn out more tanks than the rest of the combatants put together, leaving out the amazing feats of the Russians.

This in turn created pressure to stick with the best design

available when trouble began, the M4 Sherman. The United States cranked out forty-nine thousand of them, not counting Sherman chassis converted to other uses. The War Department made something of a fetish of quality, and designs with heavier guns and lower silhouettes were rejected in favor of an uninterrupted flow of Shermans, until that tank became seriously outclassed in 1944. It also believed that fighting enemy tanks should be left to "tank destroyers" with lighter armor and heavier guns. And not least important, American equipment had to be shipped overseas to get into the fight, so the lighter Shermans were ideal for the long trip across the Atlantic.

So what did we get in the Sherman? This thirty-five-ton tank started with light but well-sloped armor, at first bolted together, then with the hull cast in a single piece. It had a sound suspension and transmission, used one of a variety of reasonably powerful gasoline engines, and mounted in its turret a useful infantry support 75mm gun. It could do 25 mph, and go where heavier tanks often could not, besides being easy to maintain, repair, and, if damaged, retrieve from the battlefield. But its armor was almost as weak as the Cromwell's against the late-war German weaponry, and its gasoline-filled fuel tanks and poorly protected ammunition made it highly inflammable.

However, in the West in 1942 it looked like a world-beater, and the British put more than sixteen hundred into service: the Free French and the Poles standardized on the type. The Sherman also grew at least part of the way into its job. Later models had better-sloped and thicker armor, better suspensions giving an easier ride, and ammunition stored in fireproof water tanks. They also had better guns—76mm in the American Shermans, and the most powerful Allied antitank gun, the British seventeen-pounder, in the British Sherman Firefly.

These did not, however, keep it a world-beater. The British and Americans reckoned that one German Panther was equal to five Shermans, and on good defensive terrain, single Tigers sometimes killed as many as sixteen of their American-built opponents before succumbing themselves. Fighting the Germans, too many Shermans were lost working their way around the flanks of their better-gunned and better-armored opponents. With them were lost far too many of their crews, giving the Sherman the reputation of a deathtrap. Agility and numbers usually won in the end, but how much consolation was that to the crews of the dead Shermans or their next-of-kin?

Germany,
or the Big Cats

The Germans went more systematically than anyone else at developing tanks and tank tactics. They did so well in the blitzkrieg years of 1939–1940 that they thought what they had was good enough for years to come. So they rolled into Russia in June 1941 with four thousand tanks that were either prewar models or slightly improved versions of them—and the most skilled tank leaders and crews in the world. In October 1941, they were driving hard for Moscow when they encountered stiffening Russian resistance. One of the stiffeners was the T–34, which outgunned most German tanks and was virtually immune to every German weapon short of the 88mm antitank gun, of which the Germans had only a few hundred, counting those that started off as antiaircraft guns. Fortunately, the Germans faced only a few hundred T–34s sent into battle in penny packets, until well into 1942.

They responded by nicknaming their standard 37mm antitank gun "the Door Knocker." They also converted practically every suitable gun (including captured French 75mms leftover from World War I) and tried it out as an antitank gun. Some of them worked. Finally, they set out to produce tanks superior to the T-34.

Their first attempt was the Tiger, rushed into battle less than a year from the drawing boards and with bugs in its turret motor, gun sights, and transmission. It was basically a large heavily armored box on wide tracks, with a smaller armored box rotating on top of it. But the armor was practically invulnerable and the turret carried an 88mm gun that could kill any opposing tank.

After the Tiger I proved itself in battle, the Germans acted on the principle of "bigger is better." The Tiger II, or King Tiger, had a longer-barreled, more powerful 88mm, and thicker and much better-sloped armor for deflecting heavier Allied antitank rounds. It was undoubtedly the most formidable tank of the war, and even the small detachments in which they were deployed could have major tactical influences. (The company-sized or smaller detachments were necessity as much as choice—total production of Tigers was thirteen hundred plus for the I and five hundred for the II.)

Apart from being few and far between, both Tigers were underpowered, the second more so than the first (fifty-six and sixty-eight tons, with the same 750-horsepower engine). This made them slow to keep up with advances and slower still to keep up with retreats (12 mph off-road, 20 mph on road). It also made them almost impossible to retrieve if they became stuck, broke down, or took crippling battle damage. Finally, their wide combat tracks gave them formidable cross-country ability but had to be taken off and narrower tracks put on so the Tiger would fit on railroad cars. Then the whole process had to be reversed at the railhead.

Needless to say, German tank mechanics earned their pay.

Much more user-friendly was the Panther, built as a direct reply to the T–34 when the Germans discovered that they couldn't just reverse-engineer the T–34 (particularly its engine) and build it themselves. At forty-five tons, the Panther had good, well-sloped armor, a 75mm gun with almost the armor penetration of the 88mm, and enough horsepower to be reasonably fast on the roads and agile off them (30 mph on roads, 15 off).

Its poorly protected fuel system always made it fire-prone, and it started off with so many quality-control problems in virtually every major system that in its first battle (Kursk), more were lost to breakdowns on the way to the front than were lost in battle. But the Panther could be and was debugged, and was a well-balanced design that didn't sacrifice any one vital quality in favor of another. The five thousand built gave the Germans good service during the war.

Allied tankers might have paraphrased Ogden Nash: "If you see a Panther, don't anther."

Their answer to both of the German giants was improving their own tanks, and also by achieving air superiority. The enemy had built mobile fortresses with thick walls—but a P–47 or a Shturmovik could strike through the thin roof. And the Germans simply had too few fortresses.

They would have been better off with no Tigers and another five thousand Panthers.

Russia,
or Keep It Simple, Comrade

The Russians did not make that German error. Had not Comrade Stalin said, "Quantity has a quality all its own"?

Stalin nearly brought down his country with the mistake of beheading his own army in the prewar Great Purges; among the victims were most of the advocates of the mobile and largely armored corps, divisions, and brigades. In those formations, even the eighteen thousand obsolete tanks the Russians fielded in June 1941 might have given the Germans a busy time.

Stalin's industrialization program did produce a lot of tractor factories and a lot of tractor drivers, easily converted to producing and driving tanks. Now all they needed was trained tank leaders and good tanks.

Enter the T–34, the product of a team of engineers in Leningrad, who liked the large road wheels of the Christie suspension, which both drove and returned the tracks and therefore allowed greater speed. So they built a Christie chassis with wide tracks for off-road mobility. On top of it they put a hull with the best-sloped armor of its day. In the rear of the hull they put a lightweight diesel engine, whose greater fuel economy increased range and whose less-volatile fuel decreased the fire risk. On top was a turret mounting a 76mm gun, the most powerful turret-mounted tank gun of 1941. And all this could roll along at 30 mph on roads. Elsewhere, the wide tracks and high power-to-weight at least let it crawl where every other tank in the world would bog down.

Perfection? Not quite. The turret held only two men, which meant the commander and gunner had their hands full. Russia was short of radios, which meant limited tactical communications nets in the tank forces (who started the war using flag signals while fighting the radio-equipped Germans). And quality control in transmissions remained so poor that T–34s often went into battle with spare transmissions lashed to the rear deck, along with the gas cans, bedrolls, and cases of Lend-Lease Spam.

Poor crew training initially reduced the combat effectiveness of the T–34. The movement of much Russian heavy industry to the Urals or beyond to be out of reach of the Germans also slowed the increase in production. Initially, many T–34s came off assembly lines working in below-zero temperatures while the construction crews finished the plant overhead.

But by 1943, the Russians had both skill and numbers. At Kursk that summer, T–34/76 met its ultimate test. In conjunction with massed antitank guns and air support, it took on the panzer's best and destroyed, becoming *the* offensive force on the Eastern Front for the remainder of the war. They used maneuver, mass, smoke and dust cover, and even ramming to put down their opponents and begin the march on Berlin.

The last chapter of the T–34 saga came with the T–34/85 in early 1944. With an 85mm gun in a three-man turret, now often equipped with a Lend-Lease American radio, it was considerably more reliable and rolled steadily on to Berlin. Manufacturing continued until the 1950s with a total production of more than fifty thousand T–34s. T–34/85s used to be center of war memorials all over the former Soviet empire and some remain in service (mostly in the Third World), but there are probably more in storage, the Russians being very reluctant to throw away any potentially useful weapon.

The tank that contains the fewest mistakes wins. This gives the Golden Track Pin Award for World War II to the T–34.

THE STORY OF THE
MESSERSCHMITT 262

Germany, 1944–1945

BY DOUGLAS NILES

Willy Messerschmitt was a brilliant designer of aircraft, and his machines played a major part in the success of the Luftwaffe throughout the course of World War II. The Bf–109 fighter set a world speed record of 380 mph on November 11, 1937. After service in the Condor Legion (Germany's contribution to Franco's fascists in the Spanish Civil War), its armament was increased and it ruled the skies in the early years of World War II, almost prevailing over the English Spitfires and Hurricanes during the Battle of Britain. Even as the war entered its final years, the Bf–109 was still claiming kills from the vast armada of heavy bombers the Allies were sending over Germany on a nearly daily basis.

But by 1944 it was essentially obsolete, outmatched by American P–51 Mustangs and supercharged British Spitfires. Even Germany had a better fighter plane in the Focke Wulf Fw–190. But the Bf–109 was far from the last arrow in Messerschmitt's quiver. As early as 1938 his company had been working on plans for a revolutionary aircraft, one that would be powered by turbojet engines instead of the traditional piston-engine, propeller-driven designs that everyone in the world was using.

A design team led by Dr. Waldemar Voight drew up plans for a sleek twin-engine fighter plane. Called Project 1065, the fast interceptor looked very good on paper, though it faced some daunting challenges before it would ever be able to fly. But Messerschmitt and Voight were ready to persevere. While engine development and production was still undetermined, a number of the aircraft's key features were present in the initial drawings: the plane would feature narrow, gracefully swept wings, with twin engines located in streamlined under-wing enclosures called nacelles. The pilot would sit high, with good visibility in all directions through a bubble canopy, and the fuselage would have a strong triangular cross section and taper toward the tail to improve aerodynamics.

Aircraft production in Nazi Germany was coordinated by the German Air Ministry, or Reichs Luftfahrt Ministerium (RLM). It had already seen a prototype turbojet built by the Heinkel corporation, the He–178, and had dismissed it as unreliable and, in fact, slower than standard fighters such as the Bf–109. However, by May 1940, Messerschmitt was ready to put forth his own plan, and the RLM was intrigued.

Several turbojet engines were in various stages of experiment and design in Germany. The Heinkel He–178 was deemed underpowered. The BMW company was working on another engine, the BMW–003, but because of the complexity of the finely honed turbines, it kept running into unexpected problems that delayed production. Junkers, however, had come up with a promising design, the Jumo–004. In early 1942, two of these Jumo engines were fitted onto Messerschmitt's prototype, and test pilot Fritz Wendel took the plane for its first flight in July of that year. He was exhilarated and impressed by the experience.

The design team confidently invited a pilot from the Luftwaffe's official test center, Flight Captain Henrich Beauvais, to try out the plane. Unfortunately, the captain didn't follow Wendel's advice for handling the tricky aircraft, and immediately after taking off he crashed the initial prototype into a manure pile on its second test flight. (Beauvais walked away a little smelly, but not seriously harmed.) A second machine was not ready until October 1942. Refinements and improvements continued for the next six months, though the RLM—directed by the conservative-minded Erhard Milch—still did not authorize production.

Finally, on May 22, 1943, the Luftwaffe general of fighters, renowned ace Adolf Galland, flew a prototype and was overwhelmingly impressed. His backing was enough to convince the RLM to issue an order for a hundred of these revolutionary fighter aircraft. Efforts to produce the Me-262, dubbed the Schwalbe ("Swallow") commenced in earnest.

But there was more trouble on the horizon. As the year 1943 progressed, the Allies had been making steady inroads against Hitler's empire. In particular, amphibious invasions in North Africa, Sicily, and Italy alarmed the führer, who was growing increasingly unhinged as he witnessed the thousand-year Reich coming to pieces around him. Allied bomber raids against German cities, too, were an affront against the Reich, and these attacks would only grow stronger and more destructive as the war progressed.

Reichsmarschall Hermann Goering was the head of the Luftwaffe and one of Hitler's favorite cronies. Together with Milch (who had come around to appreciate the 262's splendid potential), he visited the Messerschmitt factory in Augsburg on November 2, 1943. There Goering saw the jet in flight and was very impressed. When he asked Messerschmitt if the plane could carry bombs, the designer breezily informed him that it had been designed to carry five hundred kilograms of ordnance.

Goering carried word to Hitler, who saw the plane before the end of the month and asked the same question and got the same answer. The Nazi dictator was ecstatic: here was a plane that could strike Allied forces on their landing beaches, inflicting punishing damage and holding the troops in place until German ground forces could arrive to throw them back into the sea! He enthusiastically endorsed the aircraft, and eagerly awaited delivery of his new fighter-bombers.

Messerschmitt and Milch, meanwhile, basically ignored the führer's request, and continued to design the plane as a fighter. And, indeed, it would be the greatest fighter aircraft in the world when it finally became operational: using a discardable rocket booster, it could take off and reach an elevation of thirty-eight thousand feet in less than five minutes. It was a dream to handle and fly, and it could attain speeds in excess of 500 mph in level flight—so it was at least 100 mph faster than any plane the Allies could put against it. Knowing that the Americans were working on new strategic bombers, including the huge, fast B-29, Milch saw that the Me-262 could become an integral part of Germany's air defense.

Still, there were lots of problems to overcome, including delays in engine production. Allied bombing raids smashed the major Messerschmitt factory in Regensburg in August 1943, and a general shortage of resources, most especially fuel, impeded progress. Working to overcome these challenges, the Schwalbe was slowly entering production by spring of 1944.

In May, Hitler gathered Goering, Galland, Milch, Reichsminister for Production Albert Speer, and others to Berchtesgaden, where he had an official residence. The topic was the state of fighter production, and naturally enough the conversation got around to the Me–262. Hitler was surprised, since he had been considering the aircraft as a bomber. When he found out that not a single one of the currently produced jets was configured to carry bombs, he exploded. Goering hastily blamed Milch for the misunderstanding, and the director of the RLM was lucky to get out of the room with his life, even though it cost him his job.

Hitler insisted that the current production run of the Me–262 be halted, and a new version of the aircraft, to be used as a tactical bomber, be commenced at once. Galland and others tried to dissuade him, but he only became more agitated and insisted. Using the Me–262 as a bomber was a terrible idea for many reasons, and not just because it would delay the deployment of this revolutionary aircraft for four crucial months. The jet's performance at low altitude was poor, and when carrying bombs its range was limited to targets within only about two hundred miles of its base—two strikes against it as a bomber. Furthermore, when fitted with a load of bombs, the Schwalbe's speed was slowed so much that it could actually be caught by a P–51 or a Spitfire.

But mere facts had little impact on Adolf Hitler, especially by this time in the war. Nine Me–262s were configured for the bombing mission and sent to France during the summer of 1944. They accomplished little and by September the Allies had driven the Germans out of France and back to their own border. The need to attack amphibious landing forces on their beaches was no longer relevant to the strategic situation. Finally Hitler granted permission to develop the plane as a fighter. Even then, he ordered that it be configured so that it could easily be returned to its bomber role.

By the end of the war, the Me–262 was recognized as the best fighter interceptor in the world, but there were never enough of

them to make a real difference in the course of the air war—
only some 200 of the 1,400 built ever saw combat. The Allies devised tactics to swoop down and attack the jets when they were
making their long takeoff runs, and only a limited number of air
bases were available for them, since they could only operate off
of concrete—they tended to light asphalt runways on fire! The
final combat tally resulted in some 150 planes shot down by the
jets, while about 100 of them were lost in action.

Still, one has to wonder: with another four months of progress, and proper leadership from on high at the crucial moment
in the aircraft's development: what might have been?

BOOKS BY
BILL FAWCETT

HOW TO LOSE A WAR
More Foolish Plans and Great Military Blunders
ISBN 978-0-06-135844-9 (paperback)

From the ancient Crusades to the modern age of chemical warfare, history is littered with horribly bad military ideas, and each military defeat is fascinating to dissect.

IT LOOKED GOOD ON PAPER
Bizarre Inventions, Design Disasters & Engineering Follies
ISBN 978-0-06-135843-2 (paperback)

This book is a collection of flawed plans, half-baked ideas, and downright ridiculous machines that, with the best and most optimistic intentions, men have constructed throughout history.

YOU SAID WHAT?
Lies and Propaganda Throughout History
ISBN 978-0-06-113050-2 (paperback)

From the dawn of man to the War on Terror, Fawcett chronicles the vast history of frauds, deceptions, propaganda, and trickery from governments, corporations, historians, and everyone in between.

OVAL OFFICE ODDITIES
An Irreverent Collection of Presidential Facts, Follies, and Foibles
ISBN 978-0-06-134617-0 (paperback)

Featuring hundreds of strange and wonderful facts about past American presidents, first ladies, and veeps, readers will learn all about presidential gaffes, love lives, and odd habits.

HOW TO LOSE A BATTLE
Foolish Plans and Great Military Blunders
ISBN 978-0-06-076024-3 (paperback)

Whether a result of lack of planning, miscalculation, a leader's ego, or spy infiltration, this compendium chronicles the worst military defeats and looks at what caused each battlefield blunder.

YOU DID WHAT?
Mad Plans and Great Historical Disasters
ISBN 978-0-06-053250-5 (paperback)

History has never been more fun than it is in this fact-filled compendium of historical catastrophes and embarrassingly bad ideas.

HUNTERS & SHOOTERS
An Oral History of the U.S. Navy SEALs in Vietnam
ISBN 978-0-06-137566-8 (paperback)

Fifteen former SEALs share their vivid, first-person remembrances of action in Vietnam—brutal, honest, and thrilling stories revealing astonishing truths that will only add strength to the SEAL legacy.